Talk
Talk Talk

Talk Talk Talk

The Cultural Life of Everyday Conversation

Edited by S. I. Salamensky

Routledge
New York and London

Published in 2001 by
Routledge
29 West 35th Street
New York, NY 10001

Published in Great Britain by
Routledge
11 New Fetter Lane
London EC4P 4EE

Routledge is a member of the Taylor & Francis Group.

Printed in the United States of America on acid-free paper.
Designed by Liana Fredley.

10 9 8 7 6 5 4 3 2 1

Library of Congress Cataloging-in-Publication Data

Talk talk talk : the cultural life of everyday conversation / edited by S. I. Salamensky.
     p.   cm.
   Includes bibliographical references and index.
   ISBN 0-415-92170-8 (alk. paper) — ISBN 0-415-92171-6 (pbk.: alk. paper)
   1. Interpersonal communication. I. Salamensky, S. I.
BF637.C45 T35 2000
302.3'46—dc21   00032301

Contents

Chat Three: Culture Klatch

What Can I Say? Acknowledgments

For talking about talk: Barbara Johnson, Stanley Cavell, Judith Ryan, Barry Qualls, Robert Atwan, Jane Shattuc, Eric Zinner, Annalee Newitz, Carla Mazzio, Grant Farred, Laura Grindstaff, and Grace Kehler, for input and inspiration; a "dream team" of contributors—Homi, Sander, Judith, Paul, Alex, Carla, Debby, Tom, Stanley, John, Marge, Alec, Steven, Nicholas, Margaret, Jan, Avi, Sherry—for golden words, patience, strong coffee, bad soup, bad jokes, Japanese fabric, and much, much more; and Liana Fredley, Dan Geist, and Bill Germano, for transmogrifying "mere talk" into matter. This volume is offered with thoughts of Francis Barker, whose talk left us breathless, whose loss leaves us speechless.

For still talking to me: Sandra Naddaff and the Harvard University Committee on Degrees in Literature; Jonathan Lichtenstein and the University of Essex Centre for Theatre Studies; Peter Hulme and the University of Essex Department of English; my Essex hosts Jeffrey Geiger and Beatrice Han; my Oxford hosts David and Lesley Smith; Tom Cohen and the University at Albany, SUNY, Department of English; Robert Polito; my students at Harvard, Essex, and SUNY; Herr Professor Mark F. Schwartz, for insights on the *Ungesagt*; Barbara Howard; Matthew Howard, big talker, many times over; my family and above all my brother David, without whom I would not have seen the publication of this volume.

What We Talk about when We Talk about Talk (A Word in Edgewise)

Introductory Remarks

S. I. Salamensky

> Talk is like a structural midden, a refuse heap in which bits and oddments of all the ways of framing activity in culture are to be found.
> —*Erving Goffman*

> So they opened their big mouths, and out came talk. Talk! Talk!
> —*Norma Desmond,* Sunset Boulevard

Before Drama, before Media, before the Internet . . . there was Talk itself. Our lives are greatly made of talk. Our identities are composed, and daily re-composed, in it. Our friendships, loves, and social structures are built upon it. Everyday chatter supplies the basis for artistic and cultural forms that reshape talk to new forms, in turn reshaping talk itself.

People are talking, as they say, and have been since the first cave utterance. Writers and performers—one thinks of Ovid, the Elohist, Shakespeare, Austen, Dickens, James, Joyce, Eliot, Hurston, Faulkner, Beckett, Mamet, Woody Allen, Anna Deavere Smith, Busta Rhymes—have woven evanescent talk into immortal texts. Freud swore by talk in the name of science. Kierkegaard swore off it, Heidegger against it. Technologized talk hybrids—man-on-the-street opinion polls, "hype," "buzz," the "much-talked-about" *Talk* magazine, cell phone "scanner" performance, "cyberdemocratic" Internet chat, and more—are increasingly broadcast at high volume into public discourse.

Yet, strangely, scholarship to date has largely failed to address theoretical questions surrounding talk. From a critical standpoint, talk—so ubiquitous and integral to all we do, read, write, believe, and feel ourselves to be— remains, like the purloined letter in Poe's story, hidden in plain sight. If indeed, as is increasingly argued, our world functions through communications—and that communications are all, finally, that can be "read"—new discussion of all rhetorical means is merited. Common talk—and its textualized, staged, and technologized manifestations—is especially worth tracing, in that it is traditionally linked to notions of the natural, unfettered thought, and subjectivity, as well as artifice, unoriginality, and objectivity. Whether any of these characterizations is accurate—and on the basis of our knowledge of language's roles in culture we may choose to reject them all—these are vital cultural cruxes in all times, and certainly the one in which I write.

I first conceived this project when researching cultural anxieties over talk at the Western fin de siècle—the nexus moment of Freud's talking cure, the sharp rise of speculative economy, Chekhov's and Wilde's "talking" performances, the invention of the telephone, press lampoons of various gender and ethnic groups as decadently voluble, and other talk-related trends—and, to some surprise, was unable to locate a substantial theoretical source on talk. This volume represents one such as I wished to find at that time: a compendium of work on talk commissioned from an eclectic range of fascinating scholars. In this process, I have been privileged to work and converse with some of the greatest thinkers—and talkers—of our time. Some were chosen because they had written on talk—most because they had not.

Homi Bhabha and Sander Gilman start off Chat One, "Talking the Talk," with a spontaneous, freewheeling talk about talk in general, upon which I had the fortune to eavesdrop. The old friends' talk ranges across postcolonial language change, clandestine samizdat meetings, *A Streetcar Named Desire*, garrulous Indian and Jewish families, and beyond. I follow with a discussion of philosophical and cultural attitudes toward talk—contradictorily called at once "mere," "idle," and, especially, "dangerous."

Judith Butler and Paul Rabinow open Chat Two, "The Arts of Conversation," with a wide-ranging dialogue on speech and political power from *Antigone* on. Alexander Gelley enters the discussion with an examination of "talky" literature. What work, Gelley asks, is language expected to do? Why is it, then, that wordy writing is so often thought to be failing in its duties—loafing? Carla Kaplan, similarly, talks about the conversation that fails, in life and literature, and whom it fails—those disempowered to be heard. Who speaks? Who listens? Kaplan asks, tracing a case of writing in which talk is, powerfully, staged for one. Deborah Geis and I explore a related case: monologue in drama. Theatre is traditionally conceived as dialogic.

What is the sound of one voice talking? Examining early "talkie" cinema—positioned at the junctures of talk and silence, the verbal and the visual—Tom Conley traces the tensions involved in the meeting of film and voice technology and how they gave rise to film's unique narrative form. Stanley Cavell considers later movies at their talkiest, with the Marx Brothers. The immigrant brothers, Cavell argues, performing insurrectionary vaudeville, talk over, under, and around mainstream discourse to carnivalize—and, finally, cannibalize—the all-American scene. John Limon, similarly, theorizes comedy, neurosis, and cultural identity in a discussion of standup routines by Lenny Bruce and Ellen DeGeneres.

Marjorie Garber begins Chat Three, "Culture Klatch," with an expansive, and intensive, query of quotation—retalked talk—from the ancients through Monica-era legislators. Alec Irwin takes up a rather different sort of animal: the animal, discussing talk in Doolittle, Disney, and so forth. Steven Connor channels talk from Satan and Sybil (yes, *that* Sybil), listening to dissociation and possession. When we talk, who is speaking through us? Are we not, in that sense, all possessed? Nicholas Rand then talks us through Freud's "discovery" of talk as cure. Listening to Freud's inheritors, Margaret Bruzelius takes on talk shows, daily self-affirmations, and other "psychobabble." Jan Gordon puts hearsay on trial with a whirlwind historical tour of the uses of talk as evidence. Like gossip, Gordon writes, talk functions under human law as a sort of "fugitive orality"—in a sense, as criminal itself. Avital Ronell then provides a brief overview of early technologies of talk. The string-and-tin-can contraptions of our childhoods were, we learn, far from the first telephones. Sherry Turkle, concluding, takes talk into the future, telling me about technologized talk, from e-mail to living dolls.

As Ezra Pound elegizes it, talk is useless; and still there is no end of it—"no end," Pound writes, "of things in the heart."

Chat

one

Talking the Talk

Just Talking

Tête-à-Tête

Homi Bhabha and

Sander L. Gilman

Homi Bhabha: Hello, Sander.

Sander Gilman: Hello, Homi. Good to hear your voice.

Homi: Yours too. So. We're going to talk about talk. Now, who wants to talk first?

Sander: Why don't you start talking?

Homi: Well then, okay. I guess one of the things I've been thinking is about what happens if you come, as I do, from a once-colonized country, where English is still a predominant cultural and symbolic force, and you can't speak the queen's English. Then you speak what's called a "babu" English, which is a much more vernacularized English. And it immediately sets up whole registers of hierarchy, competence, capacity—ways of measuring these things, of judging oneself and the society in which one lives. Of course, this lessens when local languages emerge in a postindependence phase with great strength. But then, again, you're clobbered when the processes of globalization require a much more international lingo, which somehow happens to be English. So there's this continual move toward a foreign language which is not actually so foreign because it's a part of your own history—then being judged by that negatively, then surmounting it, then again being negatively judged by it.

And what I find fascinating lately are the conventions, not only of common speech, but of media-speak in India and in South Asian diasporic channels. For instance, television presenters will speak half in English and half in Hindi. When I first heard it I thought it was a kind of a spoof. My children, who have a very, very shaky knowledge of Hindi or Gujarati, can actually understand it, because a lot of the operative terms happen to be in English. So there are some places where you combine the rules and the misrules, and you speak out of it.

Sander: And then you get these extraordinary developments of diasporic languages. The example I always give is of the anglicization of Yiddish in the United States up to and then after the 1960s. So when you read the *Forwärts*—the *Forward*—for example, in the 1960s, people are talking about the *vindas*. Not *fensters*, right? The *vindas*, windows. You realize that no one could understand that language except people in the diaspora.

So then there's the whole question of transitional languages, what are technically called creoles—although that's a term I don't especially like. So then the question is, does this language facilitate, does it function, in defining oneself as both in a society and in transition into a society?

Homi: I think that's a very good point, and that what we don't adequately have is what you've just touched on: a way of valuing ourselves, our languages, our historical moment, our culture, as objects of—or indeed subjects of—transition.

What especially interests me here is the way in which creolized language—and like you I'm hesitant to use the term—has gained a public presence. I was watching this Hindi program in New York and Chicago, and they would literally say things like: *Jub me ghar aya*, I found that tea was already on the table—*jub me ghar aya*, meaning "when I got home." Quite literally like that. At the literary end of it, this is something that Salman Rushdie does all the time. Of course, he has to Indianize his English rather than use actual Hindi phrases, which is what is done on the television.

But, you know, what I like about this is that creolization in a way assumes that the suture is not visible, that everything is sort of turned into something else. Whereas here there really is a suture. People really do live that thing that you so perceptively call the transitional fold.

Sander: Yes, and what interests me here is our fantasy of language being fixed, fixed in such a way as to exclude the exterior. As if languages are somehow or other an interior space, when what they are, of course, is a transitional space.

Homi: Yes, but, you know, Sander, I want to take this notion of transition, about which I've been thinking a little more conceptually up to this point, and ask you something about the more quotidian notion of conversation.

Just because people can speak—just because they're intelligent people, just because they're communicative—does not mean they're conversationalists. Conversation depends on a certain kind of culture: of evocation, nostalgia, metaphor, the permission to ramble, periphrasis, peripateia—all those kinds of interesting, wandering, associative things are part of conversation, which is why those sorts of highly motivated conversations on the television screen or in the movies don't work. So we permit wandering, and we entertain transition, in the act of conversation.

Sander, can you say there were periods—X, Y, Z—with various conditions under which there was a great coffeehouse culture where people could converse, or not? Is this a historicizable thing?

Sander: Well, I think that there are moments when conversation becomes thematicized. There are moments, for instance, in which social settings are created where the rules are overt: one can think about salons in the seventeenth and eighteenth centuries. And where there is a desire, and often a realization of the desire, for transcription of conversation. The problem there, of course, is like that of the diary. You write a diary for yourself but you also hope to hell that somebody's going to read your diary at some point. You also produce a certain persona for the diary.

One question to ask is not just whether it's historicizable—of course it's historicizable—but why at any given moment a culture of conversation is seen as desirable. And at what point do we differentiate between conversation—which is always a public act, not a private act—and lying together with someone whispering sweet nothings?

Homi: A conversation, perhaps, requires not only rules of communicability, but some perceived notion of community—a felt notion, an affective notion of community—and a public sphere.

Sander: Absolutely. We tend to think about conversation as people talking; it's one level above that. It's organized speech; it is structured speech; it is structured speech in a specific environment.

And then one can ask questions such as why is it that in the eighteenth or early nineteenth century, in salons in Berlin run by Jewish women, a certain type of conversation takes place. When you look at that, you think, you know: I would feel very uncomfortable trying to engage in these kinds of conversations; I wouldn't have been invited into this sort of a setting— wrong class—right? I don't know the rules. You look at it as a sort of period piece.

And yet, when you and I have this kind of a conversation, we do know what the rules are.

Homi: Well, or we wait to discover the rules when we get the transcript.

[laughter]

Homi: But, really, I say that because there is a kind of proleptic energy in all conversations, that they're spoken for the now but they're also leaping ahead of one, so that you have to describe the rules, or inscribe the rules, retroactively.

Okay. Let me attempt a statement, and you tell me what you think: Conversation demands a culture of mutuality, a dialogical culture, a democratic culture.

Sander: Eh—

Homi: No? Yes?

Sander: Eh—

Homi: I'm just trying to see if we can discover the rules.

Sander: I think what it demands is a space in the culture in which the rules of conversation can take place. That might be the most autocratic culture possible. The French salons of the seventeenth century were hardly democratic; they may have looked democratic because you had writers and politicians conversing together, but in fact they were talking together with very specific rules in a very specific space. I would hate to fetishize conversation as something necessarily good. I think conversation is a neutral space which can be, as you've described it, the fruit of an opening. But that also can be the product of great stultification—

Homi: A sort of an artifact that has lost its real affective or intellectual purpose. I see exactly how that can happen, because you hear it in certain plays.

Sander: And novels.

Homi: And novels. The artifice, the genre of conversation without the substance. But at that point would we want to say—and clearly I'm being tendentious—would we want to say, well, that's not really conversation, that it's staged talk, whether or not it's on the stage or in the salon or on the street? I wonder whether real conversation must have a sort of ethical charge to it, that you put yourself out into the place of the other, and listen to yourself from there just as you listen to the other person.

Sander: I think it can be that. But I think what you describe is an idealized state of conversation, at one end of the spectrum. But I would also say that at the other end of the spectrum from that we see situations in which there is both what seems ethical and productive and a level of masking. I guess my problem is that I believe that language does two things simultaneously: I think it opens, but I also think it obfuscates.

Homi: Yes, and much of the most interesting stuff about listening to a conversation is to go along for the ride, for the detour. What language represses, the processes of sublimation—those are absolutely crucial, the ways in which the aim is superceded, or deflected, and you end up somewhere else. But, now, would we want to say that an exchange within an analytic setting is a conversation?

Sander: Absolutely not. Because, for instance, think of transference. I'm not conversing with the analyst; the analyst is rather in a sense that space within which I talk. I think the analytic situation is a really good example of something that looks like conversation—that is exactly not conversation.

Homi: That's why I brought it up. I thought we might trip though some of these situations, or institutions really, to try and see what kinds of rules there might be.

Now, I remember an image which has really stayed with me from the Shah's reign in Iran—and I'm absolutely sure that after the Shah's reign, in the Ayatollah's reign, the same thing happens. The bugging devices and spies were so subtly disseminated throughout the fabric of society that people used to go for long walks in the fields in the country to have their conversations. Those conversations need not have been explicitly subversive in any way. But the paranoia about conspiracy and rebellion and so on was just so intense that people who had never got their feet out of velvet bedroom slippers—as you know, Teheran was a great Francophile salon culture—would now literally put on walking boots and trump along in the sheep shit, you know, trying to have these conversations. There is a certain intensity there. I'm sure that samizdat cultures make for greatly intense conversations.

Sander: I actually had that experience. In 1976 I was one of the first exchange professors with the German Democratic Republic, and I was in Iena and Weimar for a term. And I remember distinctly walking with people through graveyards having conversations. Because you knew you could not do anything in a domicile. And you walked in a graveyard, which was by the way a very eerie setting, and it gave the conversations—most of which were in fact incredibly banal—a kind of an odd twist. The funny part is, that in thinking back upon this, I cannot remember what we talked about, but I can remember doing it.

Homi: The performance of the conversation.

Sander: Absolutely. And now we're back to the notion that conversations are staged. Those were conversations that were staged. I don't mean that in a negative sense. They were staged in that what you wanted was to have the ability to communicate, not necessarily to exchange any specific ideas or statements.

Homi: You know, Sander, so far I think we've been talking about conversation with the underlying sense of the face-to-face society. What about what we're doing now? What about telephone conversations?

Sander: Just now, talking on the phone to you, I am desperately trying to extrapolate your hand gestures, Homi, I am trying to extrapolate the expression on your face. Are you bored and looking out of the window?
Conversation is, of course, that whole concatenation of stuff, the signs of the body. It's walking next to you in that field—looking at your eyes, seeing your hands move, your physical presence.

Homi: So many of our relationships are mediated by the phone, that plastic technology. People reveal things about themselves, feel very comfortable on the telephone. Deals are made on the telephone, assignations are planned on the telephone, we can be circumspect but we can also be shameless on the telephone.
Something you said earlier about the psychoanalytic moment, the transferential issue, carries over into telephones, which is: projection. Of course face-to-face you have it too, you have your whole sort of fantasy scene before you, yet it's more controlled with the other party there. But on the telephone, it seems possible, in a funny way, to have your cake and eat it—by having neither.

Sander: Let me give a concrete example which interests me: Spike Lee's film about phone sex, *Girl 6*. The thing about phone sex is that it only works if you've got incredible projection on the part of the caller. This could be a seventy-five-year-old man in an apartment in Georgia—our fantasy is that she is twenty-three years old and desires us. But there the problem of the authentic persona versus the imagined or constructed persona is really important. We desire the person at the other end to be authentic. No matter how much we lie about who we are, we assume that the other's end of the conversation is somehow or other more truthful.

Homi: Yes, we want to have the motility and the mobility but we want the other thing to be fixed and we want it to be looking us, as it were, straight in the eye while we dodge around, you know, and make our subtle nuances and our lies and our self-deceptions and our self-projections.

Sander: Someone pointed out to me that for years, back in the 1930s, the most popular radio personality was a ventriloquist. A radio ventriloquist!
But it's because we give that authenticity to that voice or those voices, we really believe that there is this erotic object at the other end of the phone line. That's tied up with our fantasy for the need for control in the world. And I don't know that one should reject the idea that this is also part of the face-to-face conversation.

Homi: I also think the question of time is very important. Conversation takes a certain time. It takes its own time. Could we explore that? Why don't we fantasize, or project—or converse!—about the time of conversations, whether conversation needs a certain kind of commitment to the contingent, to letting things turn out as you didn't expect.

Sander: I agree with you that one of the definitions of conversation is: conversations exist over the passage of time. The difference between an exchange—good morning Homi, good morning Sander, goodbye Homi, goodbye Sander—and a conversation is that a conversation demands working out over time, and real, complicated conversations, over time with separations.
The ultimate literary conversations—Eckerman and Goethe, Boswell and Johnson—take place over decades.

Homi: No matter how deep and wide the time between them, they need power to be resumed and revised.

Sander: We all have a friend whom we may not see for a decade, but with whom we can literally pick up a conversation ten years later. I have a great friend in Australia whom I don't see but once every two or three years, and my wife is always amazed that we can literally pick up in mid-strand whatever we were talking about last time we met. It's because these conversations are, in a way, ongoing even when we're not together.

Yet that raises an interesting question of whether or not such conversations are necessarily a good thing, whether those conversations reveal rather than hide, clarify rather than obfuscate—I would be anxious about making the kind of Buberian claim that says that dialogue, by definition, will lead you onto the right path.

Homi: Right, absolutely not. Because it leads to the contingent, and futurity, and the detour, and sublimation and deflection of the aim, and projections—the performance itself of the talk, the staging of the conversation, the literal ritual of beginning it, giving it its own time, starting it, breaking it, five years later resuming it, that whole ongoing process is so important. I mean: to be committed to the transition that is conversation.

A person will talk and so quickly usurp the other's ground in conversation and end up producing a monologue. People are so unconscious of it now. And it makes me feel—well, I'm going to just suggest some conditions! I think that I enjoy conversations, and—I'm going to make a claim for myself—I think I'm reasonably good at them. I think that is partly because I was brought up in a large, and varied, and various, family. You know, it was a family with uncles and aunts—some peculiar, some entirely pleasurable, some good, some bad—stashed away all over the house.

Within my own family there were a whole range of people, a whole range of things. You couldn't survive unless you actually, at some level, gave the other person their space to speak, and to speak to you, and you to them. You had to develop a kind of ventriloquism. And I don't believe it was a ventriloquism without veracity. It was not. It was not as if one pretended.

That very condition made you talk. And the very conditions of storytelling, the convention of being able to pass a story on from person to person, across a table, or in a room, or as you go for a walk, or in a car as you drive out—these things are good preparations for conversation. Both to jump in, and to let go.

Sander: I mean, one of the interesting claims of the nuclear family is that nuclear families talk, and, in American culture, talk is by definition good: you have to talk with your children. We might see that kind of talk as a mock conversation.

When you're raised in an extended family as we both were, one of the things you learn is that talk is also a weapon, and that conversation is a way of establishing yourself—learning to tell stories but also learning to debate—especially in my family, to debate—to take a position and to defend that position—

Homi: That was very much a part of your upbringing.

Sander: Yeah. Absolutely.

That notion of conversation has to do with the power, right? And it's very different than sitting around and saying things like: What did you do in school today, Johnny?—which, by that point, the family never listens to the response.

That's a question, whether to consider our upbringing as conversational rather than debating. For years I was always amazed when I was invited to friends' homes and the decibel level was so—low!

[laughter]

Homi: Yeah, and in mine too! The decibel level rises immediately!

We had fourteen to a table at Sunday lunch. If you could hear yourself after the first ten minutes then you were doing very well. Everybody was always complaining about it all the time. Saying, Oh my God! Can't you keep quiet? What do you—I can't hear *myself*!!

[laughter]

Sander: I would see this as a wonderful variant on conversation but it would stretch the notion of conversation out from the dialogic completely.

Homi: I am wondering, stretching it out from the dialogic, whether conversations depend on a culture where a sense of the past—needing to bring the past in, or where the value of making absent things, you know, very present—I mean, isn't that true of all symbolic activities in all cultures? I'm wondering whether, in cultures where people do talk about the past, that actually encourages conversation.

I was thinking of the difference between images of conversation in Tennessee Williams or Eugene O'Neill plays, and the image of conversation in Chekhov for instance. When I listen to Chekhov, I immediately think back to holidays, summer afternoons spent with my grandparents and their cousins and their brothers and sisters and my brothers and sisters in the hills south of Bombay, you know, in a country place. I can really identify with it. And as a conversation, it makes me nostalgic for all the conversations of those long afternoons.

When I hear Williams or O'Neill—I'm generalizing here—those seem to me not to be conversations. There's something very intense about not hearing, not wanting to hear, in those plays.

Sander: Again, if one thinks about conversation on a spectrum, the conversations in Williams, of course, are to show what happens when people look like they are talking to each other—

Homi: But are not. And that's when the whole projection issue becomes so important. Now, the funny thing is that when the gentleman caller actually emerges, and a conversation takes place between him and the young woman, then the play has its real weak spot. Don't you think?

Sander: Of course it does. Because he keeps on trying to be helpful!

Homi: And the whole thing is running on his absence, about him being talked about rather than—

Sander: He just keeps on trying to be helpful! And he keeps on saying things like: You have an inferiority complex!

[laughter]

Homi: What a louse! At which point the entire symmetry, the entire mise-en-scène of the play entirely collapses!

Sander: Yes!

Homi: I think this is a very good illustration of some of the themes that we've been talking about: the necessity for a kind of projection, not only in a two-way conversation, but in a three-way conversation, or a multiply accented conversation. and how a conversation depends for its process and for its interest and for, to an extent, its depth on there not being answers, on the gentleman caller not telling you, you know: well, just read Dale Carnegie!

Sander: And it is in fact so often in the interstices, in the blanks, in the unspoken moments that we who are not taking part in the conversation see the reality. I would say that that is a perfect example of the way you would read Chekhov. It's certainly not in the three sisters' conversations, but in what the sisters—

Homi: Don't say. And then again to revert to our theme of time, the way in which Chekhov gives the silence its time—

Sander: Absolutely.

Homi: He respects the silence.

Sander: I think time is right. If one wanted to say what would be a necessary component of conversation, I would argue: presence. I would argue: rules. But I would also argue: time.

Homi: Time. Time is quite important.

Sander: Having said that—

Homi: It's time.

Sander: It's time.

Homi: Thank you, Sander.

Sander: Thank you, Homi.

Homi: Bye.

Sander: Goodbye.

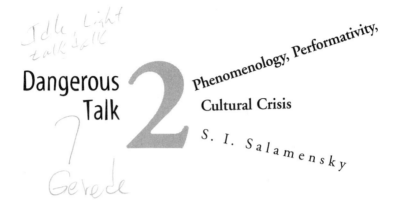

Dangerous Talk 2

Phenomenology, Performativity, Cultural Crisis

S. I. Salamensky

Idle, Light talk talk

Gerede

U nder *talk*, the dictionary says (among other things):

> Speech, discourse; familiar oral intercourse; ordinary manner of speech. *It is not enough to be full of talks. Nothing which is a Phrase or Saying in common Talk, shou'd be admitted into a serious Poem* (Dryden). *Time was too precious now for talk.*
>
> Rumor; gossip. *Their . . . talkes behynd his backe war not hydden . . . to hym. The disgrace that would follow in beeing made fabula vulgi and the talke of the towne. The talk of the conduit and the bakehouse.*
>
> Contemptuously: empty words, verbiage, big talk, idle talk, tall talk, speaking in a boastful or exaggerated style; see also SMALL TALK. *As the man is, so is his talke. That is but talk. He sort o' stands round, and spreads, and lets off all the big talk he hears. Tall talk is luckily an object of suspicion to Englishmen.*
>
> Writing of the nature of familiar or loose speech. *Columns of wild, inflammatory, and*

dangerous talk are appearing in most of our newspapers.
    Talk-stuff, matter for conversation. *For want of talk-stuffe, Out goes his rapier.*[1]

    Quite a mouthful.
    What this should say to us is that *talk* (as opposed, for instance, to *speech* or *discourse*) is traditionally coded as "familiar," "ordinary": informal, close-at-hand, common, pedestrian, everyday—more primary or originary for its proximity to us, perhaps, but seemingly also secondary, second-class, not for elevated usages. Talk is the popular discourse of the public domain; yet, free from central authority, talk may travel secret pathways, emerging "behynde" one's "backe" to render its subject a *"fabula vulgi"*—an inferior text. Ungoverned, sanctioned talk may prove catching. Talk is feared, and yet also dismissed as ineffective, ineffectual, "idle"—though on the helpful side adequate "talk-stuffe" may displace or delay the active "rapier." Talk can be "empty," or falsely inflated—"big" or "tall." "Luckily," no "Englishman" is fooled. Talk can also be "small"—less offensive, perhaps, but no more admirable. "As the man is, so is his talke": he talks the talk, but talk also bespeaks, re-speaks him.
    The verb offers still more evidence of negative—and contradictory—associations. To talk is to engage in impotent effort—"prate, chatter . . . say trivial, idiotic things," to "speak confidently or boastfully . . . without matching the word by performance"—all talk, no action, save the performance of the talk itself. Yet talk, as performance, is also akin to action: There is "dangerous talk," as they say (perhaps only in war and in movies: stool pidgin)—and there is "persuasive talk"—incantatory and finally transformative talk: "to bring to a specified state by talking."[2]
    There's "sweet talk," "pillow talk," "fast talk," and "double-talk"—all too often in the same instance. One may "talk shop," "talk turkey," "talk up," "talk down," "talk back," "talk in circles," "talk at," "talk bullock" ("to use much and picturesque bad language," 1846), "talk Miss Nancy" ("to talk very politely," 1910), and "talk into the big white telephone" ("vomit," 1978); along similar lines, there is "verbal diarrhea."[3] Talk is lame; the talker must also "walk the walk."
    Talk claims monstrous and magical qualities: You can "talk your head off," yet it remains firmly attached; you can "talk something to death," yet it lives. "Talk" appears in the *O.E.D.* after "talisman" and "talith"; this linguistic accident suggests power beyond the range of the dictionary. Like these holy objects talk works mysteriously for, and upon, us, healing charm and touchstone.
    Stanley Cavell dares to speak its name:

. . . schmooz.

. . . The Yiddish *schmooz* is taken up in German as *Schmus*. My German dictionary, after giving the derivation of *Schmus* from the Hebrew word for things heard, adduces the word *Gerede*. Now *Gerede* is the word Heidegger uses in *Being and Time* to name Dasein's everyday (hence, for Heidegger, our average, inauthentic) modes of Being and understanding, and first our everyday possession of speech; it is translated as "idle talk." (From here a path leads to one of Wittgenstein's diagnoses, or terms of criticism . . . of a certain failure of philosophy, namely that in it language is idling, something he also seems to identify, most prejudicially, with language's going on holiday. Idlers do not idle. Can engines loaf? Something Wittgenstein means by philosophical failure I find better expressed in saying that language is racing.)[4]

Schmooz or *Gerede* affronts Heidegger and stymies Wittgenstein by slithering in as simulation of, dissimulation of, supplement to, speech proper. Wittgenstein, it seems, finds the whirl of word-music simply *"seltsam"*: "queer," "occult," ineffable. When the language game comes to an end, the word ceases to signify, but we will not quit trying to trap essence with signs. For Heidegger, *Gerede* is something more: wrongheaded, disingenuous, common, vaguely evil.

As writing is to speech, in the terms of the conversation begun with Plato, talk, schmooz, or *Gerede* is to formal speech—the rhetorical or rhetoricized form of talk we might call speech-text or *Rede*—from the other end of the spectrum. As Michel Foucault writes of writing, *Rede* might be considered the "'male principle' of language," seen to alone "[harbor] the truth."[5] For Plato talk implies presence, and thus greater proximity to the real. But for Heidegger, talk's is a pedestrian presence, not Presence, far from Essence:

> Discourse, which belongs to the essential state of Dasein's Being and has a share in constituting Dasein's disclosedness, has the possibility of becoming idle talk. And when it does so, it serves not so much to keep Being-in-the-world open for us in an articulated understanding, as rather to close it off, and cover up the entities within-the-world.[6]

Gerede—literally that-which-has-been-spoken; useless, unoriginal discursive junk—is pretense at what Heidegger hears as speech in its purer form.

Gerede stands as ersatz *Rede*—negligible, fatuous, second-hand, derivative, adulterated speech—nonoriginary, *hors-texte*, beside the point, insuffi-

cient yet wasteful, excessive. It is at once "idle"—seemingly impotent, inef-
fectual, static—and powerful, harmful, communicable in the sense of disease:

> The fact that something has been said groundlessly, and then gets passed
> along in further retelling, amounts to perverting the act of disclosing. . . .
> This everyday way . . . is one into which Dasein has grown in the first
> instance, with never a possibility of extrication. In it, out of it, and against
> it, all genuine understanding, interpreting, and communicating, a re-
> discovering and appropriating anew, are performed. . . . "[S]aying" some-
> thing . . . is uncovering something. . . . [I]dle talk is a closing-off, since to
> go back to the ground of what is being talked about is something which it
> leaves undone."[7]

Rede alone is licensed to drive meaning: stalwart chauffeur for Being, as
against *Gerede*, lunatic joyrider, errant word. While both attempt to convey
meaning, *Gerede* is unlikely to follow the route, or ever to arrive at the destination intended. *Gerede* flits around Being, skirts, flirts, cannot be pinned
down, hems and haws, interrupts itself, constantly changes the subject. It is
all about, but only about, encircling, obfuscating Being.

Everyday talk cannot represent Being, because Being lies, for Heidegger,
at a vast remove from the everyday. This opposition is of some interest in
that while Heidegger classes the everyday as inauthentic—a forgetfulness, a
blindness, a fallenness from Being—he lauds anxiety, in the metaphysical
sense, as Being's most authentic experiential mode. A certain well-rounded,
well-"grounded" discourse, as Being's expression, is permitted, but
Heidegger draws the line at discursive "scribbling." Talk, random talk, nervous, all-comprising talk—the Dasein-wracked ramblings of, in Avital
Ronell's likening, "schizophrenia"—the manic broadcast from the fray of
Being—would seem to pinpoint the pinball precariousness of our Being at
all, and would thus seem to join existential anxiety to language to form the
discourse of privilege.[8]

Rather, in Heidegger's system, *Gerede* is communistic, common—and,
of course, like all things common, talk is cheap. The tawdry talk of everyday
talkers contaminates pure speech—and through it, pure Being itself:

> The average understanding . . . will never be able to decide what has been
> drawn from primordial sources with a struggle and how much is just gos-
> sip. . . . The groundlessness of idle talk is no obstacle to its becoming pub-
> lic; instead it encourages this. Idle talk is the possiblity of understanding
> everything without previously making the thing one's own. Idle talk is
> something which anyone can rake up. . . .

Since talk is always already there, Dasein is, in the first instance, always-already corrupt:

> In no case is a Dasein, untouched and unseduced by [the] way in which things have been interpreted [in idle talk], set before the open country of a "world-in-itself" so that it just beholds what it encounters. . . . The "they" prescribes one's state-of-mind, and determines what and how one "sees."[9]

Gerede always already pollutes the "open country," usurping Dasein's *Lebensraum.*

Where Cavell proffers an affectionate name, Heidegger a damning one, and Wittgenstein simply a divine bewilderment, J. L. Austin, John Searle, and Walter Ong each provide neutral terms for talk that may elucidate the others. Searle reconstitutes Austin's "constative" statement as the "illocutionary act" (utterance stressing informational assertion) and Austin's "performative" statement as the "perlocutionary act" (utterance stressing texture or nuance contributing to the statement's effect).[10] Ong, similarly, distinguishes "information-driven" discourse—transmission in its purer, *Rede* sense—from "performance-driven" discourse—discourse that effects an additional text of texture or nuance.[11] Ong's terms are particularly useful in appending "-driven": Performative discourse may also convey information; informative discourse may also perform. What distinguishes the two discursive genres are less their imagined motivations, which imply unlikely foresight and agency, than the qualities enthusiasts find most delightful—and detractors most irksome—in each.

Cavell clearly enjoys the delays and dalliances of schmooz as performance, locating Dasein in just being there. Heidegger wants to cut through the *Gerede* to the good stuff, although—even with the most refined of *Rede* at his own disposal—never quite articulates what that might be. Wittgenstein, perhaps, enjoys talk on holiday but is anxious for everyone to get back to work. Kristeva nudges Wittgenstein's sense of language's vacation into a jailbreak, casting performative language as the primal scene of the carnivalesque, where "language escapes linearity (law)."[12]

Overall, performative language is situated as a—worrisome or glorious—site of linguistic and cultural freedom. Talk seemingly resides further along the liberatory spectrum than more formal forms of performative discourse—literary narrative, the dramatic, the poetic. Heidegger would certainly class the formal performative closer to the realm of *Rede*; Mary Louise Pratt has convincingly argued against distinguishing the formal performative from the everyday. The stigma all performative discourse might be seen to share—if by degree—is Platonic anxiety over relations of essence and representation. Discourse, seemingly, equals its mimetic function, its purpose fulfilled when it colludes with what is seen as essence to adequately, proportionately, accurately represent it. When discourse falls into disjunction or opposition with essence, a problem is located in improper or debased speech: what Heidegger calls *Gerede*, what the *O.E.D.* calls talk.

A similar Platonic schism occurs on the level of text and performance. Where some more superior form of discourse is imagined to correctly represent essence, that superior discourse may stand as, erect, or enact a text from which talk may be considered to diverge. Thus *Rede* appears as primary in regard to, and previous to, the sorts of discourse coded as talk or *Gerede* above. *Gerede*, perceived as even further removed from Essence than is *Rede*, is thus also further debased or derivative. *Gerede*—despite its perceivedly greater proximity to the act of vocalization, the spontaneous, and/or the everyday and thus, in some systems, the real—therefore supplements, displaces, reenacts, reinterprets, and re-performs what might be called speech-text discourse, and badly at that. In addition, *Gerede*'s perceived performativity, as well as the copy-without-an-original echo effects of performative repetition upon perceptions of talk's problematic relations to authorship, authority, and traceability, may also—in the sense of largely closed but interpenetrative systems—somewhat shape the cultural life of the linguistic.[13] If truth is measured against standards of materiality held irrefutable, the word's location in the realm of performance—and thus its relative immateriality—relegates it to a secondary or supplementary position. Further, all verbiage falls into lacunae between the material body and performance, where talk forms or performs an alternate or virtual self—"As the man is, so is his talk"—supplementing or competing with the material body as site of self. In all, *Gerede* threatens the carnivalizing of established phenomenological, epistemological, and thus from the view of the humor preceptor, "metaphysical" orders.

In sum, *Gerede* appears to manifest largely as discourse coded as effecting a dialectical disjuncture with an imagined speech-text, and, further, with essence, materiality, and the body—at once equating with, and failing to equate with, essence, materiality, and the body. As such, it can be considered to both succeed in representation, and to miss the mark of mimesis in one way or another (as with talk that is too "tall" or "small")—as well as to both wield ("dangerous" talk) and lack, or fail to inhabit, material power ("mere" talk, "but" talk). Talk about talk clearly addresses a construct both defined and undefinable, wielding cultural power as, perhaps, only the finally undefinable can.[14]

*   *   *

I am less concerned here with what talk is, what it means, what people talk about—or even, in Cavell's phrasing, with *how* it means—than *how it has been taken to mean* in various cultural communications; how it has been received, treated, used, and how it may be traced through our lives and productions: talk as cultural object.

Binary constructions readily blur; and all distinctions, of course, are notionally interdependent. Heidegger, for instance, critiques *Gerede* but fails to describe its other, which he champions, only negatively, as what-is-not-talk. The notion of talk as distinct from gelled or sanctioned rhetorics, like distinctions of genre or gender, appears to some extent as deriving less from structural than cultural needs or wishes. And all discourse develops dialogically—literally in dialogue—drawing from various and conflicting sources. As Bakhtin writes:

> Language, for the individual consciousness, lies on the borderline between oneself and the other. The word in language is half someone else's. . . . Prior to [the] moment of appropriation, the word does not exist in a mutual and impersonal language (it is not, after all, out of a dictionary that the speaker gets his words!) but rather it exists in other people's mouths, in other people's contexts.[15]

Talk, we might say, is like language—but more so. Whatever may be said of language adheres most to talk, which delimits itself less than formal genres.

More, the talk of what are called "complex" societies is decidedly post-oral. As Walter Ong writes, the "primary orality," of cultures "totally untouched by any knowledge of writing or print," differs at base from "secondary orality," the sphere of oral discourse in literate cultures.[16] By Ong's reasoning, we learn oral discourse both from talk and from literary and para-literary sources (film, TV, popular music). Where talk is concerned, we have many mothers, and thus many mother tongues. Our own mothers' tongues are already post-oral, influenced by literary and paraliterary sources in their own right.[17]

Still, what we call talk may be witnessed—for instance, in the case of Oscar Wilde's criminally "talky" performance on trial—to provoke considerable cultural discomfort, and to wield palpable cultural power. Thus despite the arbitrary, or possibly imaginary, quality of bounds describing talk-as-construct, it is worth investigating the general mechanics of the space within those bounds, through a few—certainly not exhaustive—lines of theoretical and cultural inquiry: problems of presence, materiality; dialogism, inscription, authorship, authority, and alterity.

Dr. Johnson's disparagement of gossip as "idle talk about people not present," for example, conveys both the sense of the primacy of material presence, and the sense that talk is that which occurs on the sly; the same words, seemingly, spoken in the referents' presence, would qualify as proper speech.[18] In this case it is as though, either (1) the signifying process—language—is to be ethically subordinate to the signified—the person of the person discussed, the body—no matter how closely approximate, valid, or true the signification might be; or (2) the identical signifying process—talk—without, and with, the material presence of the signified—the person discussed—is seen to constitute two differing significations, each of differing validity. Of course, far more than *politesse* is at stake, phenomenologically, in materialist anxiety over the propensities of mimesis to rival or, in the Butlerian sense, alter the notionally material.[19] All speech, pace Plato, may also be considered as founded on absence: the absence of the object—like that lurking at root in the obsessive talk of hysteria.

Talk is not only, like gossip, about people not present. *No* object any speech is about is fully present in any manner that would allow it to match what the speaker can do, vis-à-vis that object, with language; or for that matter what the speaker can do vis-à-vis other speakers or listeners with language; or what the speaker can do vis-à-vis her own relations as subject to the object world with language. On the level of the signifier, the speaker can manipulate the object discussed in any way and on any conceivable spatial or temporal plane. The speaker can, in communicating with another around and about the object, bond, compete, or position herself relative to the other, in any conceivable configuration. The speaker can, in talking around and about the object, assert any conceivable relation of herself to the world around her, including the simple enactment of subjectivity that the act of stated perception of an object implies.[20]

Along the speech continuum, *Gerede* manifests as even more suspect than *Rede*—less allied to materiality and presence ("It's just talk"). As Wittgenstein explains, language is inexact and thus troubling even when it's "doing work" as *Rede*, but the "confusions" are greater "when language is like an engine idling."[21] If *work* may be defined, in basic terms, as the transformation of matter from one state to another, *Gerede*'s failure to perform work, in Wittgenstein's estimation, is not only a failure to perform the work of language—representing matter—but also a failure to impact matter, to be matter, to matter itself, in the scheme of things. Yet, as with the fear of mimesis, talk is portrayed as mattering at once insufficiently and overly. As Cavell points out above, idling is also an activity; and while Heidegger casts *Gerede* as idle language he worries, paradoxically, over its effects.

A related problem involving presence and materiality lies in perceived differentials of mimesis. Of course, we know that no verbal transmission is direct, in the sense of seamless correspondence between signifier and signified, and that no matter how directed any transmission might be in intention or design, the signification process is messy and leads meaning awry. However, in Heidegger's formulation, *Rede*, the rhetorically "correct," strives toward systematics of exclusivity and closure in its attempt to screen out as much heteroglossia and dialogism as possible for the sake of clarity—to hone language, if it were possible, to monoglossia, to limit its bricolage of genres and narrative levels.[22] A police officer, for instance, making an arrest, is unlikely to wax poetic or relate deep-seated childhood traumas to the accused. Casual talk, it would seem, tends to embrace inclusion or heteroglossia in structuring its stylistic domain. The vow, for that reason, may be seen to trade in *Rede* rather than *Gerede*—a speech-act, in J. L. Austin's system, rather than a talk-act. A comparatively directed statement like *I take this person to be my spouse* is perceptibly more substantial than whatever its less-directed, less-linear, more dialogic or heteroglossic, talkier, or *Gerede* equivalent might be: *Spouse—house, mouse—I have a cat—do you like pets at all?—but sure, why not?*

The *Rede* statement's being-as-action, as well as its more legally binding status—its power in the material realm of property and so forth—is predicated, not only on its following a standard form accepted by all as meaning more or less the same thing, but in its spareness, its presumably tighter correspondence of the signifier to the matter signified. The *Gerede* statement should, perhaps, be considered more trustworthy—less repressive than the vow formula, it might be heard to reveal more of the speaker's actual thought process, allowing the spouse-to-be more knowledge of the speaker's cerebration regarding the process of wedlock; but the *Rede* statement elides confusing variables such as impromptu musing, rhyme, and eccentricities of personal expression. The greater the number of variables in a statement, the more possibility there is that the statement has more than one meaning—either different meanings for the talker and the listener, or more than one interpretation as a statement in general. For instance, in the *Gerede* statement, *spouse* is used both to signify a person and to signify its own surface qualities as a rhyme; *sure* fails to carry the sense of subjective agency implied in *I take*; the interjection *I mean*, in its very accuracy, acknowledges particularly well the possibility of what Wittgenstein calls "the problem of private language," suggesting an interpretability loophole.[23] Meanwhile, the *Rede* statement projects the impression of having eliminated the open-ended character of talk. This is illusionary, in a sense, as all language may, of course, be seen as operating through language game systems; the references suggested by the signifiers *I*, *take*, and so on, as well as the signification suggested by grammar at all, are hardly essentially constructed, but rather dialogically constructed, and thus still multivalent. Yet the *Rede* statement at least enacts a veneer of totalization, rendering *Rede* more conducive to comprehension—in both senses of the word—than *Gerede*, and more amenable than *Gerede* to notions of cultural order. Linkage of talk's dilatory space to notions of excess suggests that a central aspect of cultural unease with notions of *Gerede* as offering a higher proportion of words to subject matter than *Rede*, and thus as more mediated or mediating than *Rede*. If *Rede* is felt by Heidegger and others to adhere more closely to presence, as discussed above, talk may be considered as calling more absence into presence, absence—associated with death, the unseen, the unnameable, dark, lack, repressed psychic elements, and so forth—being a nervous-making state in cultures founded largely on presence, materiality, and having.

Thus it seems that the closer we stick to *Rede* locution, in the Wittgensteinian and Heideggerian formulas, the better we are considered to represent matter. In John Wayne movies, for instance, the hero is a man of few, relatively direct words, which, the viewer is given to believe, are thus to be trusted. His statements follow as linear a progression as language will allow, and his words correspond fairly tightly to the object world—"town," "gun," "sunset." The viewer comes to learn, as well, that his words correspond to material power—the town is his territory, his gun is the fastest, he really can evict the villain by sunset; the viewer has had opportunity to intuit this all along, through both verbal and visual clues, but until the final showdown, the hero's power has been demonstrated almost solely on the discursive level. The villain, by the same logic, is indisputably coded, by the final showdown, as untrustworthy, "weak," or even "feminine"—"lily-livered" being the operative term—by the indirection of his discourse. The viewer's suspicions are confirmed as the villain at once proves impotent on the level of action—and begins to talk in nervous circles around and about the situation, providing too many words in proportion to an object world whose salient features are "town," "gun," "sunset," rather than taking his punishment tersely, "like a man." The filmic fool, Jerry Lewis or Don Knotts, is also largely coded as—if lovable—ineffective in the material realm, on the basis of his chattiness. The final violence in Martin Scorsese's *Mean Streets* is all the more shocking because its garrulous gangsters ("I've always wanted a tiger . . . Y'know, William Blake and all that . . .") seem incapable of bodily action or effect, and because it interrupts the endless mimetic, or antimimetic, deferral that is talk.[24]

In Howard Hawks and George Cukor films, the hero—Cary Grant, for instance—is very chatty, but he's a mediocre hero, a deeply flawed, human man, lovable but not entirely reliable in the material world. The talky screwball antihero, however, problematizes *Rede/Gerede* associations. For he might be, like the garrulous spouse-to-be above, more trusted in providing information regarding his own thoughts; in *His Girl Friday*, for instance, the chatty Walter Burns, presented as a somewhat known and knowable quantity, turns out to be a better bet as a husband for Hildy than is Bruce, whose unrevealing *Rede* discourse turns out to hide flaws even less attractive than Walter's. As manifesting greater consciousness of his own cerebration than Bruce, Walter also proves more interesting and imaginative. *Gerede* here appears more, rather than less, revelatory of truth—more candid, purer, in the Voltairean sense—than *Rede*, at least in matters in which the truth of the speaker's own mind is at issue. In this case, the state-of-the-speaker's-mind replaces the state-of-matter as referent, and in fact as matter; in this case, *Gerede*, reflecting the true state of the mind in its indirection and disorder, may be considered more trustworthy than *Rede*. Walter's intrigue and imagination also help project the impression of power in the realm of the matter of the mind, concepts and language, which, in the talk-driven farce of the Hawks film, replaces the matter of the greater object world—"town," "gun," "sunset," Bruce's money—as what really matters. Indeed, Walter and Hildy's world trades largely in talky intangibles, "rumor, distortion, falsehood"; even for the criminal whose story Hildy scoops, the bottom line is not "town-gun-sunset," but rather a good verbal defense, which Hildy gleans from his *Gerede* discourse.[25] What Walter Burns lacks in command over his own material realm, he makes up for in finesse, or performs into materiality; Burns literally fakes $450 when Hildy needs money, but his counterfeiting generally takes the word as its coinage. Heidegger, similarly, suggests *Gerede's* power as a sort of counterfeit, a shady misrepresentation of the Platonic real by the imaginary, with real results. Walter Burns is a sort of talk-terrorist, in Anthony Kubiak's sense of the theater as terrorism, summoning resources—including Hildy's heart—through performance.[26] That it is talk, more than action or looks, that finally (re)wins Hildy over to her ex, is emphasized in that she "suffers her rebirth of feeling," as Cavell puts it, in response to "talking to Walter over their special distance of the telephone."[27] Walter does not have as much to offer as Bruce in terms of money, and may or may not have as much to offer in terms of physicality, but he makes it seem so, and in effect be so, as he excels in the testosteroned gladiatorial pit of the newsroom, and triumphs over Bruce in Hildy's attraction through talk.

Vocal discourse—like all performance, and unlike written texts, time-bound—leaves no permanent trace, no residue, no record of its brief existence or content, other than that now offered in the age of mechanical reproducibility—though, even then, awareness of talk's mechanical inscription may remove it from the everyday to other forms of performance. Peggy Phelan's description of the problems of the unmarked in performance in general applies to problems and cultural receptions of talk as well:

> Performance's only life is in the present. Performance cannot be saved, documented or otherwise participate in the circulation of representations *of* representations. . . . To the degree that performance attempts to enter the economy of reproduction it betrays and lessens the promise of its own ontology. Performance's being . . . becomes itself through disappearance. . . . Performance occurs over a time which will not be repeated. It can be performed again, but this repetition marks itself as "different." . . . Without a copy [it] . . . disappears into memory, into the realm of invisibility and the unconscious where it eludes regulation and control.[28]

To say that talk is traceless is not to say it leaves no trace at all—for as seen, for instance, in the example from *His Girl Friday*, it leaves its impression in the moment of its hearing, and in the form of very real effects. Yet *Gerede*'s inscription is preserved only in memory and in retelling, and thus more imperfectly than that of *Rede*; if writing is, in Derrida's formulation, a Nambikwaran road, one might say *Rede* is the road in a mild dust storm, and *Gerede* is the road in a raging flood.[29] The seeming untraceability and irreproducibility of *Gerede* appear to stem from its irreducibility to more directed meaning, to *Rede*.

Ong cites the link of speaker to spoken word, echoing Plato, as better than a trace. An oral statement's proximity to its source gives it authoritative and evidentiary strength, in Ong's reading, in that a speaker can be questioned where a text, which appears as a sort of autonomous entity, cannot.[30] In fact, cross-examination may be seen as the effort to squeeze the trace out of talk; if a statement may be reproduced repeatedly from different angles while maintaining its integrity—that is, without changing—it takes on the virtues of writing. Still, in court, material evidence in the form of real writing—a contract, a will, a letter—is touted as the ultimate trump. As another example of the problematics of tracelessness, the fast-talking Hawks hero gleans success from his ability to cover his *Gerede*'s traces, even in the moment, with other *Gerede*; cultural fear of fast talk may reside in the fact that the listener can't reproduce for herself the path of statements leading to an apparent conclusion, and capitulates to the speaker's constructed "truth" out of confusion. As another example, the *Rede* bride-to-be in the wedding-vow scenarios above stands to be rebuked on the basis of her words if, for instance, she claims in court that she did not take the person in question to be her spouse; in the *Gerede* bride-to-be's case, it is hard to pin down the "truth" of what was said because *Gerede*'s irreducibility to *Rede* prevents its full reproduction.

Gerede's waywardness provides additional texture, self-referential to how it is meaning. Peter Brook's directorial dictum regarding divergences between text and performance—"If you just let a play speak, it may not make a sound"—suggests a similar tension between speech-text and talk. *Gerede*, as performance, disseminates messages supplementary to those of the speech-text as texture. It is *Gerede*'s textural textuality that serves as guarantor of talk's virtual irreducibility, and thus irrepeatability, and thus untraceability. Anne Ubersfeld's characterization of all performance might well be applied to *Gerede*, that it is "at once both eternal (infinitely reproduceable and renewable) and momentary (never reproducible as identical to itself)."[31] Short of a mechanical reproduction—in which case *Gerede* may be received as and thus on some level rendered *Rede* by goal-directed, narratizing, spy- or detective-type listening, listening, to resituate Brooks, "for the plot" or key or answer—no retelling will be identical in form, and thus content, to the originary instance.[32]

Heidegger and other detractors are concerned that, while *Rede* is already ersatz, supplementary, fallen, as a simulacrum of Being, *Gerede* is a simulacrum of a simulacrum, irrevocably removed from Essence, in content comprised rather of endless echoes of itself. Certainly, repetition, hearsay, and repetition of hearsay comprise the content of much or most talk, and talk, in form, may repeat itself and be influenced, in form, by other talk; dialogue is founded on this, as an endless and originless process. However, in straying from the ostensibly directional form of *Rede*, *Gerede* appears to make its own way; each instance of *Gerede*, even when different instances are based on identical subject-matter, is bound to be somewhat original in form, and thus content—as formal qualities largely determine meaning. Meanwhile, the aspects of *Rede* significant to the illocutionary project—for instance, a scientific formula—remain fairly consistent across different instances.

Phelan locates the essence of performance in its irreproduceable traceless texturality: "Performance honors the idea that a limited number of people in a specific time/space frame can have an experience of value which leaves no visible trace afterward." Like performance at large, *Gerede* constitutes itself as such—and draws cultural suspicion to itself—through its qualities of traceless, textural, nonreproductive self-enactmentment. While Heidegger mourns *Gerede*—literally that-which-has-been-spoken—as nonoriginary, Cavell celebrates *Gerede*'s wayward, weedy growth as fresh regeneration, recasting "originality in speech" as "the rediscovery of speech." For Cavell, richly textured *Gerede* is a return to and renewal of the intrinsic capabilities of language. As Cavell observes, Marx Brothers audiences who ignore the texture of Groucho's talk miss the proximity to "madness, or hysteria, of so much of what he has to say . . . the sheer range of reference of his uncontrollable thoughts"—the sort of talk that, in its freshness and fulsomeness, in fact provides the most truly appropriate discursive register for Dasein, pace Heidegger:

> *Woman:* You can't stay in that closet.
> *Groucho:* Oh, I can't, can I? That's what they said to Thomas Edison, mighty inventor, Thomas Lindbergh, mighty flyer, and Thomas Shefsky, mighty like a rose. Just remember, my little cabbage, that if there weren't any closets, there wouldn't be any hooks, and if there weren't any hooks, there wouldn't be any fish, and that would suit me fine."[33]

As Phelan describes performance in general, so might it be said of talk that it "refuses [the] system [of substitutional representative economy] and resists the circulatory economy fundamental to it."[34] Similarly, talk's problematic ties to inscription pique problems involving authorship and authority.

Heidegger worries that when "anyone" can talk, "anyone" might be believed, disrupting what he situates as authoritative discourse, or what might otherwise be called dominant discourse. Heidegger's trouble with public discourse is related in part to problems of *Gerede*'s authorship—what Jan Gordon calls talk's "crisis of credit."[35] Just as a conversation, as a text, has at least two authors, talk at large issues from a decentralized provenance, with a diffusion of sources impossible to certify or monitor. Further, Heidegger is concerned that the very act of enunciation carries with it the aura of authority; thus unsanctioned *Gerede* displaces truly authoritative *Rede*.[36]

As Cavell points out in the example of the Marx Brothers, their ethnic schmoozerei, like their antic, anarchic physicality, does in fact intrude into and subvert the established speech-mode of their host milieu. Hyper-heteroglossic *Gerede*, as marker or source of cultural alterity, decenters, destabilizes, disorders, and reorders dominant—as well as, in the cases Cavell cites, patriotic—*Rede*. In particular, the dialogic nature of their *Gerede*—in contrast to their host milieu's fairly straightforward, homoglossic *Rede*—drawing as it does schizically from a plethora of sources, raises questions of origin, particularly in terms of the Jew as cultural bricoleur; the Weird Brothers cannot be pinned down to their words, as their words cannot be pinned down expressly to them. Althusserian or Marcusean questions of locatability of power and political authority are also raised, as in Groucho's reordering of the axiomatic facts of American history into, simply, fodder for wordplay, and in the "bastardization" of the grand into what is familiar to their own New York immigrant experience:

> *Groucho:* I'll show you a few things you don't know about history. Now look . . . [*Drawing a circle on a globe*]. Now, there's Columbus.

Chico: That's-a Columbus Circle. . . .
Groucho: Now, Columbus sailed from Spain to India looking for a short cut.
Chico: Oh, you mean strawberry short cut.[37]

While reflecting and/or affecting political naiveté, the Marx Brothers' punning deflects dominant-culture signification, spinning signifiers off to divergent signifieds, as well as to the surface level, at once enacting multiple meanings while suspending decisive meaning altogether. The dominant milieu, as typified, in the films, by the ever-present Margaret Dumont dowager, does not know how to interpret these others. Are they simpletons or masterminds? Are they marginal, like their comments, or have they actually hijacked the center of meaning, and thus discursive primacy, to the margins? Are they risible or powerful? The heteroglossia of the Marx Brothers' discourse mirrors dominant anxieties over discursive authority on the part of the cultural other—through versatility and heterogeneity.[38] As has been noted elsewhere, the three better-known brothers represent a spectrum of differently threatening "stages" of assimilation—all of which manifest through talk, "from silent, childish dumbness (Harpo), through the accented, expressive, speaking, and marketeering adaptation (Chico), to the clever, manipulating and insulting mock professional (Groucho)."[39] Zeppo, verbally indistinguishable as other, holds perhaps the most menacing post of all. Groucho, in his character as the most acculturated and thus most "sophisticated" of the immigrant brothers, and the fastest "fast-talker," represents the most powerful discursive threat in his ability to confuse and seduce Margaret Dumont, as the high-class Anglo matron, who invariably capitulates—as Hildy does in *His Girl Friday*—if not into outright sex, than into willing miscegenation of his talk and her speech. These cases confirm Heidegger's worries, as talk assumes authority. Heidegger's fears of *Gerede's* disruption of dominant *Rede* point to *Gerede* as not only the other discourse but the discourse of the other—an other whose identity at once constitutes and is constituted in lack of sanctioned authority.

Cavell's name for talk is telling; *schmooz* is an affectionate term for chat from a people of the "Word"—repeatedly, historically, dispossessed of much else. It would be tempting to venture that the discomfiture of Heidegger, the German, or the ambivalence of Wittgenstein, the lapsed and perhaps self-hating Jew, echoes some complex, abstract ambivalence or discomfiture not just toward the performative threat posed to material orders by schmooz, but toward the keepers of it. (That's one thing talk can do: venture while refraining from it.)

Talk appears as effete, uncertain, excessive, inward, narcissistic, decadent, sneaky, threatening, neurotic. In some murky light, Semitic. Feminine, immigrant, low-class, queer, of color—too much color, coloring outside the lines. Historically, talk has been linked to alterity via tropes like "women's gossip," "chattering natives," and so forth. The tendency, then, of the right-thinking scholar would be to defend talk as salutary, liberatory, and all other good things. But is that right? Or even left?

Numerous protomodern sources link unrestrained talk to women's liberation and gender confusion; one 1894 London *Times* editorial complains that:

> The leading doctrine of the New Woman school, which contains a certain number of effeminate males, is that the thing worth living and working for is the free discussion of unsavoury subjects by men and women.[40]

From a later perspective, Patricia Spacks hails *Gerede*'s radical potential:

> It provides a resource for the subordinated (anyone can talk; with a trusted listener, anyone can say anything), a crucial means of self-expression, a crucial means of solidarity. (An account of women in the Muslim harem reports that they "exchange experience and information, and critically analyze . . . the world of men. The general tone . . . is one of satire, ridicule, and disrespect for males and the ideals of the male world." That's what I mean about "the subordinated.")[41]

Carla Kaplan echoes Spacks in positing talk as a feminist form, hoping to balance its seductive "erotics" with an ideal or "ethics" allowing fuller inclusion of marginalized voices.[42]

Certainly, talk does promote a sense of liberation on a valuable level. Where talk feels subversive, empowering—by very vital criteria it is. Silence has equalled death in many contexts. Talk may also, of course, lead to more talk into the right ears, or to grassroots bonding, or to action and the righting of a problem at its source. Jane Shattuc, analyzing television talk shows, finds that, though they are not feminist in every way, they do give voice to underrepresented women and may spur some form of women's solidarity and action.[43] Even where talk is "just talk," where no action is possible, where the cause of suffering is beyond reach, ubiquitous, indefinable, or absent, talk may relieve the pain of despair, need, ugliness, inequity—when nothing else will do, when nothing else remains.

Yet any untroubled assertion of the antireifying character of talk within a subordinated class—for instance Luce Irigaray's wishful assumption that women, objects, together, "commodities among themselves," will automatically speak as subjects—optimistically oversimplifies both the multiplicitous natures of what Lacan calls "je" and "moi" dynamics, as well as the "voice" and "the subject" altogether.[44] The term "girl-talk," recuperated as hip, to denote a tête-à-tête comprising anything from a firm feminist setting-straight, to an intimate outpouring, to talk about "boys," to gossip, to hair tips—like the pop use of "girlfriend" as a form of affectionate heterosexual female-female direct address (or queer male-male address, or . . .), or the recuperation of "nigger" between African Americans—illuminates precisely how complex subject-object relations, as tied to talk, can be. What talk cannot do, or not as simply as Irigaray would have it, is resolve the subject-object dialectic informing language, as system of signs, and constituting the impulse toward communication itself. Further, phenomena like hate speech on talk radio and the Internet provide examples of ungoverned subjectivity more difficult to call emancipatory.

Psychoanalytically, what appears a "talking cure" may well be a placebo or at best a deeply craved, addictive painkiller. "Catharsis" may merely equal temporary displacement, a notion on a parallel of curing death with aspirin. Moreover, being-able-to-say does not necessarily equate with knowing; J.-B. Pontalis, for instance, mourns the therapeutic failure of the great talker impervious to cure, the patient in whom talk, rather than aiding cure, functions as disease, the analysand who is an expert "at coding and decoding, prolific with word, dream and interpretation games, skilled at all kinds of combination," who at first dazzles, then finally bores the analyst with endless talky displacements, prevented from reaching "cure" precisely by these brilliant insights.[45] And yet further—even if there were some reliable bond between "meaning" and "saying"—as Wittgenstein notes in terms of testimony, even the most intentionally "frank" of talk, the most intentionally "true" of confessions, is cognitively structured by "what one is inclined to say," what occurs to one as essential to communicate.[46]

Politically, *Gerede*, especially in the hybridity of its post-oral bricolage, might be just as prone to re-reify as to liberate. We can only put out, arguably, some permutation of what we've taken in. In the Foucauldian formulation, all speech that involves a listener—not to mention an imagined listener, or previous exposure to narrative-form expectations: that is, all talk—cannot help but reflect and reproduce various dominant societal influences, including prevailing power relations. The talk-partner or listener is "not simply the interlocutor but the authority," the fact of whose presence calls talk into being, and who is situated to witness, and in doing so also to "judge, punish, forgive, console, and reconcile."[47] Although each instance of talk tends to take its own general shape, the talker—schmoozer, *bavard*, Gereder—is not any more linguistically self-determining than any other participant in language. *Gerede*, as a discursive practice that commonly appears as a *façon de parler* of our *être*, in fact may merely stand as one part of our constitution-by-and-in-language—our *parlêtre*—our thrownness-into-language in which being and talking, identity and otherness, are inextricably interwoven.

An ethical question might be raised, as against any blithe declarations of talk as formally, and thus by some dint politically, radical, in terms of calls for "vocativity"—a thorough implication of and intercourse with the "du" in the discourse of the "Ich." The "unproductive" self-referentiality noted by Phelan of performance might also be viewed as effecting some degree of formal solipsism antagonistic to the ideal communicative communitarianism envisioned by Buber, Levinas, or Habermas. All in all, it is clearly a grand error to consider all talk "free expression" in either the hawkish or hippie senses; there are numerous counterweights to the neo-Foucauldian impulse to assign political rectitude, or leftitude, to all seemingly "liberatory" forms.

On a pragmatic political level, while talk may on the surface appear an alchemical assumption of phallic power—the naming-and-judging role—on the part of the disempowered, the space of material lack, filled by talk as if by placebo, is still, in the final analysis, material lack. While *Gerede*, perhaps, powers culture and cultural politics—we may think of "buzz," "hype," Internet opinion polls, and the collision of talk, speech, and constitutional text in the Clinton impeachment fiasco—equal possibilities may be heard in *Gerede* and *Rede* for the reinscription of power dynamics, as well as the re-reification and commodification of communicative functions. Blowing off steam, arguably, co-opts revolutionary energy. "Free speech," perhaps, is most free where talk is cheap. Though Lukacsian warnings against formal fragmentation as conducive to maintenance of dominant political structures have long been dismissed out of hand, experience of the talky disorientation of the "cyberdemocratic" information age would seem, if intuitively and perhaps erroneously, to bear them out. Total discursivity appears, on some order, a totalization as well.

Poison, remedy, drug, "beneficent or maleficent" substance/nonsubstance/antisubstance: talk may be taken as a form of what Derrida codes the *pharmakon*. Drug and medicine, addiction and cure, talk is potent. The danger of the draught—like the one Alice drank or the one Plato couldn't swallow—is that it seduces one to "stray from one's general, natural, habitual patterns and laws . . . [it takes one] out of his proper place and off his customary track."[48] Of course, it may be harnessed, like the atom—yet, as with the atom, not likely mastered in full.

Notes

1. *Oxford English Dictionary* (Oxford: Clarendon Press, 1987). All emphasis mine. *Talk* is said to derive from the Danish *tal*, to count, hence perhaps the relation to "telling"—

in the sense of notes or votes—and notions of talk as "retelling" (reminiscent of Heidegger's *Gerede*, roughly "that which has already been spoken," to indicate talk as something retold or rehashed).

2. *Webster's Dictionary of English Usage* (Springfield, MA: Merriam-Webster, 1989).

3. James T. Rogers, ed., *The Dictionary of Clichés* (New York: Facts on File Publications, 1985).

4. Stanley Cavell, *Themes out of School: Effects and Causes* (San Francisco: North Point Press, 1984), xi–xii.

5. Michel Foucault, *The Order of Things: An Archaeology of the Human Sciences* (New York: Vintage Books, 1994), 39.

6. Martin Heidegger, *Being and Time* (New York: Harper and Row, 1962), 213.

7. Ibid., 212–13. It is, seemingly, possible to "say something," but not to "talk something"; it is possible to *dire quelque chose*, but not to *parler quelque chose*; it is possible to *etwas sagen*, but not to *etwas reden*. "Saying" seems to have a stranglehold on life as direct object.

8. Avital Ronell, *The Telephone Book* (Lincoln: University of Nebraska Press, 1989)—beyond value here.

9. Heidegger, Being and Time, 212–13.

10. John Searle, *Speech Acts: An Essay in the Philosophy of Language* (Cambridge: Cambridge University Press, 1969).

11. Walter Ong, *Orality and Literacy: The Technologizing of the Word* (London and New York: Routledge, 1982), 3.

12. Julia Kristeva, *Performance: A Critical Introduction* (London and New York: Routledge, 1996), 79.

13. See Niklaus Luhmann, *Social Systems*, trans. John Bednarz Jr. with Dirk Baeker (Stanford, CA: Stanford University Press, 1995).

14. See Pierre Bourdieu, *Language and Symbolic Power* (Cambridge: Polity Press, 1991).

15. Mikhail Bakhtin, *The Dialogic Imagination: Four Essays*, ed. Michael Holquist, trans. Caryl Emerson and Michael Holquist (Austin: University of Texas Press, 1981), 56.

16. Ong, *Orality and Literacy*, 8. As one example, Ong characterizes oral culture as favoring additive constructions ("and . . .") over more complicated conjunctions ("meanwhile . . .") It might be noted that novelistic discourse involves more in the way of these complicated conjunctions than, for instance the medieval. Seemingly, then, Ong's notion of secondary orality describes less a binary than a relative condition. As another note: discourses of primary orality can be considered at once spontaneous and informed by other oral textual structures; and just as speakerly discourse informs writerly discourse, speakerly discourse is informed by written textual structures (see also Henry Louis Gates, *The Signifying Monkey: A Theory of African-American Literary Criticism* [New York and Oxford: Oxford University Press, 1988], 131).

17. Certain oppositions of orality to literacy are fairly identical to those in Heidegger that pit *Gerede* against *Rede*. As Ong demonstrates, orality may be seen to bear even more problematic relations to presence, and thus authority and evidence, than its rival (*Orality and Literacy*, 78). Orality, in comparison to textuality, may be received as disordered or even threatening to law and order (174). It appears undetached from the personal and thus may be characterized as at once more reliable, less reliable, deeper, and more trivial (78, 48, 14, 178–79). In most regards, *Gerede* is to *Rede* as orality is to literacy, with the greater burden of cultural prejudice—despite philosophical privileg-

ings of speech over textuality—falling upon the former in each case (110).

18. Patricia Meyer Spacks, *Gossip* (New York: Knopf, 1985), 26.

19. See Tom Cohen, *Anti-Mimesis from Plato to Hitchcock* (Cambridge: Cambridge University Press), 1994; and Judith Butler, *Bodies That Matter: On the Discursive Limits of "Sex"* (New York: Routledge, 1993).

20. All language, as compared to the materiality it purports to signify, is thus in the Platonic sense already fallen, ersatz, supplemental in relation to the presence for which it is an inferior stand-in ("seeing is believing"). Writing involves the absence, which implicates it, for Plato, as debased simulacrum; however—despite Plato—writing's materiality may lead it to be perceived as more allied to the object, on the basis of its own status as substitute object. Writing, in fact, may be more privileged over speech in certain contexts in our time ("get it in writing") as more material, closer to the "truth" represented by matter, which, in turn, trades on presence. *Rede* would also seem to carry the stigma of absence; a strict scientific statement in a formal lecture still describes and manipulates matter not-present-in-the-same-capacity-as-language-can-render-it, and still establishes particular relations between speaker and audience and speaker and world. Since the object is not present in a form that can provide indisputable "proof," many factors are open to question: the truth of the statement, the authority of the speaker in relation to the audience, the authority of the speaker in relation to the world of objects, and so on.

21. Ludwig Wittgenstein, *Philosophical Investigations*, trans. G. E. M. Anscombe (Oxford: Blackwell, 1972).

22. In a related notion, sanctioned rhetorics appear to reside in the unreachable, idealized, static realm of linguistic structure—the *enoncé*, or what Noam Chomsky calls "competence"—rather than in the accessible, flawed, variable realm of language-in-use—*énonciation*, or what Chomsky calls "performance."

23. On Frege and assertion, see Wittgenstein, *Philosophical Investigations*, 154.

24. See Cohen, *Anti-Mimesis*.

25. Stanley Cavell, *Pursuits of Happiness: The Hollywood Comedy of Remarriage* (Cambridge, MA: Harvard University Press, 1981), 79. As Cavell notes, there is a certain optimism in Walter and Hildy's world, in that, despite all its brutality and dross, its social conditions are improvable through the sorts of communication these reporters provide.

26. Anthony Kubiak, *Stages of Terror: Terrorism, Ideology, and Coercion as Theatre History* (Bloomington: Indiana University Press, 1991), 1–3.

27. Cavell, *Pursuits of Happiness*, 172. As Cavell notes, their intimacy, even during marriage, seems always to have been relegated to the office and a certain restaurant—uncomfortable, unhomey, even *Unheimlich* spaces. Sex is not the prime currency, or current, between couples in public; verbal intercourse is, and Walter's skill exceeds Bruce's in this.

28. Peggy Phelan, *Unmarked* (New York: Routledge, 1993), 148–53.

29. Jacques Derrida, *Of Grammatology*, trans. Gayatri Chakravorty Spivak (Baltimore: Johns Hopkins University Press, 1976), 123.

30. Ong, *Orality and Literacy*, 78. At later points, Ong also convincingly argues the opposite, that writing, in offering enduring, repeatable proof—its trace—is the more reliable (48).

31. Anne Ubersfeld, *Lire le théâtre* (Paris: Belin, 1982), 13; translation mine.

32. *Rede* may be seen to carry this same problem to an extent, for instance, when intonation matters, as in a political address, but then it is the "chat" aspect of the address—the motion toward *Gerede* within *Rede*—that is at issue. The reproduction of the con-

tent of a scientific lecture for informational purposes—unless there is some more sub-jective interpretive or cultural content to be divined—is less troubled. As long as all data, formulae, and such are accurately recorded, the speaker's manner of presenta-tion—any texture as may be involved—matters little.

33. From *Monkey Business*, quoted in Stanley Cavell, "The Marx Brothers' Immigrant Talk," in this volume. Cavell identifies "Thomas Shefsky" as Boris Thomashevsky of Yiddish theater fame.

34. Phelan, *Unmarked*, 148–49.

35. Jan Gordon, *Gossip and Subversion in Nineteenth-Century British Fiction* (London: Macmillan, 1996), ix.

36. See also Kierkegaard's wish to regulate his neighbors' chitchat: "Its subject matter is nonexistent from the ideal point of view. It always consists of some trivial fact such as that Mr. Marsden is engaged and has given his fiancee a Persian shawl; that Petersen, the poet, is going to write some new poems, or that Marcussen, the actor, mispro-nounced a certain word last night. If we could suppose for a moment that there was a law which did not forbid people talking, but simply ordered that everything that was spoken about should be treated as though it had happened fifty years ago, the gossips would be done for, they would be in despair." In Spacks, *Gossip*, 71–72.

37. From *A Night at the Opera*, quoted in Cavell, in this volume.

38. Similarly, the disruptive Wildean aphorism has been noted as Irish "guerilla" subversion in form of Anglo discursive dominance via insistence on stereotypically Irish tropes of blarney (see Declan Kiberd, "Oscar Wilde: The Resurgence of Lying," in *The Cambridge Companion to Oscar Wilde*, ed. Peter Raby [Cambridge: Cambridge University Press, 1997], 277; and Jerusha McCormack, "Wilde's Fiction(s)," also in Raby, *Wilde*, 98). The sterotype of the "shifty" subaltern may be seen to reside largely in notions of propensity toward shape-shifting and significance-shifting; the Marx Brothers' talk, as Cavell argues, plays into these cultural anxieties.

39. Claire Pajaczkowska and Barry Curtis, "Assimilation, Entertainment, and the Hollywood Studios," in *The Jew in the Text*, ed. Linda Nochlin and Tamar Garb (New York: Thames and Hudson, 1995).

40. Quoted in Alan Sinfield, *The Wilde Century: Effeminacy, Oscar Wilde, and the Queer Moment* (New York: Columbia University Press, 1994), 77.

41. Spacks, *Gossip*, 5.

42. See Carla Kaplan, "Talk Ethics and Erotics," in this volume, as well as her *The Erotics of Talk: Women's Writing and Feminist Paradigms* (New York and Oxford: Oxford University Press, 1996), 162.

43. Jane Shattuc, *The Talking Cure: TV Talk Shows and Women* (New York and London: Routledge, 1997), 136.

44. Luce Irigaray, *This Sex Which Is Not One* (Ithaca, NY: Cornell University Press, 1985), 192.

45. J.-B. Pontalis, *Frontiers in Psychoanalysis: Between the Dream and Psychic Pain*, trans. Catherine Cullen and Philip Cullen (London: Hogarth Press), 163.

46. Wittgenstein, *Philosophical Inquiry*, 156.

47. Michel Foucault, *The History of Sexuality, Volume One* (New York: Pantheon, 1978), 61–62.

48. Jacques Derrida, *Dissemination*, trans. Barbara Johnson (Chicago: University of Chicago Press, 1981), 70.

Chat

The Arts of Conversation

two

Dialogue 3

Antigone, Speech, Performance, Power

Judith Butler

and Paul Rabinow

Paul: So Judy. What are you working on?

Judith: Well, right now, I'm working on *Antigone*. I'm trying to figure out the ways in which Antigone stands up to Creon and what sorts of language she uses to stand up to him.

And I'm struck by the fact that her language, in fact, tends to replicate his. And that she's more profoundly implicated in his language—and, in particular, his invocation of sovereignty—than one might expect. Because, I think, conventionally—perhaps most paradigmatically in Hegel—Antigone is understood as simply opposing Creon and as standing for a wholly different principle: the principle of kinship over and against the principle of the state.

And I guess I want to start with her speech acts, which are significant because we get no evidence that she's actually *buried* her brother; all we get is her saying: Yes I did it, or, I will not deny that I did it. And it seems to me that the confession that she did it is as bad as the deed that she did, and it's unclear whether her verbal act is tantamount to the criminal act that she performed.

I'm interested in this question of how a verbal act can be understood as criminal.

And then I'm also interested in the broader question of whether one can actually separate questions of kinship from questions of the state. I want to suggest that they are more radically implicated in each other than conventional readings of the play would allow. And that one might use *Antigone* as a point of departure for thinking about those problems as they're being experienced—not just nationally, but globally, where the question of family is being administered quite intensively, I think, by international and state apparati of various kinds. So that gives you a couple of things—

Paul: Does it ever. But how did you get there? Why there? I mean, this is in some ways a jump—

Judith: In some ways yes, in some ways no. I recently published a book on hate speech, called *Excitable Speech: A Politics of the Performative*.[1] There, I was looking at the problem that has emerged as a result of hate-speech regulation within the U.S.—but also, I think, within the European Union—the problem of whether speech wounds and how it wounds, what's the status of its wounding power.

Some, for instance Catherine MacKinnon, would say that speech wounds, or is approximate to a wound, and ought to be understood—in certain contexts where it's hate speech—as discriminatory conduct. And that the speech/conduct distinction ought not to hold where we are considering speech that is directed against minorities, speech that is directed against women. Because that speech can effectively undermine their capacity to function in the world, in the same way that discriminatory conduct can affect one's capacity to function in the world, or at least in the public sphere.

I take this description very seriously, and do agree that language has its own quite pointed, hurtful power. I do, however, have some questions as to whether it's the same injury as physical injury and whether it ought to be modeled on that, legally or otherwise.

I'm also interested in the insurrectionary power of the speech act, its power to produce conceptual shifts that are politically consequential. I think that there is in the U.S. an emphasis on the speech act—for instance, the speech act of coming out as a homosexual—as a powerful act. It's considered injurious and offensive by some—the military, for instance, understands coming out as, virtually, hate speech. And then the question becomes, well, who's going to decide when and where this language is hurtful and offensive, and who's going to decide when and where it's insurrectionary and crucial for opening up an episteme that has been closed to what is being said.

Antigone is sort of great in this regard because she does perform a speech act by claiming that she did the deed. She owns the deed that she did, which is in itself a somewhat awesome thing: she's asserting that she's a sovereign subject who performs an act, and that it is her act and hers alone. And she won't let anyone else take credit for the act. Ismene tries to come in, claim solidarity, says: I'll say I did it too. Antigone says: No, no, *you* didn't do it. So it's not a notion of feminist solidarity that one derives from Antigone! I think that's one of the misappropriations one sees in Luce Irigaray and others.

I do think that the owning of the deed is a radical act, and that it's a punishable act in her case. And yet, I think that the power of utterance is not hers alone, even though she claims it is. I think, in fact, it's mimetically related to Creon's language, in the same way that he wants his sovereignty to be absolutely unabrogatable, absolutely powerful, unilaterally powerful. She wants her language to have that same effect, and I think they are both engaged in what I understand as a certain kind of fantasy of sovereign power within the speech act.

Paul: But nonetheless one with consequences as well.

Judith: With enormous consequences. And this is part of what I criticize in the sovereign speech act, part of what I tried to accomplish in *Excitable Speech*. So I suppose I'm furthering that in this other domain.

I think that one thing that actually happens in the play is that Creon condemns Antigone to this cave where she's locked in alive, and she actually describes herself prior to being condemned to this living death as somebody who has been serving death her whole life. Of course, Oedipus's curse is upon her as it is on his children. And his curse is, of course, that they shouldn't have to live.

And then the question is: What is the sphere of living or not living? It's linked, of course, to what Orlando Patterson described as social death, like the situation of slavery, where death again is—I'm hesitant to call it—metaphorical.

Paul: That's a good question: it's not quite metaphorical, but it's not quite literal either.

Judith: It's as if it's a different zone of death, its own ontological register of death. I think what interests me is the way in which—because Antigone is already at the border of the intelligible, after all; her father was her brother—she's already defied kinship, she's already slightly monstrous, she's already at the edge of the human because she's at the edge of kinship. The questions whether her speech is speech, her life is life, her death is death, all, I think, become really quite crucial.

Similarly, I think that there is a zone—Giorgio Agamben describes this well in *Homo Sacer*—of, say, stateless persons who are and are not persons.[2] And are and are not living, and are and are not recognizable as such. And then the question is how do you go about describing that kind of liminality? And what language is available for that? And what language is available to them? Which may even be the more important question.

What I'm interested in is the language of the insistence that a given family is a family even if it doesn't accord with the accepted laws of kinship. It's at the edge of kinship; it's an aberration of kinship. It's an aberration, yet at the same time it is yet a further instance of it. A person who is not a citizen is still a person, even though we know that citizenship exercises this conceptual constraint on our thinking of personhood, politically. It seems to me that there's a moment where the person who's not a person, the family that is not a family, has to use the dominant lanugage and use it in a way that misuses it and contaminates it in order to allow it to mean something else or something different.

Fredric Jameson is one who, I think, would say, look, any attempt to do that simply culminates in the domestication of the claim. It will end up being an assimilation of the claim; that claim will be contained within the dominant power. That there's no way of entering into using that language, misusing it, opening up something through it because no such resistance is possible, no such subversion is possible. That language is more powerful than any of those speakers and will contain and domesticate it and vitiate their claim.

I think that view of power, that kind of systemic totality that eats things—I think that that's not quite right. So I guess what I'm interested in is what happens to speech at that border.

Paul: Let me ask you a thing on that: One of the foundational self-styled human claims—I'm thinking of Luc Ferry, whom I particularly detest, so I'll use him as an example—is that people as persons immediately recognize other people—

Now, anthropologically, of course, I think that's wrong. So in this discussion of both anthropology and violence—which is really in one way what we're talking about—how do you react to that? These liminal zones are ones in which these boundaries get articulated—so—

Judith: I think recognition continues to be an important category. And—I mean—I have some friends who are more strongly Nietzschean than I am, who actually think that the language of recognition as it comes from Hegel is a slave morality, that to want recognition is to want a certain kind of subordination to an already existing norm. I actually think that even reading Hegel you don't need to accept that notion of recognition because I think that even in Hegel that recognition also brings into being what it recognizes—that it's not just a recognition of what is already there, but that is has—

Paul: —a productive—

Judith: Yes. Dimension. That's crucial. What I've sought to do is think about the struggle for recognition, that the capacity for recognition and what is recognizable is given to us through various discourses that constrain the recognizable as such: what will and will not be a recognizable person, what will and will not be a recognizable gender, what will and will not be a recognizable sexuality, what will and will not be a recognizable race—which is most interesting given the way in which it exceeds the binary in every moment. And whether categorization even works in the service of recognition.

Paul: And the various regimes which have been in place to do that. We're probably on the edge of some new ones.

Judith: When the Beijing Woman's Conference happened a couple of years ago, there were two interesting, related feminist centers of organization. One was something called "women's human rights," and another one had to do with lesbian human rights. And it was really strange, this strange redundancy: woman/human, lesbian/human. Why?

Why, because, on the one hand, those terms—*women, lesbian*—have not been conventionally admitted into the human, or what is recognizable as the human, as the human has been mandated by, not simply United Nations regulation, but international law at some level. And yet it wasn't a call for assimilation, it wasn't just human rights, it wasn't just: Okay, let's all gather a meeting for all of the human. I think by staging these political movements in this way, it also exposed something about the contingency of the human, the contingent definition of the human, what it excludes and what it has excluded in order to achieve the coherence that it has. And how the mechanisms of its exclusion and the contingency of its definition can be brought into light and called into question.

I thought that was good, I thought that was useful precisely because it disturbed people, and it disturbed them, I think, at the level on which they were thinking the human. They thought, like Ferry, that they know the human when they see it. They don't want to think that their capacity to recognize other humans is itself profoundly mediated by discourses that, in fact, efface.

And not just a simple effacement, right? They don't just efface, but they condemn—I actually think Creon is good here—they condemn a part of the population to living in that liminal place where they are and are not human. On the one hand one would say: Of course they're human! You know: Of course they're human! I see them on the street; they're human! Right? But on another level, where the normative constraints of the human are operating perhaps more fiercely—they're not. We're not talking about groups that are simply erased, or simply effaced, or simply rendered invisible. They are visible, they are there, but they are there in an ontologically suspended mode.

Paul: Indeed. But then you're in this situation, as you've been describing it, of where to push that. Is this this Habermasian notion that we need to extend the public sphere further? Obviously you have a more troubled position than that.

Judith: I do. Although my Habermasian friend Seyla Benhabib says, No, no, I'm moving in the exact same direction that she is! So what do I do with that? I'm nervous.

I think that what I'm trying to do is develop a way to put the language of ontology into crisis and to make clear that when we endow somebody with the status of being a citizen, when we endow somebody with the status of being a gender, that there is an attribution of ontology that issues from that institutionalized act of recognition—

I actually don't want anyone to *be* anything. Okay? I suppose that's where I differ. I actually don't want anyone ever to actually achieve or be *anything*! It's a terrible thing to say! I know! I can just hear my detractors. But I think that once we recognize, as it were, that this ontological status is produced, retracted, suspended by various kinds of institutionalized, discursive regimes, that the question is how we mobilize those regimes and for what purpose. I think I'm not just interested in passing out—making sure that everybody has, now—a badge of ontology.

Paul: Or complete deconstruction for its own sake, either. There are dangers, clearly, in that.

Judith: That's right, no. It's politically nonsensical to call for that. I think that's an impossibility. . . . There was a conference in Santa Cruz called "Left Conservatism." I thought: Oh, well, this is interesting, there are some conservative trends on the left; we could talk about that. I actually thought it might be an intellectual discussion in which we'd talk about, you know, how it is that people can be on the left and oppose certain other movements on the left and, in fact, have quite conservative feelings about them, and the shifting of balance within the conservative; like, Who's conservative? Of course it was not an intellectual discussion because the conference flyer named people as being exemplary; without my knowing I arrived at a scene with everyone angry because their friends had been named as left conservatives by the organizer.

Now what became interesting was that there are a whole lot of people who work in cultural studies, cultural theory, diasporic studies, contemporary race, ethnic studies, who probably think there's an old left, and they would say that kind of older left is conservative. It might be conservative epistemologically; it might hold to certain foundationalisms this more sort of postmodern group wouldn't hold to; it might be conservative in the sense that it thinks we ought to return to class, or Todd Gitlin's notion of a common world. The more postmodern group is saying: No, no, we're all a bunch of differences; how are you going to make a coalition out of all these differences?

But the folks who are part of a more entrenched left and who write for *The Nation* and so forth maybe have no idea that they're being talked about as conservative. And some of the folks who are part of this ostensibly postmodern movement also have absolutely no idea of how deeply they are despised for claiming the mantle of leftism and even being recognized culturally as leftists when these other folks in fact have been involved in leftist politics and work for a very, very long time. And there are not just two camps; there are a whole lot of people in-between, there are a lot of people whose main point in life is to prevent a division between those two, right, and who can't bear the idea of this kind of split—for whom it is utterly painful.

What seemed to me very interesting was the use of the terms "conservative"—"*Do not* call me conservative!"—and "leftist": "*You're* not a leftist!" In some ways it just boiled down to that; it was like fourth grade! "I *am not* a conservative!" "You *are not* a leftist!" The real questions seemed to be: *What* do those terms mean; *who's* going to own them; *who's* going to be excluded by virtue of that ownership? Can the title "left" be mutually owned by groups who do not always see eye to eye with one another?

Unfortunately, the discussion never got to that. It never actually became an interesting discussion on how such terms travel. I do think, for instance, that the term "liberal" has undergone an enormous transformation in the last twenty years—and not simply by being travestied by the right. Certain things are now called and affirmed as liberal that were twenty years ago just patently centrist or even right-wing. This is the travel of the word; it's not exactly the same as historical change on the broader level. But I do think it's an index of something.

Paul: It's energy-draining. When you constantly have to talk about definitions of terms—"postmodern" is another one, trying to explain to people who should know better that it doesn't mean anything—

Judith: An empty term—

Paul: It keeps you back. It takes up an incredible amount of time.

Judith: Huge. But I do *like* the moment when the terms don't work. Or where the epistemological unceatainty, the semantic uncertainty of the term is brought into light in the way that makes people think: Well I'm not quite sure I can use that word anymore, or, I'm not quite sure what I mean when I say X. And that's, I think, a very creative moment, an intellectually interesting moment.

If only this event had, in fact, produced that: Oh, what do I mean by left? What do I mean by conservative? How is it that others couldn't see it that way. . . . But there was an inability to occupy the perspective of the folks who were using the term in a way that they couldn't quite see. I had no interest in a war. I was going to try to look at this as something that I thought was really interesting and that needed to be opened up so there might be some kind of dialogue about it, but I was naively liberal. I was naively hopeful about the possibility of dialogue. Those lines were really deeply drawn.

But this is what I think: I think that on some level people know that they don't own those words. And here it brings us back to the question of sovereignty and speech. At some level, I think that people on the left know they do not own that word, "left." And that people who are called "postmodern"—even though they don't know what postmodernism is (they maybe think it's an architectural style . . .).

Whatever these terms *are*, they are enormously loaded and people really want to use them and consolidate them through their use, and use them precisely by drawing lines: *You* are and *you* are not. And I think it's a way to shore up a sense of sovereign command over a language that one cannot control.

And I do think it is of the character of political discourse, perhaps of our time. I don't know how to generalize this—I don't know how generalizable it is—but I would say that at least for those of us who are still living under the weight of sovereignty and in the shadow of sovereignty and in the wake of sovereignty, whatever this is, that it is out of our control, that there is no way to rein it in.

In the same way I think one can't say in hate-speech legislation: Come up with the utterances that we know to be unequivocally hurtful. Because those utterances are also in the process of being reappropriated and being— It's part of the temporality in the life of language that one is trying to in some sense paralyze or stop short in order to regain the sense of control.

Paul: And positioning.

Judith: And positioning. I actually think that to live politically now means to find a way to affirm that temporal dislocation and to affirm the dislocation of sovereignty. Which is why I say these folks are not—they may think I'm the enemy, I can't help that, but these are—not my enemies. These are not my enemies.

I think that what I do rail against—Antigone-like, perhaps—is the smugness of those who think it's all come to an end. The smugness of those who think they know what community is, who think they know what universality is, who think that it's already been defined, and that we have it, and that we have access to it, either a priori or through some kind of European historical achievement—God forbid. And that those who resist this, who say that in fact there's an open future or that these terms are in crisis—and good that they are—are nihilist, decadent, relativist, and that the consequence of their relativism is a paralysis of politics.

Paul: One of the conversations that I've had a number of times on this theme has been with friends in Paris who are very adamant that gay couples must be raising psychotic children. And these are thinkers, people who are socialists or communists or Trotskyites or leftists of all friendly bourgeois sorts who are defending all the right things in every other realm. It is particularly striking to listen to that—and hence I provoke it all the time when I'm in the mood—and I say: Well, I don't know, I'm an anthropologist and live in California and I haven't noticed more or less psychotic kids running around with gay couples—

It's the question of the boundary—watching where the boundary is and where people are invested in drawing the zone and saying that beyond this you are not any longer a member of the moral community. . . .

Judith: Your question brings us back to the sphere of liminality. What would it mean for the psychotic to speak and to make a claim, and to go to school, and—

I do think boundary lines shift when certain kinds of contradictory formations emerge, and where a certain kind of really intense dissonance emerges. I think that when you hold that view that such kids would be psychotic, and then the putatively psychotic kid comes over to your house—and wants a cookie, wants to play with your kitten, tells you about his feelings about balloons—there's a certain kind of insistent mundaneness that, I think, undermines that highly phobic relationship, maybe even lives in some kind of tension with it until it breaks open to something else, until it becomes unsustainable in some way.

Paul: So you are mildly optimistic.

Judith: I am mildly optimistic about it. Because I think I've seen this work. . . .
I do actually see this, I think I've seen this happen again and again over generations. I do think that there are times when over and against certain kinds of phobic responses to this kind of family, to that kind of citizen, there is the possibility of asking: What kind of community do we want to be? What kind of world do we want to live in? What kind of university do we want to be? Do we really look like the University of Alabama in 1954? What kind of state do we—I mean there's a normative question that opens, where the question of who we are and what we want to be is not yet decided, and where there is a decision to be made.

Paul: I'm rather pessimistic about that these days.

Judith: I am too. But I continue to see ways in which people do retreat from their positions of extreme phobic exclusion because they are so deeply proximate to precisely those they would exclude, or they find that they love them—inadvertently!—or they need them or their kid does, or shopping—
There's just this force of mundanity that I think is actually working against the logic of exclusion even as it's enormously powerful. I am interested in those moments of crisis.

Paul: But there seem to be two registers here. One is the level on which the forces of societal segregation—particularly racial segregation—are strong and would be working against that. For instance, in the case of many of the public schools, where there's de facto desegregation through immigration—but also endless microredrawing of separation on both sides, a schizmogenic sort of mechanism in which the kids are not interacting much at all. Then at the same time there's the normative discourse you're affirming—that there's an enlarging sphere both of rationality and of some normativity, of minimal normativity and citizenship. . . . I think there are narratives of progress, but others which seem particularly grim these days.

Judith: No, I agree, it's more grim than I ever thought it could be, there's just no question about that. There's no logic I'm pointing to that will magically reverse that grimness. . . .
One of the reasons I think someone like Cornel West is as powerful an orator as he is is that he knows damn well what the grimness is. But he invokes—as I think Jesse Jackson did in a different register—a posture of hope, of utopianism, of the future which goes against all the odds.

You know, folks on the left will say: Ugh. I don't want to hear about *America*. Everything that's wrong has been done under the rubric of America. And he'll say: No, no, we have to *seize* this term; we have to seize this legacy, America, and make it mean and emphatically change what it's been. He opens it up and—

I mean, it's a rhetorical gesture which one might say feels good while you're listening, but can't really do anything—yet I do think he goes for that moment of contingency. Where what has been, what is, is not the extent of what will be. . . .

Paul: It very much seems to me that fixed ontologies are an important locus of, and have a very long history of, being the sites of violence that we know about.

Judith: And the institutional—I would even say the institutional fixing— of the ontological to the point where one no longer sees the trace of the institution in the ontological effect that it produces. And this is also why the Santa Cruz arena ended up taking this quite vicious turn, at least after the event. Because, I think it was this wanting to hold on to the term, the meaning of the term: The term means this, I am this, you are this.

Paul: So it's the fixedness and the sovereignty dimension of it.

Judith: Yes, and the notion that one might be able to fix a term to its ontological referent through a masterful sovereign act, which then makes it yours and which makes it yours to control. So I think it's the fixity of the ontological in the service of this fantasy of sovereign control.

And I actually do believe it is a more nonviolent way to live, not insisting on having the control of those terms. Which is not the same as giving them over to institutions that will control them more forcibly than you ever could—reinscribing race, reinscribing sexuality as these naturalized phenomena—I wouldn't say that.

But I think there has to be an active effort to open those kinds of reinscriptions up, in fact reenter them into an ontologically liminal zone, because there I think the point is not that you take the ontological liminality of Antigone, or the citizen who's not a citizen, and say: Okay, make them real. You must, I think, expose the apparatus by which the real is produced, reproduced, et cetera. . . .

Well. That's all I have to say. . . .

Judith: Oh, I'm sure that's not true, but. . . .

Notes

1. Judith Butler, *Excitable Speech: A Politics of the Performative* (New York: Routledge, 1997).
2. Giorgio Agamden, *Homo Sacer: Sovereign Power and Bare Life*, trans. Daniel Heller-Roazen (Stanford, CA: Stanford University Press, 1998).

Idle Talk

4

Scarcity and Excess in Literary Language

Alexander Gelley

The noun "talk" implies a kind of empty state of language, a condition more pronounced in locutions like "just talk" or "idle talk." The implication is that proper talk is "about" something or else "doing" something. Is there a way to measure language practices in which the issue of efficacy, of what the utterance is supposed to accomplish, is suspended? My aim in this essay will be to examine instances of fictional narrative where language, and notably spoken language, dialogue, and first-person narration, is operative at a minimal level, not "saying much" but still active.

In literary usage, talk, speech, dialogue, and other such modes of oral articulation are, of course, conveyed in writing. The premise of narration is the *enactment* or representation of speech, a point that is implicit in the French term *discours*—the act of telling, with special reference to the source or agency—as it has been used in narrative theory. This concept has been developed by Emil Benveniste and others in opposition to *récit*—the story told or narrative content.[1] As Gérard Genette has claimed, this differentiation (or "frontier") within narrative is not always easy to make, but it has its uses at a theoretical level. *Discours*, according to Genette, is a pervasive phenomenon whereas *récit* or narrative proper, at least in the more traditional literary forms, is more restricted and can be isolated on the basis of internal stylistic criteria. But more recently the tendency of fiction, Genette continues, has been to "absorb the *récit* in the present discourse of the writer in the process of writing. . . . In this sense it appears that literature has exhausted or moved beyond its own representational resources, and has sought to enfold itself in the indefinite murmur of its own discourse."[2]

How might we specify what Genette terms the "indefinite murmur" of literature? Could this be a "noise" that is not merely a flaw but a component of the system?[3] What does speech in narrative do when it is not conveying the content or substance of a narrative? What I am looking for are instances where there is a hollowing out of *what* is said, but the act of talking remains. One way to focus on this issue is to pay particular attention to language that is deemed low, formulaic, or "empty"—gossip, chatter, prattle, *idiotismes*. It is this kind of inadvertence in language that I think of as speech in an "idling" state. Philosophers and critics have not often turned their attention to this question, being more concerned with fully realized language practices.

Peter Fenves's *"Chatter": Language and History in Kierkegaard* is one of the few works of criticism that is seriously concerned with the issue at hand. Fenves distinguishes his undertaking from that of various disciplinary approaches—in psychology, sociology, anthropology, media studies, philosophy, literary criticism—that evaluate gossip "according to its ambivalent social function: it can be an instrument of social control as well as a means of resistance to authority."[4] To the extent that they do so, such approaches underwrite the traditional goal of rhetoric, namely, to further the functionality, the pragmatic effectiveness of language. But Fenves focuses on "catastrophes" that take place in talking, catastrophes "to which the subject is exposed when its speech, including the statement 'I think,' can no longer be said to shelter it from an ungraspable and unappropriable, always altering outside."[5]

Apparently meaningless talk has often been analyzed in terms of group idiolects, as a mechanism for the maintenance of social cohesion. But such approaches must assume a givenness of language and then argue that a kind of group-speak is deficient or misses the mark. Fenves claims that the idea of a collectivity in this sense, far from avoiding the problematic of the subject, postulates the possibility of gathering "the subject into a whole, even when the speech of the collective is somehow uncollected, indeed distracted and dissipated." Such a detour cannot resolve the problematic: "Chatter 'itself,'" writes Fenves, "can be clarified only if emptiness and idleness command respect, if they are treated as traits of language in its retreat from the task of fulfilling functions and contributing to already established operations, if the very concepts of emptiness and idleness disengage themselves from symmetrical opposition to fullness and proper functioning."[6] Fenves is right to insist that the kind of negativity in language that he terms chatter cannot be specified with reference to a fully realized communicative functionality. One cannot presume a plenitude of language in relation to which chatter or idle talk represents a lapse, and yet something like a lapse can be instanced. The aim of this essay is to examine certain texts in which talk is explicitly marked as deficient in meaning, whether through lack or excess. Such a feature may, of course, be understood in terms of traditional narrative functions such as characterization or social setting; that is, idle talk or gossip may serve as a trait of character at the level of the individual or the collective. But in works such as those I consider, it seems to me that another principle is at work, one designed to disclose fault lines or "catastrophes" in the structure of language and meaning.

In Louis-René des Forêts's novel *Le Bavard*[7] the exhibition of bavardage as a social pathology serves as point of departure for a testing of the reader, a testing in which the status of literature is balanced between fascination and boredom. In Henry James's "In the Cage" the setting of the narrative—the meshed cage of a telegraph office situated in a grocery store—is replicated in a play of concealment and disclosure in which multiple systems of coding—private, telegraphic, social—play their parts. Finally, in James's *The Sacred Fount* the reader is presented with a narrative persona whose obsessive interest in the amorous ties of fellow guests at a house party is far more compelling than the objects of his scrutiny. In each of these examples I will try to demonstrate that the dimension of meaning, the putative narrative content or diegesis, is subject to a slippage or eclipse, and that what remains is a discourse of evasion, a species of idle talk.

While the title of des Forêts's novel *Le Bavard* might suggest a character sketch in the manner of La Bruyère's *Caractères*, the work is an extended monologue *by* the bavard, and constitutes, in effect, a demonstration rather than an illustration. The title indicates in the first instance not "character" in the sense of a bundle of traits but rather the kind of action or effect to be expected from such an agent. And the goal of this agent will be less to draw attention to itself—to a "self" that underwrites the speaking voice—than to bring to the surface the condition that sustains it, namely, the repeated invocation of a self by means of the utterance of the locution *I*. "[H]ow can I disguise from myself the fact that I am utterly undistinguished?"[8] the bavard writes at the start of the narrative. Yet this does not in the least inhibit the accumulation, the sheer mass of self-reference in the text.

Benveniste has argued that the usual form of denotation—that is, the function of nominal expressions to refer to a given content—undergoes a decisive shift when language is "actualized in the instance of discourse." What is termed "the instance of discourse" is "the discrete and always unique act[s] by which the language is actualized in speech by a speaker."[9] And one must add that "speaker" here is not to be understood as limited to oral discourse but designates a speaker function, and further, that this speaker function is marked by the mobile sign of the first-person singular, *I*.

Now this function, Benveniste continues, "is a very strange thing. *I* cannot be defined except in terms of 'locution,' not in terms of objects, as is a nominal sign. *I* signifies 'the person who is uttering the present instance of the discourse containing *I*.' This instance is unique by definition and has validity only in its uniqueness."[10] Further, the instance of discourse not only invokes a field of reference that is parceled out through words that mark a relation in time and space to the speaking subject, but in doing so it repeatedly stipulates a *present* in terms of which such a field exists.

In *Le Bavard* the repeated "reinvention" of the self by way of the articulation of the *I*, normally implicit as an accessory of self-presentation, gains prominence to the extent that other indices of identity are minimized. In this sense Maurice Blanchot has commented of the novel: "The self who recounts, crumbles no sooner than a world has begun to take on solid shape around him. The more he convinces us of his reality . . . the more he is derealized; the more he is derealized the more he is purified and thus affirms himself in the mode of authenticity which is uniquely his own."[11] And this mode is of a phantom self that holds apart, to the greatest degree possible, the signal in discourse *that* it speaks from the content, *what* is spoken. Further, it is by means of this signal, the reiterated *I* and the correlative invocation of a *you*, that this self ensures its hold on us, the readership. For the narrator's *I* repeatedly evokes its addressee, insisting in this manner on the reciprocity of the channel thus established. But the *you*, the reader addressed by the bavard, though formally required, is existentially indifferent to the speaker, a point that the bavard reiterates repeatedly.

This text works like an experiment in which the motivation for address is attenuated as much as possible without being altogether eliminated. And that is precisely what *bavardage* consists of—the generation of talk that appears to be motivated by nothing but its own exercise. In the process the voice of the *I* necessarily implicates an addressee, a post or site occupied, in this instance, by none other than the reader. The narrator in *Le Bavard*—like those in Dostoevsky's *Notes from Underground* and Sartre's *La Nausée*—undertakes to force the reader to submit to a discourse whose content or referential focus becomes increasingly dubious.

The premise of *Le Bavard* is quite explicitly stated: the reader is to think of himself in the position of someone who has been buttonholed by a bore:

a companion whose only function is to lend an ear, without any obligation to utter a word; . . . This fellow [the bore] . . . doesn't really mind whether his interlocutor agrees with or dissents from him, and yet he cannot do without him, although he wisely requires from him only a purely formal attention.[12]

What kind of reader is stipulated as requiring "only a purely formal attention"? One could say that what is minimally required is the act of reading. The reader reads and when he stops reading, he is no longer a reader. But this is not quite right, since someone who has read something can still be called its reader even after having ceased to read. What about someone who reads only half of a work, or only a page? Boredom, after all, may cause one to stop reading. But then boredom may also be a way of reading. Could it qualify as "a purely formal attention"? At a late point in the text the bavard writes, "I've already said, and I shall not reiterate, that a talker never talks to empty space, he needs to be stimulated by the conviction that someone is listening to him, even if mechanically; . . . his loquacity . . . can sustain itself quite well in face of indifference or boredom."[13]

Is the bavard's talk impelled by a story, a plot? To be sure, there are incidents: thus, an attempt to impress a young woman so mocking of him that he is forced to flee; encounters with her boyfriend, who beats him up; an evocation of his childhood as he lies prostrate in the snow following the beating; finally, a moment of ecstatic exaltation veering toward suicide. But these exaggerated, self-dramatizing episodes rather put the reader on guard and, what is more, echo other narratives, from sources as divergent as Constant, Kleist, Kafka, and Bataille. In the final part, the reader's suspicion toward the text is confirmed when the narrator indulges in an extended harangue of those he is addressing. It is the readership, collectively and severally, whoever is targeted in the second-person address, the *you*, that is called to task. The bavard brings to the surface whatever suspicion, reserve, or disinterest a reader might have felt and makes that the occasion of a final peroration. In the process he puts into question the veracity of the incidents recounted earlier, and he does so in the name of what he considers a higher claim, namely, the right simply to talk. He can finally acknowledge the intense desire that has grown in him: "suddenly I realized, in a flash [*me vint cette illumination*], that what I was seeking far and wide lay close at hand. I would talk about my urge to talk." In a triumphant finale he exposes the hollowness, the insignificance of all that he had been talking *about* since, as he now realizes, this need in no way inhibit the talking itself:

> But I hope you're going to ask me why I have busied myself with such strange zeal about exposing my own frauds. . . . The truth is that, feeling

> my imagination fail and yet reluctant to hold my tongue, I could think of
> nothing better than to disclose my swindle to those who were its victims,
> and you have seen that I haven't spared you a single detail. . . . But I was
> holding my own, and that was the main thing: I was talking, I was talking,
> what bliss! and I'm still talking now.[14]

Are we, the readers, still listening, still reading? Evidently so, since to have
cited this passage is to betray my continued attention. Was it justified? Was
it worth the trouble to read this far, to read to the end? In a sense the question tests the very status of the literary. Why do we ever read to the end, even
when the work bores us or we don't see the point it is driving at? Are we not
motivated by a sense beyond the particular work, a sense of possible illumination that even failure in a particular instance endorses? This is the sense of
Maurice Blanchot's characterization of *Le Bavard* as a text of "an almost in-
finite nihilism . . . the nihilism of fiction reduced to its essence, sustained in
the closest proximity to its void and to the ambiguity of that void, . . . pro-
voking us to make a bond [*à se lier*], for the sake of a love of truth, to non-
truth, that flame without light, that tongue of fire that scorches without
illuminating."[15]

From this example of a form of talk whose abundance is the very mark
of its hollowness we turn to a contrasting instance, one where the channel-
ing of language testifies to a constitutive fragmentation and scarcity in
human expression. In Henry James's "In the Cage," the enclosure in which
the heroine—a telegraphist situated in the meshed postal station of a
London grocery store—is confined is as much a frame of language as of locale. We are introduced in the opening sentence of this novella to the young
person "in framed and wired confinement, [spending] the life of a guinea-
pig or a magpie."[16]

The unnamed heroine is aware that she is destined to remain in her confined condition yet dimly aware of another scene, a world outside. Since her
profession requires her to deal continually with coded messages, she fancies
at a certain moment, in consequence of an attraction to one of the customers, that her familiarity with such messages could allow her to gain
knowledge of that other world, even to enter it, however briefly. The only resource at her command is the language of her profession and her station,
meager enough in relation to the fashionable world to which she is drawn.
Yet the very limitation of this resource is the basis for the drama of discovery that ensues.

This drama may be taken as an exploration of cognitive capacities under
the conditions of the Platonic cave. "The problematic of cave outlets," Hans
Blumenberg has written, "is that one cannot conceive what a cave is when
one is in one."[17] And yet, as Blumenberg has demonstrated, versions of

Plato's allegory have often exploited the permeability of the division between inside and outside, or rather, the stratified nature of any inside, so that the outside—the sphere of Truth illumined by the sun in Plato's version—appears as yet another layer of illusion. In this sense, Blumenberg argues that Plato's fable anticipates the course of modern philosophy: "even where it seems to celebrate the triumph of the human spirit, [it] still for the most part consists of delineations of imprisonment."[18]

The heroine of James's tale attempts to breach her confinement by manipulating a set of interlocking codes, not all of which she is capable of negotiating. What she learns about the great world, the world of high society in which some of her clients move, is filtered through the communications that pass through her hands, and it is on the basis of these—specifically, of those involving a dashing young officer and his mistress—that she constructs her fantasy of that other world. As a transmitter of data she operates in terms of a doubling, a hypertrophy of the code function: first, the messages are transposed into the telegraphic code; secondly, those that particularly interest our telegraphist, those of the officer and his mistress, employ a set of fictitious addressees and place names designed to circumvent discovery of assignations that are being arranged. In the course of the action the postal employee fancies that she penetrates this second degree of coding, to such a degree, in fact, that she feels empowered to intervene and to correct, as she thinks, a crucial message transmitted between the lovers.[19]

Were she a perfect drudge of her class, like her fiancé Mr. Mudge, she would remain unaware of her ignorance. However, her desire to understand allows her to reach through the bars of the cage:

> As the weeks went on there she lived more and more into the world of whiffs and glimpses. . . . The nose of this observer was brushed by the bouquet, yet she could never really pluck even a daisy.[20]

There is a pathos, certainly, in the vast gap between the heroine's yearning and her resources. But there is comedy in her misapprehension of the world she fantasizes. We never lose sight of the fact that it is from the vantage of "cheese and pickles"[21] that her aspiration for truth, perhaps for love, arises.

In her one extended conversation with Captain Everard, the officer whose love affair she watches over, she claims that what she "get[s] out of it is the harmless pleasure of knowing," yet the narrative will quite clearly reveal how ignorant she is. This dialogue, which takes place on a bench outside Captain Everard's lodgings—a rare moment outside the cage in this story—, represents a kind of exchange very frequent in James's fiction in which talk serves not to convey a determinate meaning or data but rather to test and stimulate the unspoken disposition of the interlocutors. The telegraphist begins:

> "To be perfectly fair I should tell you I recognise at Cocker's certain strong attractions. All you people come. I like all the horrors."
>
> "The horrors?"
>
> "Those you all—you know the set I mean, your set—show me with as good a conscience as if I had no more feeling than a letter-box."
>
> He looked quite excited at the way she put it. "Oh they don't know!"
>
> "Don't know I'm not stupid? No, how should they?"
>
> "Yes, how should they?" said the Captain sympathetically. "But isn't 'horrors' rather strong?"
>
> "What you do is rather strong!" the girl promptly returned.
>
> "What I do?"
>
> "Your extravagance, your selfishness, your immorality, your crimes," she pursued without heeding his expression.
>
> "I say!"—her companion showed the queerest stare.
>
> "I like them, as I tell you—I revel in them. But we needn't go into that," she quietly went on; "for all I get out of it is the harmless pleasure of knowing. I know, I know, I know!"—she breathed it ever so gently.[22]

Each response reacts to the prior statement only to deflect it, to draw it into the ambiance of the recipient. The exchanges reflect an imperfect meshing, a subtle, ongoing displacement in the repartee. David Lapoujade has written of the importance of a dimension of implication (*sous-entendu*) operative in James's constructed conversations: "The *sous-entendu* is not a transgression of the principles of conversation. . . . A conversational statement is never a response to another statement but to that which the statement itself assumed implicitly. . . . Interpreting [the interlocutor] always involves penetrating a secret, because I want to perceive what the other does not intend to signify."[23] In this kind of Jamesian dialogue the overt message remains suspended as the reader looks into the interstices of the exchange for "the secret threshold of the point of view."[24] The narrative frame, with its coded messages and snatches of conversation, is devised to support a minimalist effect.

The vast disproportion between the telegraphist's quest for knowledge and its ultimate result situates her inescapably among the denizens of the cave. Her disavowal of interest ("harmless pleasure of knowing") is contradicted by the triumphant exclamation immediately following ("I know, I know, I know!"), a veritable proclamation of the desire implicit in her knowledge.[25]

The Sacred Fount resembles "In the Cage" in that both place an unnamed protagonist within a carefully delimited social setting in which that protagonist attempts to decipher forms of behavior that elude his/her understanding. This protagonist—the male narrator in the one work, the female telegraphist who functions as a reflector figure in the other—occupies a position of exclusion in relation to the phenomena under observation. Such a protagonist, as Tony Tanner has argued, assumes "for James the predicament and function of the artist . . . exclusion from participation," an exclusion that is compensated, Tanner continues, by an immense profit, "the imaginative transformation of the world.[26] But in the works under discussion this "imaginative transformation," I would stress, results in what may well be a patent mis-recognition, a contingent and quite arbitrary construction on the part of the observer. What particularly interests me in these narratives is the expression of this mis-recognition.

The subject-matter of *The Sacred Fount* was put down in a notebook entry very much as it came to be worked out in the novel:

> [The] fancy of the young man who marries an old woman and becomes old while she becomes young. Keep my play on idea: the *liaison* that betrays itself by the *transfer* of qualities—qualities to be determined—from one to the other of the parties to it. They *exchange*. I see 2 couples. One is married—this is the *old-young* pair. I watch *their* process, and it gives me my light for the spectacle of the other (covert, obscure, unavowed) pair who are *not* married.[27]

This kernel or theme is given narrative shape as the progressive testing of a hypothesis, a work of detection directed to the following conundrum: given the premise that a liaison will be signaled by an imbalance of vital energies between two individuals (the example of the Brissendens, the "old-young" couple), can such an imbalance be observed in another couple—Gilbert Long and May Server—and thus testify to their being lovers? But this formulation of the theme gives no sense of the striking discrepancy in scope between the speculations devoted to the investigation and the evidence they yield. For as intense the passion and energy invested by the narrator, so elusive and insubstantial the results. The greater the investment the more remote the goal.

What I want to focus on is not this "parabolic" element, as it is termed by the narrator[28] but the form of its presentation, the voice that proffers it, elaborates it, becomes its medium to the extent that nothing else seems to exist for that voice, that it seems to operate as a disembodied agency whose existence is wholly tributary to the elaboration of the narrative germ. For the germ that James identified as the source of the work, the "little *concetto*," functions as a requisite prop in structuring the work but by no means exhausts its meaning. The narrative enigma remains unresolved at the end; we never learn whether the theory confirms the narrator's suspicion of a secret liaison between two fellow guests at the house party. What is more, we are never assured that the phenomenon of the sacred fount, the limited reservoir of vital energies shared by a couple, has any validity at all beyond the speculations that the narrator pursues and occasionally shares with other guests.

In James's notebook entry, "I see 2 couples . . . I watch *their* process," one may readily identify the *I* with James himself. But in the novel itself the identity assumed by the first-person singular pronoun is altogether different. In fact the notion of identity may seem hard to apply since the speaker is unnamed, we learn almost nothing about his appearance, his profession, his background. In short, he lacks, or rather the *I* lacks the kind of traits that are typically associated with a fictive character. What remains, of course, is a voice, a certain style of address.

With this narrator, the *I* of *The Sacred Fount,* we come upon a form of identity that is altogether tributary to the construction of a narrative discourse. In one sense this phenomenon is related to a theme that James has treated elsewhere, namely, the continuity of vision, cognition, and artistic creation in a single persona. The Jamesian reflector as most fully realized is not simply an agent of mediation within the diegesis but a means of disclosing the creative process *in actu.* In *The Sacred Fount* this is expressed in passages like the following:

> I struck myself as knowing again the joy of the intellectual mastery of things unamenable, that joy of determining, almost of creating results.[29]

Of course, such moments can be read as unconscious irony in light of the tenuous nature of the narrator's construct and the ultimate humiliation he experiences in seeing it demolished. Nonetheless, however fragile the web he spins, it is a web that sustains a very lengthy discourse.

What precisely is its content, its subject-matter? At one level it may be characterized as the circulation of a rumor among a small group of guests at a house-party regarding the nature, and in part the very existence, of certain marital and amorous relations—the most commonplace topic of social gossip. This flow of talk—hearsay, suppositions—circles and circles and apparently yields no definitive truth, no disclosure. Much of the talk is precisely about this process. Further, the standard of social success in this social gathering is quite openly determined in terms of talk—not necessarily talk *about* anything, but only talk. Judgments regarding this point by the participants are quite categorical. Here is the narrator discussing one of the guests, May Server, with Guy Brissenden:

> "Do you mean haven't I talked with her? Well, scarcely; for it's a fact that every man in the house *but* I strikes me as having been deluged with that

privilege: if indeed," I laughed, "her absence of topics suffers it to be either a privilege or a deluge!"[30]

The capacity that May Server allegedly lacks is just what the narrator boasts of in the following remark to Mrs. Brissenden:

> "It could not but be exciting to talk, as we talked, on the basis of those suppressed processes and unavowed references which made the meaning of our meeting so different from its form. We knew ourselves—what moved me, that is, was that she knew me—to mean, at every point, immensely more than I said or than she answered; just as she saw me, at the same points, measure the space by which her answers fell short."[31]

Over and over, the capacity or the incapacity of talking is invoked not just as a standard of the kind of person one is, but as a measure of one's very existence. Not to talk is to shrink and approach nullity.

In that sense, the narrator's discourse (and of course the novel consists wholly of a first-person account) serves not in the first instance to convey a narrative substance—a coherent, verifiable story—but to attest to the speaker's very existence. The narrator's "smash" at the end[32]—that is, his humiliation by Mrs. Brissenden in their final dialogue—is coincident with the crumbling of the narrative, its exposure as an untenable supposition. In the concluding scene the narrator is forced to concede the hollowness of the narrative that he has constructed regarding the relationships of his fellow guests:

> "I seem myself to see it again, perfect in every part," I pursued, "even while I thus speak to you, and to feel afresh that, weren't the wretched accident of its weak foundation, it wouldn't have the shadow of a flaw. I've spoken of it in my conceivable regret," I conceded, "as already a mere heap of disfigured fragments; but that was the extravagance of my vexation, my despair. It's in point of fact so beautifully fitted that it comes apart piece by piece—which, so far as that goes, you've seen it do in the last quarter of an hour at your own touch, quite handing me the pieces, one by one, yourself and watching me stack them along the ground. They're not even in this state—see!" I wound up—"a pile of ruins! [. . .] I should almost like, piece by piece, to hand them back to you."[33]

But this defeat of the narrator at one level is balanced by an achievement at quite another. The rejection of his hypothesis by Mrs. Brissenden still leaves in its wake the verbal artifact that he has produced. The more hollow its substance the more noteworthy his success in captivating his auditors—and his readers—by it.[34] It is in this sense that the narrator's characterization to Mrs.

Brissenden of his "frail, but . . . quite sublime structure" is both a concession and a self-vindication.

I began this essay by referring to Gérard Genette's suggestion that recent narrative has tended to undermine the traditional opposition of *discours* and *récit* in favor of a kind of hybrid mode where the *récit* is absorbed "in the present discourse of the writer in the process of writing." But in place of writer I have focused on the narrating agent, whether first-person narrator or reflector. What is common to the three works discussed is that they at once evoke and evade the question "Who is speaking?" In each, and in very different ways, a practice of language tends to unsettle the agency of narrator or reflector, the subject status, and the reader is left pondering how such creatures of chatter can bring forth a construct intermittently compelling and dubious.

In place of an opposition between *discours* and *récit* I have tried to work in terms of an interplay of concealment and disclosure. If *récit* is taken as the narrative core, as data that needs to be brought to the surface through an act of narration, whatever seems to interfere with such disclosure will be valorized negatively, as verbiage, mere talk. But my contention is that it is precisely at the level of idle talk, of discourse operating in a mode of distraction, dissimulation, or indirection, that nodes of narrative, of *récit*, emerge. What is often taken to be a plot, a narrative core or substance, would be an interpretation or elaboration of such a node. *Discours* is often taken as merely a means of enabling *récit*, as an accessory, but in fact it seems to follow quite different laws than *récit*. Stories are not stories until told, but every act of telling is subject to a law of displacement and dispersal. And this interference, this "noise" that keeps the story from finding its proper form, is in fact a means of its generation and continuance.

Notes

1. Emile Benveniste, "Les relations de temps dans le verbe français," in *Problèmes de linguistique générale* (Paris: Gallimard, 1966), 237–50.
2. Gérard Genette, "Frontières du récit," in *Figures II* (Paris: Seuil, 1969), 68.
3. I am alluding to Michel Serres's development of the concept of "noise" as derived from communications theory, in his *The Parasite*, trans. Lawrence R. Schehr (Baltimore and London: Johns Hopkins University Press, 1982).
4. Peter Fenves, *"Chatter": Language and History in Kierkegaard* (Stanford, CA: Stanford University Press, 1993), 253.
5. Ibid., 8.
6. Ibid., 4.
7. "Le bavard" translates loosely as "the big talker."
8. Louis-René des Forêts, *Le Bavard* (Paris: Gallimard, 1973), 11–12. In English: *The Bavard* in *The Children's Room*, trans. Jean Stewart (London: Calder, 1963), 12. In the subsequent notes, the first page reference is to the English version, the second to the

French.

9. Benveniste, *Problèmes*, 217.

10. Ibid., 218.

11. Maurice Blanchot, "La Parole vaine," an essay appearing at the rear of the 1946 edition (but not in the 1973 edition) of *Le Bavard* (Paris: Gallimard), 169.

12. Des Forêts, *Bavard*, 12/11.

13. Ibid., 95/148.

14. Ibid., 99–100/155–56.

15. Blanchot, "La Parole vaine," 167.

16. Henry James, "In the Cage," in *In the Cage and Other Tales*, ed. Morton Dauwen Zabel (New York: Norton, 1958), 174.

17. Hans Blumenberg, *Höhlenausgänge* (Frankfurt/M.: Suhrkamp, 1989), 89.

18. Ibid., 752.

19. The precise significance of the telegram that the telegraphist recovers for Captain Everard, one she had earlier herself altered when Lady Bradeen submitted it, remains opaque. Ralf Norrman argues that the telegraphist's intervention misses the point and is of no aid to the lovers: "The Intercepted Telegram Plot in Henry James's 'In the Cage,'" *Notes and Queries* 24 (October 1977): 425–27. Cf. also John Carlos Rowe, *The Other Henry James* (Durham, NC, and London: Duke University Press, 1998), 160f.

20. James, "In the Cage," 186.

21. Ibid., 203.

22. Ibid., 226.

23. David Lapoujade, "Politique de la conversation chez Henry James," *Critique* 607 (December 1997): 948–63; here 955, 958.

24. Ibid., 955.

25. On knowledge as a function of power and desire in James see Mark Seltzer, *Henry James and the Art of Power* (Ithaca, NY, and London: Cornell University Press, 1984), 77f.

26. Tony Tanner, *The Reign of Wonder* (Cambridge: Cambridge University Press, 1965), 318.

27. Henry James, *The Notebooks of Henry James*, ed. F. O. Matthiessen and Kenneth B. Murdock (New York: Oxford University Press, 1947), 275.

28. Henry James, *The Sacred Fount*, with an introductory essay by Leon Edel (New York: Grove, 1953), 29.

29. Ibid., 214.

30. Ibid., 113.

31. Ibid., 272.

32. Ibid., 318.

33. Ibid., 311.

34. There is an analogy here, perhaps, to certain sculptures by Jean Tinguely, objects that are devised to fall to pieces at calculated intervals and then to reassemble again. The narrator acknowledges his defeat to Mrs. Brissenden at the end, but in doing so he seems to reserve the right to play the game again in the future.

"Talk to Me"

5

Talk Ethics and Erotics

Carla Kaplan

Talk is like a structural midden, a refuse heap in which bits and oddments of all the ways of framing activity in culture are to be found.
—*Erving Goffman*

A language is first and foremost someone talking. But there are language games in which the important thing is to listen, in which the rule deals with audition. Such a game is the game of the just. And in this game, one speaks only inasmuch as one listens, that is, one speaks as a listener.
—*Jean-François Lyotard*

Being listened to is one of the few real aphrodisiacs left.
—Ms. *magazine*

We know intuitively that how we speak, whom we listen to, who listens to us, and how we are spoken to all say a great deal about our place in culture. "Language reflects . . . [an] individual's place in society," as Peter Burke puts it in *The Art of Conversation*.[1] To be socially marginalized is to be linguistically marginalized, hence our contemporary rhetoric of the silenced and the muted. Silence challenges our basic presumptions of being because subjectivity is intersubjectivity, a coconstitutive, discursive phenomenon contrived of all our different forms of talk: argument, confession, gossip, dialogue, apology, joking, soliloquy, and so on. In literature, of course, the soliloquy is always meant to be heard, or at least overheard; no literary speaker can properly be said to be speaking to herself.

Self-talking may be our most socially resonant symbolic for status. Erving Goffman, for example, argues that no form of talk is as self-effacing, humiliating, or damaging to social standing as is talking to ourselves.[2] Self-talking demonstrates—or performs as we would now say—our lack of a

proper and appropriate interlocutor. Lunatics and children talk to themselves. Schizophrenics and cast-offs talk to themselves. Homeless people and
drunks talk to themselves. Hence, the compulsion to produce a listener is
not only a strong one, but is also motivated by a number of negative associations. And an important form of social power is the performative power to
turn speakers into "self-talkers" by denying them a hearing. "A summons [to
talk, to respond] that is openly snubbed," Goffman writes, "can leave us feeling that we have been caught engaging in something like talking to ourselves." Such performatives not only mute the speech of those who are
transformed into self-talkers, they render their very subjectivity suspect by
associating them with those whom society has already effectively marginalized. And it is not enough to simply have *some* kind of interlocutor. We can
be considered guilty of self-talk merely by addressing others like ourselves,
by being caught in such devalued discourses as "girl-talk" or "gossip," by
being caught in a "hen party" of imputed meaninglessness.

Given all of this, it is hardly surprising that conversation and dialogue
have been heavily freighted with positive, even utopian images of equality,
reciprocity, and deep satisfaction. Consider, for example, the highly charged
language with which Jane Eyre describes the fulfillment she experiences in
talking with Rochester or Diana and Mary Rivers. It is "exhilarating pleasure," she maintains, a "delicious pleasure," a "paradise of union." Or the way
that listening to Janie, and being listened to in turn, affects Pheoby in *Their
Eyes Were Watching God*: "Ah done growed ten feet higher from just listening
to you." Celie, in Alice Walker's *The Color Purple*, even measures the worth
of a newly transformed Mr. —— by whether or not he is now "somebody I
can talk to."

The feminist critique of social and political discourse theorists has cen-
tered largely on whether the possible pleasures and transformative powers of
conversation are understood as attainable under current social conditions or,
alternatively, as utopian constructs revealing the gaps and impossibilities in
the current situation. Both Richard Rorty and Jürgen Habermas have been
challenged for presuming the transformative power of discourse without attending sufficiently to the differing "footings" or social status of its participants.[3]

Rorty proposes that we adopt conversation, or "cacophony and disorder," as a model for cultural practice and social change. For Rorty, "keeping
a conversation going" is a sufficient aim in itself because the conversational
process is presumed to transform those participants who negotiate the "disorder" to which they are exposed. As a cultural model, this conversational-
ism aligns itself with both the work of feminist poststructuralists and the
demand for a plurality of voices and social vocabularies that we can now associate with multiculturalism.[4]

But how does this model explain the pathway to its own fulfillment? Some feminist critics point to an unacknowledged utopian strain here that fails to practically or adequately address questions of access and footing, the ways in which our social positions inflect the very possibility of getting in on the cultural conversation, let alone helping to sustain it as a politically worthwhile project: "Conversation on Rorty's terms would only reinforce previous power relations," Nancy Hartsock writes. Insofar as we are not "all in a position to participate as equals in a conversation," she argues, then a conversational model of cultural change is "in fact, dangerous to those of us who have been marginalized."[5]

But why "dangerous"? Just as Hartsock shows that there is no reason to presuppose that getting in on the cultural conversation will prove liberatory, so we might ask if it is always the case that doing so will necessarily prove "dangerous." If talk, as Goffman maintains, is our "structural midden," if it is our "refuse heap in which bits and oddments of all the ways of framing activity in culture are to be found,"[6] we do need, as Hartsock compellingly suggests, to be cautious about assuming that merely getting in on the conversation or helping to sustain it (something that has been traditionally "women's work" to begin with[7]) will guarantee the reframing we seek. But at the same time, we need to acknowledge that we do not really have an option of opting out of the cultural conversation because of these dangers. Even our silence, after all, would be part of that conversation, rather than a move outside it or a transcendence of it, a point to which I will return shortly.

The problem is not only, as Hartsock claims, that "Rorty ignores power relations."[8] Both Hartsock and Rorty construct a false opposition between celebrating dialogue as emancipatory and liberatory on the one hand and vilifying it as dangerous and oppressive on the other. Rather than attend to categories of difference such as gender and race, or better yet concretizing practices of cultural conversation, Rorty theorizes the transformational effects of language in the abstract. But Hartsock, after attending to those very categories, also generalizes and universalizes the efficacy of conversation. What if neither abstraction can suffice? What if it is only by engaging in actual cultural conversations—social struggles, texts, readings, discourses, collective enterprises, debates, and so on—that we can determine how "cacophony and disorder" come out?

Habermas argues that a procedural norm of truly participatory democracy in which everyone would have a "voice" must replace our conception of disembodied, putatively transcendental, and universal norms of justice and the social good. This "communicative ethics" provides the grounds for a critique of existing norms and institutions, not by appealing to a transcendental set of values, but rather to a process—hence Habermas's emphasis on the "procedural"—by which both social norms and "normal" discourse can be

reasoned discourse

challenged and adjudicated.[9] A just norm, a fair social policy, a legitimate social practice, consequently, is one that is communally determined to be so within an "ideal speech situation," "free of external pressures and internal distortions, in which participants would respond to the force of the better argument alone."[10] Because such procedures, clearly, can operate only under social conditions in which everyone has a voice and is able to express it freely, both institutions and individuals need a commitment to consensus, or at least to the principle of fruitful disagreement. Habermas most certainly recognizes that such commitments are not always present. He writes:

> As a matter of fact we can in no way always (or even often) fulfill those improbably pragmatic preconditions, from which we nevertheless begin in communicative everyday practice, and indeed, in the sense of a transcendental necessity, *must* begin. For this reason, socio-cultural life-forms stand under the structural limitations of a communicative reason which is *simultaneously denied and laid claim to.*[11]

This appears to be a crucial circularity or hedge in Habermas's theory. Do we—whether as individuals or groups—face an imperative to behave as if an "ideal speech situation" exists when it manifestly does not? Although Habermas's model of "communicative ethics" is a very productive blueprint for social relations, this apparent slippage from a diagnostic model of how things are to a programmatic one of how they should be appears to be grounded in a presumptive view of the inherent character of discourse, one that can certainly be opened to interrogation. In failing to take account of gender or race or other categories that effect our "footing," this "normative ideal of self/other relationships," its presentation as an ideal, leaves open the question of how such a blueprint might be realized under given social conditions, how discourse might transcend or help transform its own inscription in social axes of subordination such as those based on the categories of difference we've been discussing. As Iris Marion Young points out, "only if oppressed groups are able to express their interests and experience in the public *on an equal basis with other groups* can group domination through formally equal processes of participation be avoided."[12]

Nancy Fraser, who shares Habermas's commitment to the ideal of rational consensus despite social obstacles to its realization, also points out the gender-blindness of his model. "It does indeed seem doubtful," Fraser writes, that all existing material inequalities could be overridden or transcended by the conversational process. Situations in which "the power that structures discourse is hierarchical and asymmetrical" (incarceration, the bourgeois patriarchal family, compulsory education, the military) suggest "manipulation and control of linguistic behavior" rather than "the project of reaching agreement." However, "the fact that the humanist ideal of autonomous subjectivity is unrealizable, even co-optable," may be seen primarily as "an argument against hierarchical, asymmetrical power."[13] But how do we produce symmetrical power relations in a manifestly asymmetrical society? And what role can dialogue play in that transformation?

As Fraser points out elsewhere in her writing, discourse is a particularly gendered practice. Dialogic competency is deeply gendered and is, indeed, one of the principal ways in which gender itself is learned and maintained. "Capacities for consent and speech, the ability to participate on a par with others in dialogue," Fraser writes, "are capacities that are connected with masculinity in male-dominated classical capitalism; they are capacities that are in myriad ways denied to women." Hence, Fraser argues, femininity comes to be conceptually opposed to citizenship or to civic life in the public sphere. Because these sorts of gendered conceptions structure all aspects of social life, merely moving from "normatively secured contexts of interaction" (based in taken-for-granted conventions and cultural traditions) to "communicatively achieved ones" (based on "explicit, reflectively achieved consensus, consensus reached by unconstrained discussion under conditions of freedom, equality, and fairness") will not intrinsically make the public sphere more amenable or accessible to women. "An emancipatory transformation of male-dominated, capitalist societies, early and late, requires a transformation of those gendered roles and of the institutions they mediate."[14]

In a liberal, democratic society, we tend to imagine that transformation as proceeding discursively. But discourse cannot be both the means and the outcome of the transformational goals that we seek. Although communicative ethics might help transform unequal social relations, transformed social relations are prerequisite to any viable practice of such ethics. The apparent viciousness of this circle might lead one to eschew utopian ideals and imagine opting out of the cultural conversation altogether.

In a homologous reading of the structural inequalities at the heart of liberal theories of contract, Carole Pateman seems to suggest that the structurally disadvantaged try opting out of those forms of cultural converse and exchange they cannot enter as equals. As a balanced, voluntary, "free and equal" exchange between individuals—"exchange is at the heart of contract"—the ideal of the liberal contract is one of mediation between people that inherently contains the power to transform social relations between those it mediates, a construct reminiscent of calls for the transformative power of cultural conversation. The problem, Pateman argues, is that the "universal freedom" upon which the liberal contract depends is "always an hypothesis, a story, a political fiction." Individuals are not, in reality, all equally "free and equal," and contract, Pateman argues, masks this crucial fact by positing that there must have been a moment, or moments, when formerly free and equal individuals agreed—or contracted—to domination in exchange for safety or other goods. Contract, by this logic, is always reequalizing and transformative; inequality is thus a form of equality. Pateman argues that not only do individual contracts fail to provide their own equalizing preconditions, but that contract works, in part, by excluding many people from its emancipatory machinery. Hence, Pateman implicitly suggests that the only option available to the excluded is a wholesale rejection of all contracts, a refusal to engage in that which pretends to equalize while it maintains inequality.[15] "Every conversation," Hans-Georg Gadamer writes, "presupposes a common language, or, it creates a common language. . . . To reach an understanding with one's partner in a dialogue is . . . a transformation into a communion, in which we do not remain what we were."[16] Can such a description be taken as axiomatic? Or should we, rather, be focusing on that process of presupposition, on the way in which conversation hopes, as it were, to effect transformations, communions, and changes in who we are that cannot necessarily be achieved by the particular conversation, exchange, dialogue, or text in question?

It may seem obvious that the answer to that question is "Of course." However, the tendency to see discourse as both the means and the outcome of the transformational goals that we seek is hardly unique to social and political theory of democracy. Indeed, it may be literary criticism, particularly recent literary criticism interested in textual strategies of resistance and liberation, that is most deeply wedded to a utopian tendency to celebrate dialogue, qua dialogue, as evidence of something progressive and positive. Drawing on Bakhtin—whose work currently enjoys a revival of interest—much literary study has come to stress the textual "dialogic": identifying multivocality or "heteroglossia," documenting a text's multiple discourses and the "cacophony and disorder" between them, discovering conflicting discourses. In what amounts to a simplification of Bakhtin's complex mapping of narrative structures, his theory of textual dialogics has sometimes been taken programmatically, as if the mere identification of "heteroglossia" is itself a cause for celebration and proof of liberatory or subversive counterforces in a text. The mere presence of the dialogic, indeed the mere copresence of both text and reader, can become cause for celebration when we assume that narrative exchange can be the means of the very social transformations it seeks to reflect and represent.

It is relatively commonplace to assert that desire is the driving force behind all narration. Narrative desire, in Peter Brooks's account, for instance, is the desire to "seduce" or "captivate" a listener, to transform a listener from antagonist to conversational partner. "Narration," Brooks writes, is:

a form of human desire . . . that seeks to *seduce* and to *subjugate* the listener, to implicate him in the *thrust* of a desire that can never quite speak its name—never quite come to the point—but that insists on speaking over and over again its movement toward that name. . . . Narrative may first come to life as narration, as the inchoate intent to tell. . . . It is in essence the desire to be heard, recognized, understood, which never wholly satisfied or indeed satisfiable, continues to generate the desire to tell, the effort to enunciate a significant version of the life story in order to *captivate* a possible listener.[17]

Brooks's rhetoric of "seduction," "captivation," "thrusting," and "subjugation" reveals an understanding of narrative desire that is not only fundamentally male and heterosexual, but also antagonistic, suggesting that the movement of narrative is like a battle or contest, a battle in which the "seducer" can be virtually guaranteed partial, if not complete, success. Narrative appears as a desirable conversation, but this conversation takes shape like a rape.

Interestingly enough, other critics who describe narrative as seduction sometimes do so with specific reference to ideals of contract. Ross Chambers, for example, describes narrative as a "transactional" or "contractual" practice that "mediates human relationships," "has the power to change human situations," and is therefore an "'oppositional practice' of considerable significance." If we are progressive-minded critics it is our job, Chambers implies, to reconstruct the mechanisms of that transformation and reveal how texts transform the power relations they code between themselves and their readers. The key mechanism of that transformation Chambers calls "seduction." Narration as seduction, he argues, "wins narrative authority" from "a situation in which power is itself absent. . . . The narrator, who is situationally condemned to operate without preexistent authority and to earn the authority to narrate in the very act of storytelling, must be a *master* of certain 'tactical' devices." Such seduction, Chambers goes on to explain, is contractual: narration

depends on social agreements, implicit pacts or contracts in order to produce exchanges that themselves are a function of desires, purposes, constraints. It is only on the strength of such agreements [or contracts] that narratives can assert their impact and produce change. No act of narration occurs without at least an implicit contract, that is, an understanding between narrator and narratee, an illocutionary situation that makes the act meaningful and gives what we call a "point."[18]

Writers and readers—like speakers and listeners—contract to exchange the narrator's authority for the audience's interest. This speaker-listener contract functions to naturalize narrative as a process while it guarantees one possible outcome as a constitutive feature *of* that process. Like classic liberal contract theory, it obviates the need for explaining persistent inequality.

Given this cultural privileging of conversation and the dangers and disadvantages of being seen as a "self-talker," one might well expect a potential speaker's lack of social power to correlate directly with her willingness to accept any legitimizing listener at all. Social norms mandate intersubjectivity and appropriate engagement in social commerce, but while failing to provide the necessary conditions for equal exchange, social values also tend to ridicule, deride, or marginalize the discursively disenfranchised subject, accusing her, in effect, of failing to engage—proof, then, of her inadmissibility to the public sphere and the spaces of social commerce.

One response, then, might be to pursue a listener at all costs, to seduce—or even captivate—one if necessary. Yet another response might be to performatively dramatize the failure, inaccessibility, or ineptitude of potential listeners, to dramatize the difficult double bind in which the marginalized speaker finds herself. Here self-talk—silence, muttering, gossip, "girl talk"—functions as a form of refusal and critique. This is not necessarily a matter of opting out of the conversation, but of dramatizing a kind of "what if" of that very (im)possibility. Self-talk, as Goffman points out, poses a "threat to intersubjectivity; it warns others that they may be wrong in assuming a jointly maintained base of ready mutual intelligibility among all persons present."[19] Many texts featuring the voices of disempowered speakers engage in just this sort of performative self-talk, one that involves simultaneously elevating discourse's desirability and undercutting its effectivity. What I call "the erotics of talk" is the textual topos—a signature feature of much so-called minority writing—that takes the specific shape of heightened desire for an ideal listener, a listener whose existence is passionately desired but doubted at every possible turn.

An erotics of talk, in other words, is a figuration for both personal desire and social critique, projecting "normative possibilities unrealized but felt in a particular social reality," as Iris Marion Young puts it.[20] An erotics of talk is not so much the successful seduction, captivation, or subjugation of the ideal other as it is a political allegory about the social conditions for that idealized reciprocity. The narrator who longs for an ideal respondent who never comes or who finds that respondent under only the most limited and temporary circumstances, holds a critical mirror up to the failures of her fictional world and, hence, the reader's world as well. Such mirroring says, of both the private and the public sphere, that "it does not have to be this way, it could be otherwise."[21] As an openly utopian figuration of a better world, an erotics of talk is a kind of poetic justice, a "political language"[22] for personal and social equality. As Audre Lorde has argued, the erotic is a kind of ethical Geiger counter we can use to determine "which of our various life endeavors bring us closest to that fullness. . . . As women, we need to examine the ways in which our world can be truly different."[23]

Given what sociolinguists have taught us about the extraordinary amount of responsibility women have taken for keeping conversations going,[24] perhaps it should not be surprising that this trope of an "erotics of talk" often, though not always, seems to find its most nuanced and subtle realization in the work of women writers constructing female protagonists. And few novels render this performative strategy as clearly and dramatically as Zora Neale Hurston's *Their Eyes Were Watching God*—a novel that has, ironically enough, often been misread for flattering the very reader whose competency is frequently called into question. *Their Eyes Were Watching God* is the story of a young woman in search of fulfillment. From the moment Janie is "summoned to behold a revelation,"[25] and witnesses (in what may well be one of the most erotic scenes in all of literature) the "panting," "frothing," "ecstatic" "creaming" fulfillment of a blossoming pear tree, her quest is set; she wants, as she puts it, "tuh utilize mahself all over."[26] As the novel opens, Janie is forty years old and has just settled down on her old back porch to tell her best friend Pheoby the story of her marriages and her third husband's tragic death. This conversation with Pheoby is the frame that opens and closes the novel, and while it has generally been understood as a mechanism for getting Janie's life story told, it also works the other way around. Janie's life story is also a medium for her final conversation with Pheoby, the conversation that lets her, at last, experience that "self revelation" she had sought. The meaning of Janie's pear tree "revelation," it turns out, is not marriage or a husband or sex, but talk itself, the experience of conversation, the act of storytelling, self-narration, and dialogue. Janie wants to narrate her own story, exercise her voice, and participate in what Brontë's Jane Eyre describes as "joyous conversational murmur." It is only in telling her story to Pheoby that Janie is finally able to satsify "that oldest human longing—self revelation."[27] Telling her story to Pheoby turns out to be the erotic fulfillment Janie misunderstood as "marriage," and in this sense, Pheoby, whose "hungry listening helps Janie to tell her story" is the "bee" to Janie's "blossom."[28]

To dramatize even further the importance of Janie's ideal listener to the fulfillment she finally achieves, Hurston has her tell her story in a very different setting: on trial for the murder of her husband. Juxtaposing these two scenes helps explain why Hurston seems at once to privilege dialogue and talk and at the same time to doubt its social and personal value. This trial scene serves as a microcosm for the novel as a whole, an allegory of the dilemma Janie (and Hurston as well perhaps) faces in seeking the audience with whom she might satisfy her longing for self-revelation. In the court-room, Janie faces nothing but hostility and misunderstanding. The black community is there "with their tongues cocked and loaded." The jury is all-white, "twelve strange men."[29] And for the most part, Janie is silent, being spoken for by a string of white men who usurp her story from her: the sher-iff, the doctor, and the lawyer. By the time Janie herself is called to testify, her testimony has already been undercut. And importantly, Hurston chooses not to render it in the novel. Instead, we are told *that* she testified, although she doubted the possibility of understanding because her audience lacks the necessary "understand' to go 'long wid [her story]"[30] and that "she had been through for some time before the judge and the lawyer and the rest seemed to know it."[31] Hurston makes it deliberately ambiguous whether her story has moved her audience deeply, given them the "necessary understandin'" for hearing it, or, on the contrary, whether given their lack of understanding, they have been paying no attention to Janie at all, having already made up their minds based on the testimony of the white men who precede—and au-thorize—Janie's speech.

Immediately following the courtroom scene, Hurston returns us to the framing conversation between Janie and Pheoby in order to juxtapose their nonjuridical dialogue to the juridical one we have just witnessed and to con-trast the strong effect Janie's story has had on Pheoby to the questionable ef-fect it had in court. But the topic, at this point, of Janie and Pheoby's conversation is, appropriately enough, the singular importance and the du-bious value of talk:

> "Lawd!" Pheoby breathed out heavily, "Ah ain't satisfied with mahself no mo'. Ah means tuh make Sam take me fishin' wid him after this. Nobody better not criticize yuh in mah hearin'."
> "Now, Pheoby, don't feel too mean wid de rest of 'em 'cause deys parched up from not knowin' things. Dem meatskins is *got* tuh rattle tuh make out they's alive. Let 'em consolate theyselves with talk. 'Course talkin' don't amount tuh uh hill uh beans when yuh can't do nothin' else. And listenin' tuh dat kind uh talk is jus' lak openin' yo' mouth and lettin' de moon shine down yo' throat. It's uh known fact, Pheoby, you got tuh *go* there tuh *know* there. Yo' papa and yo' mama and nobody else can't tell yuh and show yuh. Two things everybody got tuh do fuh theyselves. They got tuh go tuh God, and they got tuh find out about livin' fuh theyselves."[32]

You can't, Janie concludes, approximate experience with story. Janie does not respond to Pheoby's "hungry listening" by reaffirming the positive effects of talking and storytelling. On the contrary, in spite of how the story has af-fected Pheoby's growth, self-esteem, feelings of worth, Janie reiterates the message of the courtroom scene: that talking is mostly a waste of breath, that there is no real relation between storytelling and experience, that talking doesn't really count as experience because you have to "*go* there tuh *know* there."

In making Pheoby, and Pheoby only, the listener who can fulfill Janie's lifelong desires, Hurston dramatizes the impossibilities and limits of the social conditions Janie faces. And she resists what Fredric Jameson describes as literature's ideological task: "inventing imaginary or formal 'solutions' to unresolvable social contradictions."[33] The presence of multiple and mostly failed listeners in the novel reminds us that there are also multiple narratees, implied readers, and historical readers. And that there is no reason to assume, out of hand, that all of these are either successful or ideal. Any given reader may as easily resemble what Janie calls "Mouth-Almighty" as resemble Pheoby, the "hungry" listener. By Hurston's account, the necessary condition for an ideal speech situation is not merely, as Habermas might have it, adherence to a coherent and fair set of procedural norms. Instead, she seeks a homogeneity in her audience sufficiently strong to ensure that such procedural norms, in fact, probably would not be needed. Janie's ideal listener is ideal because of who she is, not because of the dialogic skills she masters or the discursive rules she respects. This is not an image replete with optimism and promise. And to make matters even more complicated for us readers, it is only by including ourself in the novel's blanket indictments of those to whom speaking is a waste of time that one can learn to listen, to listen differently, and to help create, thereby, the conditions under which a longing for talk such as Janie's might, someday, reasonably be fulfilled in a larger public sphere.

Of course, such attention to the vagaries of social discourse proves particularly acute for writers who experience a relative absence of other forms of social recognition and belonging—access to resources of power and privilege, for example—and have no reason to think that their entry into the cultural conversation will prove itself different. The paradox that these examples all stress is that avoiding that cultural conversation is also not an option. Instead, every attempt to address an ideal listener remains a persuasive or seductive performance, an audition, a tryout that hopes for audience appreciation it cannot take for granted, that hopes for a constituency that may not yet exist, without being able to take for granted, either, that the gesture of such auditions will bring that constituency into being. As a figurative and performative trope for intersubjectivity that mediates between the demands of the textual on the one hand and the limits of the social on the other, an erotics of talk works by contradictions. It highlights—or performs—the disjunction between the implied promise of dialogue and narrative exchange and the actual social, discursive, and material conditions faced by disadvantaged speakers, the conditions in which any dialogic exchange must actually take place.

Because they work by "citations" that must be "witnessed" as making reference to an already constructed chain of significations and norms, performatives are always mechanisms of hoped-for consensus building and, hence, of social consolidation. Performatives work by invoking—and creating—a presumption of consensus between the speaker and the listener/viewer who recognizes what she or he sees as parody or exaggeration. If that consensus and recognition can be successfully marshaled, the performative succeeds. If not, it fails. A successfully subversive performative would make its audience over, would marshal a new consensus, a differently oriented community of witnesses. It would create a new critical community. In the case of Janie's trial, for example, her performance of social exclusion would change the jury such that inclusion and participation become meaningful possibilities. It might do that by bringing more women into the room, feminizing the "twelve white men" Janie's stuck with, by making her black audience less hostile, or all of the above. It would change who "we" are, witnessing whatever it is that "we" see.

Celebrations of performativity as a new modality of social critique and political action, like celebrations of dialogue qua dialogue, tend to take for granted that any instance of "speaking up" will work as an instance of "talking back."[34] But the value of the conversational performative—or performativity in general—can never be fully theorized in the abstract nor reliably predicted in advance. The outcome will always have to do, ultimately, with who "we" are in participating in that process, and with how "we," that most difficult and promising of all performatives, is—provisionally, changeably, and always differently—being marshaled and understood.

Notes

1. Peter Burke, *The Art of Conversation* (Ithaca, NY: Cornell University Press, 1993), 23.
2. Erving Goffman, *Forms of Talk* (Philadelphia: University of Pennsylvania Press, 1981), 109.
3. "Footing" is Erving Goffman's word. See *Forms of Talk*.
4. Richard Rorty, *Philosophy and the Mirror of Nature* (Princeton, NJ: Princeton University Press, 1979), 389, 157, 378.
5. Nancy Hartsock, "Rethinking Modernism: Minority vs. Majority Theories," *Cultural Critique* 7 (Fall 1987): 200–1, 199.
6. Goffman, *Forms of Talk*, 87.
7. While the literature on how language use is inflected by gender is much too vast for a comprehensive listing, see work by Nancy Henley, Barrie Thorne, Robin Lakoff, Dale Spender, Deborah Tannen, and others.
8. Hartsock, "Rethinking Modernism," 199. To be fair, one would have to concede that Rorty's privileging of cacophony, disorder, and "abnormal discourse" is an attempt to turn the tables of what has passed for normal (i.e., normalizing) discourse.
9. Jürgen Habermas, *The Theory of Communicative Action, Volume I: Reason and the Rationalization of Society; Volume II: Lifeworld and System: A Critique of Functionalist Reason*, both trans. Thomas McCarthy (Boston: Beacon Press, 1987).
10. Peter Dews, *Logics of Disintegration: Post-Structuralist Thought and the Claims of Critical*

Theory (London: Verso, 1987), 221.

11. Jürgen Habermas, *Der Philosphische Diskurs der Moderne* (Frankfurt, 1985), as cited by Dews, *Logics of Disintegration*, 221, emphasis in original.

12. Iris Marion Young, *Justice and the Politics of Difference* (Princeton, NJ: Princeton University Press, 1990), 34, emphasis mine.

13. Nancy Fraser, *Unruly Practices: Power, Discourse, and Gender in Contemporary Social Theory* (Minneapolis: University of Minnesota Press, 1989), 46–47.

14. Fraser, *Unruly Practices*, 126, 120, 128.

15. Carole Pateman, *The Sexual Contract* (Stanford, CA: Stanford University Press, 1988), 56, 57, 8.

16. Hans-Georg Gadamer, *Truth and Method* (New York: Crossroads, 1982), 341.

17. Peter Brooks, *Reading for the Plot: Design and Intention in Narrative* (New York: Vintage, 1985), 53–54.

18. Ross Chambers, *Room for Maneuver: Reading (the) Oppositional (in) Narrative* (Chicago: University of Chicago Press, 1991), 4, 7, 212, 214, 9. See also Ross Chambers, *Story and Seduction: Narrative Seduction and the Power of Fiction* (Minneapolis: University of Minnesota Press, 1984).

19. Goffman, *Forms of Talk*, 85.

20. Iris Marion Young, *Justice*, 5–6.

21. Ibid., 6.

22. Nancy Armstrong and Leonard Tennenhouse, *The Ideology of Conduct: Essays on Literature and the History of Sexuality* (New York: Methuen, 1986), 2.

23. Audre Lorde, "Uses of the Erotic: The Erotic as Power," in *Sister Outsider* (Freedom, CA: Crossing Press, 1984), 55.

24. See, for example, work by Nancy Henley, Barrie Thorne, Deborah Tannen, and others. Some recent research has begun to challenge the long-standing finding that men talk more than women, interrupt women more than women interrupt men, and, in general, exercise strategies of control and dominance in mixed-sex conversational settings. See, for example, work by Deborah James, Sandra Clarke, and Janice Drakich. In place of potentially essentializing categories such as gender, race, and age, sociolinguistic researchers are increasingly beginning to work in terms of varied forms of differential status and power.

25. Zora Neale Hurston, *Their Eyes Were Watching God* (Urbana: University of Illinois Press, 1978), 24.

26. Ibid., 169.

27. Ibid., 18.

28. Ibid., 23.

29. Ibid., 274–75.

30. Ibid., 23.

31. Ibid., 278.

32. Ibid., 284–85.

33. Fredric Jameson, *The Political Unconscious: Narrative as a Socially Symbolic Act* (Ithaca, NY: Cornell University Press, 1981), 79.

34. "Performance is thus a kind of talking back," Judith Butler writes. This discussion of performativity draws on Judith Butler's *Gender Trouble: Feminism and the Subversion of Identity* (New York: Routledge, 1991), as well as Andrew Parker and Eve Kosofsky Sedgwick, eds., *Performativity and Performance* (New York: Routledge, 1995). For a longer critique of current theories of performativity, see my *Erotics of Talk: Women's Writing and Feminist Paradigms*.

The Talking Stage

6 Drama's Mono-Dialogics

Deborah R. Geis and

S. I. Salamensky

Dramatic speech, as scripted, formalized talk, would appear inherently dialogic—and may be, if more in Mikhail Bahktin's than the common sense of the word. As a model for conversational etiquette, it is less than ideal. As in our everyday talk, one character may command more linguistic space than another present on stage. He or she may also speak alone on stage, or—within or without a conversant's hearing—directly address the audience. Further, the presence of audience members, posed as (usually silent, usually unacknowledged) interlocutors, renders any dialogical relationship, on stage, a "trialogical" one, and even theorizing the audience itself as "one" body is problematic. Intricate theatrical, narrative, and epistemological questions arise from talk—actors', as well as our own—that goes less, or more, than two ways. Much has been written on avant-garde theater's employments of multiple and/or marginal voices. Yet even at its most traditional, dramatic talk contains multitudes.

Staged talk—like the unscripted version—is far from a singular form. Even monologue takes many shapes: it may be delivered as an aside or to other characters, overtly to an audience, indirectly to an audience, and so forth. It may serve to reveal some type of internal story, backstory, memory, or secret. It may be a presentational device for providing narration or exposition in a play, especially through a "narrator" figure who addresses the audience at structured intervals, as in a Greek chorus—simultaneously, as Keir Elam points out, calling attention to the play's performativity and inviting the audience further into suspension of disbelief.[1] Monologue may serve as a structural device, counterpointing a second level of dialogue or serving as climax to a piece. And, of course, an entire play may take the form of a monologue, alone or punctuated by dialogic scenes. Soliloquy—as a form of monologue addressed by the character to him- or herself—may also suggest introspection, and often entails revelation impossible within the standard theatrical framework, allowing the audience what would be, in everyday talk, a sort of mind reading. Soliloquy's metatheatrical implications have historically brought upon it charges of implausibility. William Congreve, for example, characterized it as a crude, provisional device, bearable only in such circumstances as revelation of a villain's plans to the audience:

> when a man in soliloquy reasons with himself, and pros and cons, and weighs all his designs, we ought not to imagine that this man either talks to us, or to himself; he is only thinking, and thinking such matter as were inexcusable folly in him to speak. But because we are concealed spectators of the plot in agitation, and the poet finds it necessary to let us know the whole mystery of his contrivance, he is willing to inform us of this person's thoughts; and to that end is forced to make use of the expedient of speech, no other better way being yet invented for the communication of thought.[2]

Monologue—like the everyday "self-talk" Erving Goffman characterizes as largely adherent to the heightened states of childhood, drunkenness, and madness[3]—is recognizable because it often serves as the vehicle for some type of extraordinary discourse. Ken Frieden makes a case for the "uniqueness" of dramatic self-talk:

> Monologue may be understood either as a static opposition to communicative dialogue or as a dynamic swerve away from prior conventions of discourse. . . . [It] signals the active break from norms of ordinary language and is thus allied with innovation, deviant discourse, and creativity. Monologues often strive to evade norms, although pure monologue, in the sense of a linguistic mode that has entirely freed itself from otherness, is an impossibility.[4]

One major "narrative power" of the monologue is its capacity for manipulating time, or our sense of time, in the drama that unfolds before us. As Susanne Langer suggests, theater takes place in a kind of "perpetual present" consistently energized by a sense of the as-yet-unrevealed.[5] But monologue allows the playwright to dislocate, fragment, and otherwise transform this perpetual present into other temporal modes—thus enacting a multiplicity not just of presences, but presents. The monologuist may compress time by narrating a series of events; suspend time entirely by offering words that do not affect the time elapsed in the play;[6] move either forward or backward in time (and, sometimes, move the ensuing narrative with him or her as well); and/or alter time by changing our perception of the rate at which time moves in the play. In fact, it is not unusual for all of these effects to occur in the course of a single monologue or series of monologues, particularly when the action of the play itself is established as occurring within the speaker's head, as in Arthur Miller's *After the Fall* (1964), or when the action is conveyed primarily through the words of a central storyteller, as in David Mamet's *Prairie du Chien* (1985).

Monologue may also enact a multiplicity of spaces or dimensions. Elam argues that the "theatrical text is defined and perceived above all in spatial terms";[7] and Langer has proposed the useful idea that drama relies largely on our sense of "virtual space," the "intangible image" the viewer receives as the result of seeing the relationships suggested by the set, characters, and words of a play and the "world" these establish.[8] "Speech is like a quintessence of action," writes Langer;[9] and, although the monologue may be accompanied by physical actions of the speaker and/or other characters, its dominant characteristic is still the compression of action into words, of stage space into "narrative space." This is most evident when the monologue eclipses or substitutes for a series of events in the past or present of the characters whose actions we had, up to that point, witnessed onstage as part of the narrative of the play, as in David Rabe's *Streamers* (1976). But even the "psychological" monologue calls for such a transformation of space (again, e.g., Hamlet's soliloquies).

A result of the monologue's propensity to warp time and space, then, is that it creates types of narrative fluidity permitting the dramatic work to transcend the physical limitations of the playing space. That is, theater has certain material limits that affect its narrative form: it is confined to a particular space, time, number of players, and so forth, and thus its ability to appear to extend beyond these boundaries must depend primarily upon manipulation of the spectators' imaginations. This manipulation may, of course, take place through the use of lights, sound, and other techniques to transform the playing-space itself. But the monologue serves as a device by which non-"theatrical" leaps through time, space, and "logic" may occur with the same fluidity onstage as in written narrative or film montage. Susan Sontag has claimed that the "irreducible distinction" between film and theater lies in the idea that "theatre is confined to a logical or continuous use of space," while film "has access to an alogical or discontinuous use of space."[10] Sontag's distinction may be accurate in a literal sense, but perhaps less of an "irreducibility" exists than she would contend, for the monologue allows access to alogical or discontinuous space in the performed narrative.

Monologue allows the playwright to create at least the impression of narrative perspective or point of view, which in a novel might be accomplished with the guiding narratorial voice and in a film with a subjective camera angle. This is not to imply that a parallel point-of-view mechanism is possible, or even desirable, in drama. But the monologue does permit what might more accurately be termed "hypothetical points of view"—as in Bernard Shaw's *Too True to Be Good* (1932)—forcing the audience to decide how to delineate boundaries between the speaking subject and the dramatist who speaks through that speaking subject. In other words, the speaker of the monologue tends to take on an "authorial" or "authoritative" role, especially if he or she functions as narrator. Yet this very "authority" can serve as an opportunity for the playwright to manipulate the audience's judgment, for instance in cases of unreliable narrating characters, or monologues by more than one character that compete for the spectator's sense of which speaker to trust, as in Harold Pinter's *No Man's Land* (1974).

At the same time, the speaker of a monologue supplants the dramatist as storyteller because it is, after all, the speaker who brings the playwright's words to life. As Elam notes, "The actor imposes the histrionic subcodes regulating his performance as a whole and so his combining of messages into discourse. The actor, from this point of view, is the main agent of transcodification on stage."[11]

Unlike written narrative, in which the storyteller's words are conveyed immediately to the reader, then, drama (in performance) involves a displacement of the narrator(s) from the author to the actors. It is therefore not surprising that while the speaker of a monologue often seems to be ventriloquizing the playwright's narrator, the actor also, paradoxically, assumes narrative authority surpassing that which seems to inhere to the dramatist's "rights" as creator of the monologue.

At the heart of the paradoxical quality of this dramatic talk is its simultaneous focusing and interruption of stage action; it forces spectators to imagine things they cannot see, yet is accompanied by the invisible exhortation that they "see" the speaker as a character in (or at least in the context of) the onstage action they have been witnessing up to that point. It inevitably involves, then, the redirection of the audience's attention. This redirection may be an acknowledged one, as in the Brechtian monologue. More often, however, it is more subtle. In the process of deroulement, as the spectator gradually realizes that the dialogue has transmuted into a monologue, it is as if a form of seduction has taken place: the monologue has surrounded us before we have quite realized what has happened.

Where a monologic speech appears to address the audience directly, the paradoxical position of the audience in respect to the speaker intensifies. It is possible to argue that this type of utterance simultaneously involves the audience most directly, and reasserts the spectator's very powerlessness. The audience seems to be addressed, yet its members are not (except in certain forms of experimental theater) in a position to respond, for doing so would, in Goffman's words, occasion a "frame break."[12] This indicates that the spectator has chosen to accept a role as helpless, frozen, powerless (at least in a traditional theatrical setting); yet, for the duration of the monologue, the spectator is granted a privileged, or pseudoprivileged, status as confidant to the character.

Just as the playwright may choose to manipulate the apparent authority of the monologue's speaker, he or she may also take advantage of the schismatic position that ensues when characters talk to spectators face to face. Peter Handke's *Offending the Audience* (1966) is an example of a piece that plays directly upon this uncomfortable position in which the audience finds itself:

> Because we speak to you, you can become conscious of yourself. Because we speak to you, your self-awareness increases. You become aware that you are sitting. You become aware that you are sitting in a theater. . . . Try not to blink your eyelids. Try not to swallow any more. Try not to move your tongue. . . . Try not to smell anything. Try not to salivate. Try not to sweat. . . . Try not to breathe. Why, you are breathing. Why, you are salivating. Why, you are listening. Why, you are smelling. Why, you are swallowing. Why, you are blinking your eyelids. Why, you are belching. Why, you are sweating. Why, how terribly self-conscious you are.[13]

In Handke's play spectators become the "actors" and are subjected to verbal assaults of this kind in the monologues of the performers (qua "spectators"), who mock and deride the actors' (audience's) feebleness and inability to "act"—and, of course, inability to speak.

More recently, solo performance artists have taken further leaps over the apparent narrative boundaries of traditional theatrical discourse. Spalding Gray, for instance, mines "autobiographical" material to create a public persona as a storyteller whose rambling, hypnotic, "talky" anecdotes (though, with time, increasingly more scripted and directed)[14] in such pieces as *Gray's Anatomy* (1992) blur the distinctions between performance and talk, fictional and nonfictional narrative, character and performer. Anna Deavere

Smith, in *Fires in the Mirror* (1992), *Twilight: Los Angeles 1992* (1993), and other works, has developed a technique that juxtaposes her documentary-like (but stylized) replication of the voices and bodies of others (in *Fires*, for example, she summons a range of interview subjects from Al Sharpton to a Lubavitcher woman) with the audience's awareness that she, solo, is the sometimes-incongruous figure who is doing all of the talking.

Drama, seemingly drawn from talk, retalks talk, and—in the postmodern context—effects a revitalized, and revivifying, return to talk. And it remains to be seen what new performers might do further with it: talking within themselves, at each other, to an audience; talking excessively, outrageously, illogically, monologically . . . out from the electronic screen—or across the boards of the plain wooden stage.

Notes

1. Keir Elam, *The Semiotics of Theatre and Drama* (London: Methuen, 1980), 90.
2. William Congreve, *The Double Dealer*, in *The Comedies of William Congreve*, ed. Eric S. Rump (Middlesex: Penguin, 1985), 123.
3. Erving Goffman, *Forms of Talk*, (Philadelphia: University of Pennsylvania Press, 1981), 109.
4. Ken Frieden, *Genius and Monologue* (Ithaca, NY: Cornell University Press, 1985), 20.
5. Susanne K. Langer, *Feeling and Form* (New York: Charles Scribner's Sons, 1953), 307.
6. Peter Szondi claims that "if soliloquies followed one another without any dialogue, time would stand still" (*Theory of the Modern Drama,* ed. and trans. Michael Hays [Minneapolis: University of Minnesota Press, 1987], 83).
7. Elam, *Semiotics of Theatre*, 56.
8. Langer, *Feeling and Form*, 72.
9. Ibid., 314.
10. Susan Sontag, "Film and Theatre," in *Film Theory and Criticism*, ed. Gerald Mast and Marshall Cohen, 2d ed. (New York and Oxford: Oxford University Press, 1979), 366.
11. Elam, *Semiotics of Theatre*, 85. Elam defines transcodification as the phenomenon of the translation of semantic information from one system to another, or as one whereby the information can be supplied simultaneously by different kinds of signals (84).
12. Erving Goffman, *Frame Analysis* (Boston: Northeastern University Press, 1974), 371.
13. Peter Handke, *Offending the Audience*, in *Kaspar and Other Plays*, trans. Michael Roloff (New York: Farrar, Straus, & Giroux, 1969), 20–21.
14. For further discussion of Gray's work and the issue of spontaneity, see Deborah R. Geis, *Postmodern Theatric(k)s: Monologue in Contemporary American Drama* (Ann Arbor: Univeristy of Michigan Press, 1995), 154–60.

The Talkie

7

Early Cinematic Conversations

Tom Conley

Most baby boomers recall the word "talkie" from conversations overheard between parents discussing how they felt when they "went to the movies" in childhood and adolescence. A "talkie" was a "movie," but it was a movie of a certain kind, a movie distinguished from a "silent," an experience that still stood strong on the horizon of memory. No doubt the keystone of the edifice of the talkie was its derivation from the "movie," the noun with which it had been destined to rhyme. It could remain in proximity to what might, if a word inhabiting the world of semiotics of years past can be disinterred, be called its *genotype*. The phenotype of the talkie was based, if we are to believe in its affiliation with the "movie," on the way that words were sensed to move in and about the image. Just as a "movie" was rooted in things moving, a "talkie" could be construed to be a new form in which words, detached from what they were said to designate, began to move across the field of the image.

In the early talkie spoken words and sounds literally had a life of their own, especially in narratives built from exchanges of conversation. Our parents told us that in the early years of the Depression, in addition to finding a warm place to sleep away listless hours of unemployment, as spectators they paid money to watch words materialize in and about the moving image. They went to see words, as it were, take form and move about the confines of the frame. Speech had the bonus of being detached from any real origin and, as I will argue in this essay, its drift had a tactical virtue that conferred the viewing and study of the early talkie with a political dimension. The latter was especially obvious, we can surmise, at the beginning of the sound era, because speech and noise that were apparently located in the image-field were never taken as given. Synchrony, when it was not *naturalized*, was seen as a construction of technology, not as the essence of the moving picture. The state of detachment that inhered in synchrony in the early sound picture conferred upon the narrative and the image a condition of distanciation and of mobility. The spectator who lived at the cusp of two technologies no doubt sensed an especially attractive mobility in speech that went along with its own mechanical and inorganic virtue.

Not that speech and the image had ever been divorced from each other. At the turn of the twentieth century Alice Guy and a host of vanguard filmmakers produced shorts that offered synchronous sound emanating from recording machines that were meticulously timed to be in concert with the flow of images. These films were of short duration and set in the context of miniature narratives built around the wonder given to hold in synchrony. Some were built for well-known performers to sing arias among groups of picnickers on the shores of the Seine outside of Paris. Others were static takes of orchestras playing familiar tunes.[1] Even if film first saw light without speech, it nonetheless was located in worlds where conversation was amply present, as shown by the use of sound cues from its beginnings in nickelodeons.[2] Before its invention there was the cabaret, and the café—a *locus amoenus* in silent film, where the film seemed to enact in dialogue an instant replay of the vital inanities of everyday life. There were, too, the conversational spaces where time was, in the words of Henri Lefebvre, forever "mediated," such as in the tramway, the horse-pulled bus, and the new subway, in whose wagons people, pushed into each others' noses, if they knew each other, could "talk" about the movies they had seen.[3] The aubible conversations of people going to the movies had, in an immediate and crucial effect of ideology, to be reproduced in silence in order, after the films were seen, to be reanimated in life. The silent din of conversation in the pre-talkie years no doubt set early standards of what had been called, in the early years of the printed book, the manual of "civil conversation." The spectator could go to the movie in order to learn how to talk in the imagination, and how, too, to revive dialogue within his or her own body, in mimesis of a new panoply of silent types, without the need of interlocutors.[4] What Benjamin called the shock of modern life was no doubt alleviated by the conversation that chimed with it, especially in areas were cinema could be "talked about" for the sake of a common practice of everyday life.

But in the "talkie," in the genre that now has a marvelous historical specificity, conversation seems to take some different turns. We can assume that "talkie" now belongs to the cusp of the silent and the sound traditions, at an intermediate or even amphibious stage where the silent style continued to be at odds with the new and strange invention of sound synchrony. It may be for at least two reasons that critics as far afield as André Bazin and Kevin Brownlow have adduced. First, by the time of the mid-1920s, the silent film had devised many ways of incorporating speech into its visual rhetoric—intertitles were used as overt and covert agents of oral language. Whether the words were printed over basic black, or within an ornate cartouche bearing he production company's insignia, the intertitle was a signboard that could play the role of the fade or the dissolve by moving the narrative from one place to another merely by being placed where it was. References to speech, and interjections such as "meanwhile" carried an air of redundancy, stating what the spectator had usually already visually deciphered. When words were displayed that had just been, or were just about to be, spoken, the seasoned viewer was already aware of their form and content.

Spectators were so well trained in the art of lipreading that the graphic character or typographic style of the intertitles supplanted everything that had to do with their transcriptive virtue. Intertitles were not slaves of speech or of meaning. They could be elements of rhythm and syncopation that punctuated the continuity of the image track, much as might an arrangement of commas and colons the drift of a sentence in a prose poem. They could resemble parentheses as they are found in modern literature, whose form refers to an inner speech or a third voice that is pondered in writing without being said to represent "speech itself." Intertitles were also instantaneous reprieves from the labor engaged in the decipherment of images. They reminded viewers then—as they continue to remind us now—that speech *was not there*. In the silent film, conversation or dialogue was therefore affiliated with printed writing. In the sociology of spectatorship that prevailed into the early 1930s, it might be said that intertitles rivaled the voice of the living speaker accompanying the film in the music hall where films were shown. The indication that speech could not be reproduced hardly conveyed the idea that something living and vital was "lacking" in the movie.[5] Intertitles showed that talk would in no way become—its invention always imminent in the technology of progress in cinema—a "dangerous supplement" to the autonomy of filmed images.[6]

Second, silent film quickly incorporated into its rhetoric the advent and presence of sound. Its compositions included allusions to sound that were so pervasively visible in the image-field that speech, music, and noise could almost be experienced, in a Freudian way, as if emanating from within the body of the viewer, meeting or matching what was given on the screen. By locating plots in music halls, public houses, and noisy taverns the silent film could make ambient sound and conversation irrupt within the spectator's imagination and therefore engage, consciously or unconsciously, a comparison of the differences between "life" and "cinema." "Noisy" films were shot in barrooms or places where crowds circulated with animation, such as in Raoul Walsh's *The Regeneration* (1915), where long shots of a tavern in the Bowery bring forward, like the drunken din and laughter of Rabelais's *propos des bien yvres* (in the fifth chapter of *Gargantua*), an inner music of the popular convivium.

When sound technology reached the industry it was conventional to see directors making two versions of the same film. A silent film was crafted so that it could work on its own or be equipped with a soundtrack. Film historians have appealed to Marxian criteria of historiography to show how the uneven development of sound apparatus and the slow distribution of new projectors in different places could account for the brilliance of a cinematic rhetoric, mostly confined to the years 1928–32, in which the two modes work concurrently. Films of this period have the virtue of detaching speech from an origin, such as a speaking body, and as a result they show how much the human itself seems to be a function of the operation of an artificial apparatus or the illusion of habit.[7] What we call synchrony or, better, "lip synch" in the world of cinema has as its parallel the idea of "continuity" in everyday life. Today the return to the early talkie alerts us to the ideology of continuity and the quasi-unconscious—and often erroneous—affiliation we make between synchrony and meaning. Great creative works of poetry, the novel, and cinema (but for the purposes of these pages, especially the early "talkie") call synchrony into question. They create works in which the attachment of sound to its ostensive origins is extremely tenuous and, as a result, politically and ethically exhilarating. It seems hardly by chance that the most innocuous area of cinematic representation, that of conversation—and not pragmatic exchange of information or of the passage of "messages" from one interlocutor to another—cues the political dimension of the new medium. These films bring forward the vitality of the noise of impractical speech through the detaching effect of ambient silence.

One of the most powerful works in this area is Jean Renoir's first sound film, *La Chienne (The Bitch)* (1931), which he chose to direct for the purpose of experimenting with the new recording apparatus supplied by Pierre

Braunberger and Roger Richebé. Renoir's goals were contrary to what the two magnates of sound synchrony were seeking.[8] It appears that the style of the film is one in which the recording of ambient conversation and of speech underscores the strong degree of its literal *detachment* from its origins. The effect is especially striking in view of the "realism" of the style that would otherwise attempt to produce an unmediated transcription of the world. That it is a slice of life, *une tranche vie,* as well as a prototypical model for film noir does not entirely account for what it does with conversation or how it affects the future of the talkie. It clearly bears out André Bazin's seminal remarks about the way that in the "evolution of film language" the directors of real stripe, that is, *auteurs,* use the rhetoric of silent cinema to obviate the control exerted by the soundtrack. They avoid what would easily become an enslavement to the transcriptive task that devolves upon film directors when the sound era is firmly established.[9] It shows how and why "talk" of no consequence is essential to the art of cinema, and how the future adepts of the *nouvelle vague* readily avoided the studied beauty of literature in favor of the recording of conversation. *La Chienne* stands at the basis of any historical treatment of recorded conversation.

Its force is found in the way, first, it chooses to report the speech of a dinner party, of tavern banter, and street noises. Much of the contradiction of the presence of recording apparatus (a mediation) and the realistic style (that would be unmediated) is developed in utterances that bear little meaning either for their speakers or their listeners. The film exploits the disruptive element of the recording apparatus to portray conversation in everyday life. Voiceover (what in French is more felicitously called *voix-off*) gives a sense of disembodiment to personages who feel a need to converse about their lives and their fates. Wherever they speak they ventriloquize. Surely an economic history of the cinema would say that in the early era of the talkie whenever lip synch could be avoided expensive editing could be spared. But in Renoir's film that economy becomes the area in which its aesthetics are invested.

Many points in the film show why. The first shot of the narrative is set in deep focus and displays, in the distance of an illuminated banquet room in the evening, a group of men seated around a table. The shot is taken through a dumbwaiter that offers, as if by chance, the added economy of a frame given within the frame of the setting its borders do not contain.[10] In soft focus in the foreground is placed a dessert (seemingly a sugar-glazed cake topped with strawberries or, in more properly cinematic terms, a figure of the viscosity of "bad faith" that the film will later study wherever the lens attends to liquid shapes). A live waiter approaches, his hand apprehending the pie before he swirls around and brings it to the table. The action queues the movement of the narrative into the conversation filling the greater space of the banquet. The eye of the spectator is led to hover at low level, over the dark space of the dumbwaiter, and move into the illuminated area where the men are conversing. But encrusted in the image is the contradiction of a visual area given to the circulation of shards of conversation. The camera is obliged to use slight rack-focus pull in order to keep a clear view of both the foreground of the dumbwaiter and the background of the dinner party. The banter invites the eye to seek inside of the frame the origin of the conversation that in fact cannot be synchronized with the lips of the men seen at the table.

Even though the narrative will build on the theme of desire in the beginning of senescence (the men, whose bald heads were ironically replicated as reflecting globes, will soon go whoring after the party), a relation of closed spaces, greater worlds at large, and the tenuous connections of speech floating in or between areas of different proportion is already given. The din of festive conversation, of "men's talk" at a stag party, signals a colloquy by which the ritual noise does *not* serve up the illusion of a momentary silencing of social contradiction. Although it counts among many of Renoir's takes of dinners passed at long tables that define a deep space held in sharp focus, the shot seems to equate cigar smoke with speech. Noise and vapor constitute a dyspeptic and almost nauseous feeling. A tracking shot that moves along the side of the table to register mechanically the physiognomies of each of the participants signals how the banter is no less detached from the ambiance than it is from the the recording apparatus. Each of the guests is a stiff portrait in a revue that leads, finally, to that of the future protagonist, Legrand (Michel Simon), in formal attire, wearing pince-nez spectacles, sporting a sullen look shown in medium close-up. The moralizing tenor of his words, to the effect that revelry is nothing more than a panacea in place of the stern beauty of silence, is clearly "out of place" in the conversation. It signals that the sequence and, quite possibly, the rest of the film will equate the "meaning" of his speech to matters of less consequence than cinematic form. Crucial in this respect is how the gratuity of the conversation underscores the urgency of the film form. The emptiness of the aural register underscores the luminosity of shots that become paintings in black and white.

We are witnesses in optical terms to what is happening in the aural area of the film. The ambience of festive sounds near and far are shown together, jostling with one another, but in such a way that the spectator is shown to be free to choose to retain whatever he or she might wish. Conversation is nothing more than a "sign" of a new kind of sound, of a recording mechanism that cannot be invested with any ulterior meaning. In this sense the opening of the film attests to the force of an artifice that calls into question the very nature of realistic effects, all the while constructed from them. When the conversation indicates that it amounts to less than its performance by accomplished players (Renoir sought to de-dramatize all oral expression while directing the film), it also underscores how it empties itself of its trans-missive function. It is a "sound-sign" that anticipates the location of future film in quotidian activity. It is an "aural" essay in the way that Godard, an avid viewer of *La Chienne*, later launches "visual" essays in the name of Renoir.[11]

Effects of empty speech may indeed be the content of the men's after-dinner talk in the sequence that appeals to the noble literary tradition of the gentle colloquoy or its inverse, the *propos de table licentieux*.[12] Or it might be the charm of the clinking of glasses and clatter of plates mixed with the vital function of "noise" understood to be a circulation of energies in which a so-cial order is given to function. Or else it might be the aspect of a delay, in which as spectators we seek to find—to see and to hear together—signs that will emplot us: the conversation on the soundtrack does not yet yield evi-dence about the drama built on a scenario of "the physiology of marriage," one of the topoi of both *La Chienne* and its sequel of 1932, *Boudu sauvé des eaux*. Although the men in the sequence seem to banter over Legrand's sorry condition of a *mal marié*, the image track exceeds the narrative frame by in-sisting on the free circulation of "sound-signs." The initial sequence does not allow the narrative to inaugurate a passive viewing relation by which the story might encourage the viewer to choose to register certain sounds and images at the cost of setting others aside. The visual and aural fields, mixed together, continually detach each from the other so as to produce a critical relation with both sound and image.

In the noise and confusion of the first shot is designated the area where the "talkie" begins to work in the field of the image. The disembodiment of voice and image is all the greater for the bilingual spectator who sees in the figure of the "dumbwaiter" that which is given to be mute, without speech, or even that which records the event within the event being recorded. For a French viewer the dumbwaiter is a *monte-plats*, a mechanism driven by a set of pulleys and an elevator lined with cogwheels, sprockets, and rails. It is a sort of vertical articulation of the dolly used to obtain horizontal movement in tracking shots. But here the movement comes by way of the imaginary penetration of the spectator's eye into a space punctuated with men's after-dinner conversation. The darkness of the framed foreground stands in strong contrast to the illuminated room in the background, shown in *contrejour*. Almost implied is that the space in the *monte-plats* resembles a dark room, a *chambre obscure*—that is, an object related to the mechanism recording the film. The framing device of the narrative in the first shot is indeed an icon of the apparatus producing the film, but it is unsettling by being set forward, in a "repoussoir" effect, at once immediately before our eyes and before the narrative takes hold.

In the film that follows, the dumbwaiter never returns, but a plethora of dumb characters soon fill out the rest of the story. Implied by the mechanical device in the first shot is that a mechanical aura will prevail, and that the general stupidity of the situation and the characters who play out their destinies in this "slice of life" are related to the tenuous synchrony of the sound and image tracks. Herein the politics of Renoir's first talkie then, in 1931, and now, in 1999. The dumbness that is given in the tensions of sound and image is also a residual muteness that underscores the autonomous relation that the prevailing conversation of the film—ordinary, everyday, of tenors and tones that are anything but literary or related to printed writing—will hold with its characters.

The conversation is uttered as if detached from a context that would confer with psychology, or else it is marked only to have a strange but strongly cinematic effect in the visual field. On the basis of the first shot it can be hypothesized that the apparent realism of the film, in which are concerned personages of a level of standing equal to or lower than that of the viewer, is guided by its attraction to things "dumb," dumbness understood here less in terms of a quotient of intelligence that might be ascribed to the characters (in what most viewers would take to be a descending order from Legrand to Lulu) than in terms of the silence or the visual compositions that envelop the conversations. From the beginning the conversation prompts a break or a deviation from meaning.

The rupture is emphasized in almost all of the conversations in the ensuing narrative. Speech becomes, as the names of the characters—"Lulu," "Dédé"—suggest, something like baby talk or the discourse of marionettes. Everyday exchanges appear devoid of interlocution. Utterances are made, but they rarely find "receivers" in their listeners. Messages tend to be minimal quanta of expression that only identify the speakers or their ambient worlds. Legrand speaks an affected, moralizing French in a deadpan voice that in the sequences in the office makes his coworkers snicker. Adèle intones exclamation and vituperation that place her beyond even a parody of the most degraded species of shrew. Lulu, the agglutinated name given to "Lucienne," the bitch ("la chienne" herself), engages Dédé and Legrand with words yielding an entirely mechanical expression of both affection and duplicity. Everywhere spoken words either fall short of the mark or bring attention to their own beauty as clichés. The sequence attests to an overriding ventriloquism.[13]

Where communication does take place, it seems to be in the mute areas where personages in the frame regard objects within its purview. They stare at paintings and seem, in their ostensible deaf-and-dumb relations with them, to whisper pleasure in silence punctuated by street noises. Inner conversation, created in part by the amphibious quality of this film as both a "silent" and a "talkie," seems to advance in a strange, almost hieroglyphic language that by chance—and as if by chance alone—attaches voice (mostly out of frame or not localized in shots of long duration and in deep focus) or noise to objects in the visual field.

The double nature of *La Chienne* as a silent and as a talkie confers it with an unlikely but telling critical dimension. The disaffected and purely gratuitous effect of conversation—carefully registered in the first shot of the narrative—brings forward the points where the film theorizes its effects built upon the autonomy of sound and image. That very autonomy calls attention to the presence of speech in places where, in all actuality, it cannot be found or where it is anything but "present" or authenticating. In Renoir's film most of the conversation takes place in these intermediate areas. Like the intertitles or the fade-ins and fade-outs in black, speech seems to move inwardly, in toward ambivalence, toward a "weakened deixis," and toward a confusion of inner and outer or visual and aural registers.[14] Yet at one crucial point the contrary would seem to be the case. At the conclusion Renoir uses a spare intertitle bearing the word "Epilogue" to extend and to keep from ending a film that has ended in the space of the courtroom where Dédé was convicted for avowing in all truth, in surprisingly *formal* speech uttered directly (with strong deixis) to a judge and a jury, that he never killed his mistress.

The epilogue gives way to an ironic sequence in which the protagonist, now a Parisian bum, meets Alexis Godard, another bum, the first husband of the notorious Adèle. One clochard meets the other. They wear identically frayed jackets closed with safety pins where their buttons have disappeared. The partners express surprise over the passage of time and fate as they "talk" about their past lives. At that moment there intervenes the mute figure of the director, Renoir himself, reflected on the mirror of a car taking away a self-portrait painted by the protagonist in his former life as a Sunday painter.[15] The mute picture appears and disappears in the shape of the "dumb listener" to conversation of both rich and hollow implication. The hero's interlocutor, upon hearing of the tribulations of his friend, notes vapidly that "faut de tout pour faire un monde" (you need everything to make a world). That snatch of conversation, of the kind that often passes for proof of Renoir's humanism in much of the criticism devoted to the director, is in fact disembodied, out of synch, and at once as brilliant and as dumb as every other enunciation or visual shape seen and heard in the film. It is both specious and fulfilling.

That is has a double valence is, it seems, a sign of its worth as a piece of conversation in a medium at a moment of its history when such productive ambivalence is possible. The return to the style of Renoir's first "talkie" serves the purpose of theorizing the greater gist of conversation in general. The return leads to a careful labor of disassembling, a labor vital for creative work with stray noise and words, the raw material of much of the cinematic art.

It might be concluded that the pieces of conversation that open the sound-track of *La Chienne* have the broader critical virtue of calling into question effects of synchrony or of transmission that naturalize the conditions and exchange of meaning. The foundations of logic and of meaning tend to be "tracked" according to points of origin and emission of speech. When early sound film—notwithstanding an economy lent to letting the aural dimension of the film float at large in the field of the image—detaches talk from its speakers, it inaugurates a political labor of the first order.

Through the lens of the early talkie it is possible to look at everyday life as a form of ventriloquism or a constructed coordination of sounds and images. Detaching conversation from emitters and receivers, this kind of film—but especially *La Chienne* and its progenitors—constitutes a tactics of invention, analysis, and practice. Reengaging the early talkie serves to move much of the recent and good work of film history into broader areas of the study of ideology at large. At a time when speech and conversation in the media have been naturalized to greater and greater degrees, and when the grounds of communication have more and more been taken as going without saying, occasional regression to the "oral stage" of cinema can only be salubrious.

Notes

1. In these films, most of which were aimed at celebrating the mechanism producing the effect, the singer was a reflection of the recording machine, at once its object and its raison d'être. Film historians have insisted over and again on the way that the cabaret was related to the birth of the movie. Myth has it that Méliès, ambulating along a Parisian boulevard, peered through the vitrine of the café in which the *cinématographie*, the invention by the aptly named Brothers Lumière, was so moving its spectators that they hid below their tables when they saw a steam-driven locomotive chug into the station at La Ciotat.

2. See Richard Abel, *The Ciné Goes to Town: French Cinema, 1896–1914* (Berkeley: University of California Press, 1994).

3. Two recent books underscore the point with clarity: Leo Charney and Vanessa Schwartz, eds., *Cinema and the Invention of Everyday Life* (Berkeley: University of California Press, 1996), especially the contribution by Margaret Cohen ("Panoramic Literature and the Invention of Everyday Cinema"); and Leo Charney's *Drift: Cinema and Modernity* (Durham, NC: Duke University Press, 1998).

4. Readers of Henry James seem to share the effect of a spectator imagining the gist of conversation in a silent film. James's stories are riddled with silent conversations that never exit the area of the inner speech of his "reflector" characters, such as that of the switchboard operator in "In the Cage," a story that merits comparison with Griffith's "The Lonedale Operator."

5. See Noël Burch, *Life to These Shadows* (Berkeley: University of California Press, 1991), on the tradition of the commentator of cinema in the cabaret.

6. We need only reflect on the relation that Jacques Derrida's concept of logocentrism, developed in *De la grammatologie* (Paris: Minuit, 1967), holds with the tradition of silent

film. What Derrida studies in Rousseau's fear of writing in his first book of collected articles is anchored in cinema. Marie-Claire Ropars-Wuilleumier showed how the logocentrism and dissemination were tied to film theory in the first chapter of *Le Texte divisé* (Paris: PUF, 1981), ch. 1.

7. In "Hearing Voices: Audition and Artistic Identity in French Text and Film" (Ph.D. thesis, University of Minnesota, 1998), Kristine Joelle Butler writes an elegant history of the detachment of voice from body in the relations of literature and cinema. Random conversation in cinema, she argues, belongs to a tradition especially resonant in the novel of realism.

8. See Dudley Andrew, *Mists of Regret: Culture and Sensibility of the Classic French Film* (Princeton, NJ: Princeton University Press, 1995), 104.

9. See André Bazin, "L'évolution du langage cinématographique," in *Qu'est-ce que le cinéma* (Paris: Editions du Cerf, 1996).

10. A crisp reproduction of the shot is reproduced in Jean-Louis Leutrat, *'La Chienne' de Jean Renoir* (Brussels: Editions Yellow Now, 1994), 80.

11. In this respect the film emphasizes, at the moment of the birth of the illusion of synchrony, a collapse of what Gilles Deleuze calls "sensori-motor concatenations" that define the classical sound film. Conversation that goes nowhere mobilizes the effect that Deleuze follows through Ozu and Godard in the opening pages of *L'image-temps* (Paris: Minuit, 1985), 23–26.

12. Mikkail Bakhtin uses the term in the "banquet genre" he takes up in his *Rabelais*, trans. Robert Rovini (Paris: Gallimard, 1970), ch. 1. Michel Jeanneret expands on it in his *Des mets et des mots* (Paris: José Corti, 1987).

13. Here and elsewhere Butler's reading of the film is pertinent (see "Hearing Voices," 251–52).

14. "Weakened deixis" is the term Christian Metz used to describe the rift between speech that indicates a speaking subject's "place" in a narrative film and its atopicality in the overall mechanism of the medium. What he says of the "impersonal geography" of cinema that is gained by the weakening of deixis may have its finest case study in *La Chienne*. In this way it would call into question the anthropomorphism of most narative cinema and allow for study of a more "mobile topography" of cinema in general. In Christian Metz, *L'énonciation impersonnelle ou le site du film* (Paris: Méridiens-Klincksieck, 1991), 25, 36.

15. See Jean-Louis Leutrat's careful reading of the sequence in "Autoportrait de l'artiste en auto," *Lendemains* 18 (1993): 4–16. In his monograph on *La Chienne* (n. 10 above) he summarizes the argument, showing how Renoir gives the view an "auto-portrait" or self-portrait on the surface of the automobile, with the greater effect of a paradoxical "portrait de l'artiste en auto" becoming visible and begging the viewer to discern a kind of filmic catachresis. It confirms what is latent in the first shot studied above.

Nothing Goes without Saying

8

The Marx Brothers'
Immigrant Talk

Stanley Cavell

Movies magnify, so when pictures began talking, they magnified words. Somehow, as in the case of opera's magnification of words, this made their words mostly ignorable, like the ground, as if the industrialized human species had been looking for a good excuse to get away from its words, or looking for an explanation of the fact that we do get away, even must. The new availability of the scripts of several Marx Brothers films—*Monkey Business* (1931), *Duck Soup* (1933), and *A Day at the Races* (1937)[1]—is a sublime invitation to stop and think about our swings of convulsiveness and weariness in the face of these films: to sense that it is essential to the brothers' sublimity that they are thinking about words, to the end of words, in every word—or, in Harpo's empathic case, in every absence of words.

Marx Brothers films, as unmistakably revealed in these scripts, are extensively explicit about their intentions. Their pun-crammed air, well recognized as a medium of social subversion, also presses a standing demand to reach some understanding—which is incomparably better avoided than faked. Someone is always barking sentiments at the brothers such as "Keep out of this loft!" to which Chico once replies, "Well, it's better to have oft and lost, than never to have loft at all," upon which Groucho pats him on the shoulder and says, "Nice work!" (*Monkey Business*). (When is to speak to do something? When is to bark to say something?) Groucho's positive evaluation is an instance of the recurrent reflexiveness in the Marx Brothers' craft, letting us know that they know that we may fall to imagining that we do not know what they are doing. A repeated example, as if to wake us from this stupor, is Chico's turning to Groucho with pride, asking, "'Ats-a some joke, eh Boss?" Groucho is complimenting Chico not only on countering a dour threat with a serene wipe-out, but on maintaining his responsiveness to a world deadened with banal and unreasoned prohibitions. (Occasionally, as in *Duck Soup*, Groucho probes to see whether the compliment is warranted, as when he feeds Chico a straight line and says in an aside, "Let's see you get out of that one.") To me it is a philosophical compliment. So I have been aggrieved to hear Groucho called a cynic. He is merely without illusion, and it is an exact retribution for our time of illusory knowingness that we mistake his clarity for cynicism and sophisticated unfeelingness.

Intention, or the desperate demand for interpretation, is gaudily acknowledged in such turns as Chico's selling Groucho a tip on a horse by selling him a code book, then a master code book to explain the code book, then a guide required by the master code, then a subguide supplementary to the guide—a scrupulous union, or onion, of semantic and monetary exchanges and deferrals to warm the coldest contemporary theorist of signs; or as acted out in Chico's chain of guesses when Harpo, with mounting urgency, charades his message that a woman is going to frame Groucho (both turns in *A Day at the Races*). But Groucho's interpretive powers achieve distinct heights of their own.

The famous packed cabin sequence from *A Night at the Opera* is simultaneously an image of the squalor of immigrant crowding and of the immigrant imitation of luxury. Groucho is outside, as befits him, ordering exhaustively from a steward (getting food is one of the brothers' standing objectives). After each item is ordered, Chico's voice from within the cabin appends, "And two hard-boiled eggs," which, after Groucho dutifully repeats it, is punctuated by a honk from within, which Groucho effortlessly responds to by adding, "Make that three hard-boiled eggs." That Harpo evidently accedes to Groucho's understanding of his honk is variously interpretable. You can imagine that Groucho has some private knowledge of Harpo's language; or you can see that Harpo's insatiability, or unsocialization, signals that he has no language (that is, that he is unable to speak in the etymological sense of being in the state of infancy). In the latter case, Harpo trusts Groucho implicitly to know his wants and to have them at heart, a trust well placed. That Harpo is shown to be asleep during Groucho's exchange with the steward suggests that Harpo is honking, wishing, in his dreams, and so with the directness of infants, preceding the detours of human desire, a possibility of dreams separately noted by Freud. Originality in speech is the rediscovery of speech. (It is, by the way, not true, as it is said, that Chico can trick Groucho. Groucho has nothing to lose and is not out to win anything for himself. He follows Chico's elaborate cons out of pure interest, to see, as if to satisfy his professional curiosity about the human situation, how they will come out. One outcome is as interesting as another. Of the thinkers I know fairly well, I believe only Thoreau is Groucho's equal in this capacity for disinterested interest, or unattachment.)

The familiar, or familial, relation between Groucho and Harpo in the arena of food suggests a relation in their sharing of certain gestures of lechery. If they were really lecherous they would no longer be funny. (Adam Gopnik made such a point about Woody Allen in the *New Yorker*.) Being parodies of lechery, they enact claims on the part of each human creature ("All God's chillun" is how they name them in *A Day at the Races*) to be loved, for no reason. Harpo would not know what to do if one of the women he chases stopped running; for him the instincts of hunger, of sex, and of the destruction of whatever can be snipped or chopped, seem equal in imaginary satisfaction. Groucho, the opposite of innocent, is a lover, but one who thinks it just as hilarious as anyone else might think it that he should be found lovable. It does both him and Margaret Dumont an injustice not to see that he wins her love and is a faithful husband to it; he courts her as fervently as, and much more persistently than, he does any other woman—he amuses her, shocks her, tells her the truth, expresses contempt for the boring and brutish flatterers in her second-rate world who would deceive her for their private purposes, and with good spirits survives her doubts about him and her faiths in him. How much can one ask for?

I see no good sense in being reasonable in my admiration for these achievements. Thinking recently about the conditions of opera, as mysterious and as initially contrived as the conditions of film, I asked myself why it was, when the Marx Brothers' thoughts turned to opera, that they proposed or inspired others to propose to them, in *A Night at the Opera*, *Il Travatore* as their example. In their realm, nothing goes without saying. It turns out, in this juxtaposition, that Leonora's initial mistaking, as it were, of her love of one brother for that of the other becomes a fundamental issue: it is to the villainous brother, in the early shadows of the drama, that she declares "my love." Perhaps she was not wrong about herself that initial time. Then one remembers that the Marx Brothers are brothers, and declare their family resemblance in one of their greatest turns, in *Duck Soup*, when Groucho and Harpo all but become mirror images of each other: and then one considers that these brothers, famous for their absurdities, may be taking on, as a grand enemy, the famously dark fixations of *Il Travatore* that just about anyone regards as exemplary of the supposed absurdities of grand opera; and so consider that their competition with that darkness, absurd only in its terrible lack of necessity, is to use the power of film to achieve the happy ending in which the right tenor gets the part, the film concluding triumphantly with the opera's most famous, ecstatically melancholy duet.

Other speculations about their choices of routine keep finding confirmation; these brothers are dashing way ahead of us. Thinking more or less blankly one time of the ships on which they approach America, quite early in *Monkey Business* and quite late in *A Night at the Opera*, I think further: Of course! The films present America as requiring discovery and as providing a home for immigrants. Then not only am I swiftly embarrassed at having forgotten that the elaborate finale of the first half of *Monkey Business* is just about the anxiety of needing a passport to enter upon the American streets of gold, but I am soon rewarded by finding Groucho conclude an exasperatingly contentious exchange with Chico by looking at the camera and declaring: "There's my argument! Restrict immigration!"; and rewarded again, or piqued, when—in response to Chico and Harpo's attempt to thwart the woman's plan to frame Groucho (to compromise him in Margaret Dumont's eyes) by hanging, so to speak, new sheets of wallpaper over Groucho and the woman seated cozily on a couch, thus concealing them from the entering suspicious one—Groucho pokes his head out of the sticky sheets to observe, "I must be a citizen. I've got my second papers"—that is, the final documents in an alien's naturalization process (as if any process could naturalize this alien).

Until my father died, seventy years after arriving on America's shores as a young man, and not many fewer than that after naturalization, he never fully shook the feeling that something might be wrong with his "papers." Perhaps helped by this knowledge, I go further into the sequence with Chico that leads to Groucho's momentary wish never to have been cast together with him. It opens in the Captain's cabin, where Groucho is so to speak impersonating the Captain:

> *Groucho*: A fine sailor you are.
> *Chico*: You can bet I'm a fine sailor. . . . My father was a-partners with Columbus.
> *Groucho*: Columbus has been dead for four hundred years.
> *Chico*: Well, they told me it was my father.
> *Groucho*: I'll show you a few things you don't know about history. Now look . . . [*Drawing a circle on a globe*] Now, there's Columbus.
> *Chico*: That's-a Columbus Circle . . .

> *Groucho*: Now, Columbus sailed from Spain to India looking for a short cut.
>
> *Chico*: Oh, you mean strawberry short cut.

And it gets still further afield. It is some mimesis of the shattered tiles of facts and interpretations, the urgent implacement of which had to prepare masses of arrivals for citizenship, learning who their fathers are, the fathers of their new country, and searching to put old and new names to unheard-of objectives. And when Groucho lets it out in disgust, "Do you suppose I could buy back my introduction to you?" I again find myself speculating: the comedy is that of outrage, of exhaustion, of the last straw. And again I feel rewarded. I'll come back to say how in a moment.

The sense of culture as something overheard, and probably as tales or plots of uncomprehensible manias, comes out also in those asides of Groucho's that fill the space of responses to impossible situations and incomprehensible demands:

> *Woman*: But I haven't any children.
>
> *Groucho*: That's just the trouble with this country. You haven't any children, and as for me . . . [*Dramatically*] I'm going back to the closet, where men are empty overcoats.

Or again, also from *Monkey Business*:

> *Same woman*: What brought you here?
>
> *Groucho*: [*Dramatically*] Ah, 'tis midsummer madness, the music in my temples . . . *Kappellmeister*, let the violas throb. My regiment leaves at dawn!

Or again:

> *Same woman*: You can't stay in that closet.
>
> *Groucho*: Oh I can't, can I? That's what they said to Thomas Edison, mighty inventor, Thomas Lindberg [*sic*], mighty flyer, and Thomas Shefsky, mighty like a rose. Just remember, my little cabbage, that if there weren't any closets there wouldn't be any hooks, and if there weren't any hooks, there wouldn't be any fish, and that would suit me fine.

To speak, as I believe is still common, of Groucho's "one-liners," as if this were his characteristic genre of response, is not helpful, not just because it is so incomplete, even inaccurate, but because what it omits reaches from the closeness to madness, or hysteria, of so much of what he has to say, to the sheer range of reference of his uncontrollable thoughts—from some memory of Russian or Cartesian melancholy about overcoats and empty men, through wisps of operetta, to a string of heroes that the natives seem to name Thomas, for the moment missing a Jefferson but including a figure from the Yiddish theater otherwise known as Boris Thomashevsky, associated, compulsively if not altogether surprisingly, with some association of Abie's Irish Rose with the teary mother's song "Mighty Like a Rose," all sometimes addressed to imaginary characters, here one called "Kappellmeister," later one called "Your honor." This delirium is to be compared, not identified, with Harpo's closeness to madness, as when, in his frantic search for the frog who has jumped away from his place in Harpo's hat, Harpo hears a man confess that he has a frog in his throat, grabs the man and prises open his jaws to retrieve his companion. It touches the madness of childhood. And it enacts an unexpected understanding of Wittgenstein's perception, in *Philosophical Investigations*, that Augustine, as characteristic of philosophers, "describes the learning of language as if the child came into a strange country and did not understand the language of the country; that is as if it already had language, only not this one." This is illuminatingly implausible if taken as about the condition of infancy, with no language yet in the picture; but illuminatingly plausible if taken as about an older child, with a certain budget of words, all due for unforeseen futures, hence against an idea of the condition of immigrancy, between languages.

What is this humor? If we take Bergson's theory of comedy as bespeaking a form of madness, of men behaving like machines, and vice versa, then we can say that the Marx Brothers turn this theory on the world, showing themselves to remain improvisory, original, in a setting of absolutely mechanical reactions to them ("This is an outrage"; "I've never been so insulted in all my life"; "Beat it!"; "Oh!"; "Just what do you mean?"; "Hey. Hey. Hey"; "Are you crazy or something?"). Their madness is a defense against madness, and neither is something over which they claim control; it is a struggle to the finish, in which the question is which side will create the last word, or destroy it.

Let's accordingly go back to the idea of a comedy of the last straw, or rather of a comedy about the last straw, about the sometimes fatal whimsicality with which people announce the judgment that a straw is the last. In *Duck Soup*, Ambassor Trentino (played by the Caesaresque Louis Calhern) says to Margaret Dumont, "Mrs. Teasdale this is the last straw! There's no turning back now. This means war!"—words Groucho may well be imagined somewhere to dispose of in his own person, if perhaps he decides to take an imaginary slight as directed to the entire regiment. When later in *Duck Soup* Groucho uses the words "Gentlemen, this is the last straw," it is in response to picking up a straw boater with its crown flapping, from among the rubble of war. Then what, if anything, do we make of Harpo, in *A Day at the Races*, attacking a mattress with a knife, pulling out the straw, and then feeding it to a horse he discloses in a closet. I would like to take this in conjunction with the line of Groucho's that closes *Monkey Business*, when after events in an old barn in which a wagon wheel becomes an imaginary wheel of fortune, a cowbell becomes a time bell in a brawl, and a watering can and then a buggy lamp are talked into as microphones, Groucho turns into a pile of hay and starts pitching strands into the air. Asked what he's doing, he replies: "I'm looking for a needle in a haystack." Now some moments earlier we had seen Groucho rise from under this hay and ask: "Where's all those farmers' daughters I've been hearing about for years?" and then disappear under the hay again. It strikes me that Groucho's self-interpretation of looking for a needle in a haystack undertakes to transfigure the coarse genre of farmer's daughter gags into a search—almost hopeless, with just room for good spirits to operate—for a heart's needle of pleasure somewhere within the dry medium of this world (like the bereft husband in *L'Atalante* diving into the river, eyes open for his vanished love).

For Groucho, throwing last straws to the wind, the world as it stands has placed its last straw, suffered its last judgment, a long time ago; yet the world as it may yet be, attested in any event in which genuine interest is shown, like a Harpo craving, a Chico scam, a young woman in love and trouble, the scandalized, ecstatic devotion of Margaret Dumont—exists beyond counts of straw.

Evidently I take the value of the published scripts of these films not to be solely or primarily that of sending us back to the films (the films themselves must do that), but also of releasing these words and deeds from a confinement to film, or to what we think of as film, or think of as a Marx Brothers film. Released to themselves, these observations are free to join the observations of, say, Bergson; or Brecht, whose *Threepenny Opera* is no more valid a development of *The Beggar's Opera* than *Duck Soup* is (it needn't be as good as the *Threepenny Opera* still to be very, very good); or Beckett, whose two barrels housing the married pair in *Endgame* make excellent sense, even of the idea of the stowaway, of the four barrels in which the stowaway brothers have set up house belowdecks at the opening of *Monkey Business*. And then we are free to think about one of Groucho's responses to the recurrent idea that a situation he's created, this time involving his medical practice, is "absolutely insane." Groucho: "Yes, that's what they said about Pasteur." No doubt the reference is to the celebrated Paul Muni film *Pasteur* made the year before *A Day at the Races*; but must one deny that Groucho is claiming his own discovery of a germ theory, this time about the disease of language, about its corruption by the communications of a corrupt world? He puts it differently, but not much differently.

I was talking about Groucho's searching for pleasure, another topic about which these films are, if asked, fully explicit. In *Duck Soup*, after Firefly (Groucho), in song, promulgates the laws of his administration as not allowing smoking, telling dirty jokes, whistling, or chewing gum, he sums it up, still singing:

> If any form of pleasure is exhibited,
> Report to me and it will be prohibited.

From which it does not follow that the brothers trust any given form of pleasure, any more than they trust any other fixation, any more than they trust; they test. Nor are their films as films exactly or purely pleasurable, any more than compulsive punning is exactly or simply funny. The unpolished air of the filmmaking, and Groucho's Brechtian objectivity, are not meant to be winning, any more (if no less) than Groucho's crawling and meowing on a balustrade.

The broad groan in response to a broad pun is a criterion of real, if a little sublimated, pain. "This is no time for puns," says Groucho, gasping with them, almost at the end of *Monkey Business*. Had someone the presence of mind to say this to Groucho, he might have answered: "Yes, that's what they said about Shakespeare." No time is the time for puns, since puns stop time, stop the forward motion of assertion, peel back the protective self-ignorance of words. Is this the pain of puns? Their pain is that of, let us say, incessant thinking—thinking among the endless things there are to say, which of them we shall have forever said, and not said, now. Their pleasure is the illusion that nothing is going unsaid.

And what is the cultural economy—say, the relation between high and low thinking—in a society that has such as the Marx Brothers in store— what is its art, its philosophy, its politics, its entertainment, its seriousness?

Let us before ending linger once more over an invitation into whose depths of implication I cannot deny Groucho perception, and, as always, without presumption, he is nothing if not tactful. It comes as part of the packed cabin sequence, cited earlier, that royal levee of services, when a woman appears to Groucho with a portable beauty tray hung before her and asks, "Do you want a manicure?" Groucho replies, "No. Come on in." I take for granted that some will be satisfied to suppose that he means, fixatedly, "No, but I want something else that you could provide." Let us suppose, however, that he has the poise with meaning, whatever command of it accrues from obedience to it, to mean or imply at least also the following: "No, but there are lots of others here; perhaps they want what you suggest"; and "Nobody really wants a manicure, but if that's all you're offering, I'll take it"; and "No, but come in since you're here and we'll see what happens." All this is quite in character for Groucho. An array of implication, like the disarray of puns, will threaten anarchy, against a demand for autarchy; but both work to make what sense is to be made of a world whose sense is stolen, in which it is to be stolen back. Both show aspects of our victimization by words, fools of them, but thereby show that there are, still, ordinary words, beyond and between us, whose lives we might imagine, which might share lives we can imagine—not simply signs and signals hovering over a destroyed landscape.

A few years ago, on a walk during a conference break, a French philosopher and I exchanged friendly regrets that we were not, as it were, culturally better prepared to do the promise of each other's work more explicit justice in our own. He reported that American friends of his had been urging him to read Emerson and Thoreau, which seemed to both of us an unlikely eventuality. I took the implication quite kindly, anyway impersonally, that no one would, or could easily, without insult, urge an American intellectual to read Montaigne and Descartes and Rousseau and Kant and Hegel . . . Culture is—is it not?—European culture. Besides, Emerson and Thoreau had read them. Had I then been fresh from reading the film scripts before me now, I might have replied—whether hopefully or not is uncertain—that to the extent he was wondering what was on my mind, hence in that tangle of American culture, an equally accurate access, and one in a sense more efficiently acquired, could be had by a few days of immersion in half a dozen Marx Brothers films. But that would have been, to borrow a self-description of Thoreau's and of Walt Whitman's, bragging.

Note

1. The Marx Brothers: *Monkey Business, Duck Soup,* and *A Day at the Races* (New York: Faber, 1993). "Film script" is not an unambiguous designation. In these editions, it designates a record of dialogue and action faithful to the finished film (supposing there is a canonical version of that). This is a sound choice and I have no quarrel with it. Other choices would have been to publish the scripts as they stood before filming, but there is apparently no surviving such text for *Duck Soup,* whose script above is wholly reconstituted from the film, and in any case such a collection would serve quite specialized purposes; or to publish original scripts together with their respective reconstitutions as filmed. This dual publication was followed by Viking some twenty years ago for *A Day at the Races* and for *A Night at the Opera.* In obvious ways this is desirable— such documentation underscores the collaboration, or mutual inspiration, of the brothers with some of the most gifted writers, and teams of writers, of comic observation and plot, of gags, and of songs during the golden period of interchange between Hollywood and Broadway. But the credits included in the above scripts should themselves suggest this. Anyway, what is mutual inspiration?

Spritzing, Skirting

9

Standup Talk Strategies

John K. Limon

The opening hypothesis is that "standup" comedy—which was named perhaps as late as 1966[1]—differs from previous forms of individual-performance comedy (on, say, the Bob Hope model) by its resemblance to talk; a corollary is that unless there is some similarity in the ways Lenny Bruce and Ellen DeGeneres talked on stage when they were doing their acts, "standup" as an art form cannot have a theory. Bruce was present at the founding of standup—the term surfaced for lexicographers the same year as his death. The beginning of standup was its high-Jewish moment (perhaps 80 percent of nationally known standups in 1960 were Jewish); almost all Jewish comedians were men; almost all Jewish male comedians were heterosexual, or made a point of performing heterosexuality;[2] and the aggressiveness of their talk—which jokes are expected to repress or displace—was often scarily explicit and direct. Lenny Bruce was the Jewish, male, hetero, aggressive comedian par excellence. Invert every term and you get Ellen DeGeneres.

If the gap between Bob Hope and Lenny

Bruce (or between Hope and Mort Sahl or Shelley Berman or Jackie Mason) is wide enough for us to assume that a new art form came into existence in the 1950s, then what of the chasm between Bruce and DeGeneres? Hope told jokes and Bruce did not; but Bruce tried one way or another to destroy his audience's sense of its integrity (threatening them if necessary), and DeGeneres seems, most of the time, to be amiably and aimlessly chatting with the crowd. Nevertheless, by considering them at their most extreme—Bruce when he verges on assault and battery, DeGeneres at her most blathering and dithering—I want to suggest that standup is a certain kind of talk, a manifestation of talking in its most disconcerting aspect, its abjectness. The premise of standup, from Bruce to DeGeneres, is that it is that which cometh out of the man, that defileth the man.[3]

What distinguishes standup from the music hall or vaudeville traditions of comedy, as they arrived at Bob Hope or Milton Berle or Henny Youngman, is that standup must, to a greater or lesser extent, sound like talk. Lenny Bruce sometimes chanted, he sometimes pontificated, he often staged polylogues in alien voices. But even at the single moment in all his career when he was most baldly—almost prelinguistically—offensive, he began his assault with talk that was as confiding and comfortable as that of Ellen DeGeneres. Here are the first three lines of the routine:

> If you've, er [*pause*]
> Ever seen this bit before, I want you to tell me.
> Stop me if you've seen it.[4]

Bruce, it seems, plays the kindly host. We are his guests, and we must be frequent guests, because Bruce is not sure whether he is repeating himself to us. He does not wish to bore us; his only aim is to please. As follows:

> If you've, er [*pause*]
> Ever seen this bit before, I want you to tell me.
> Stop me if you've seen it. [*long pause*]
> I'm going to piss on you.

Has Bruce in fact pleased us? The answer, of course, is that he has pleased us if he is joking and we get the joke. The first three lines turn out to be ambiguous in defining the event, the exact nature of which has become critical to the audience. On the one hand, the two sentences that I have divided into three lines seem not to transcend everyday talk: they are not much heightened, even in the way that setup lines in jokes are rhythmically tense.

Bruce's lines are rhythmically slack—hesitant and redundant. They create suspense only by being about it. Thus the fourth line strikes with insufficient warning, and the audience has to scramble a mental return to the first three to find evidence as to whether they are in the presence of a joke or an actual threat. What is a "bit"? Why does Bruce ask if they have seen it rather than heard it? The answer is not merely crucial to the audience but also to my essay. Only if the threat turns out to be funny does standup retain its connection to talk. (Will Bruce stop talking and commit an indecency?) The remainder of my essay will have to do the job of suggesting that that much is at stake for standup in general; the local question comes down to whether Bruce is being assaultive or amusing.

We can check off the criteria, from the inside, out. From the internal point of view of the cognitive joke theorists, we have here (almost undeniably) the form of a joke: the surprise of the punchline is an unexpected resolution of the tension—such as it is—of the setup.[5] The quatrain would seem to have sufficient quantities of sex and aggression to satisfy a Freudian account of the real content of humor.[6] Joke anthropologists would be certain that Bruce is a "ceremonial buffoon" performing "ritual humor," one form of which is "simulated defecation and urination . . . carried out with scatological overtones."[7] The problem with checking off all these criteria, seriatim, and arriving at the conclusion that there is something truly funny in Bruce's routine is that the routine does the checking off for us. First: the material is so perfectly sculpted as a joke (setup, tension, pause, punchline) as to be unique in Bruce's whole oeuvre; the joke says, "Here is a [bizarre, sick] joke," in a performance that has no other jokes at all. Thus the setup is about being setup, and the punchline literalizes the assault in that term of art. Second: the sex and aggression are very close to directly expressed, though in the Freudian diagnosis of jokes, sex and aggression are triangulated. Third: the ritual nature of the routine is proposed explicitly by Bruce as its tired justification. "Let me do a few talk bits," Bruce (after the threat) tells the audience he has told prior audiences; "No," he reports that prior audiences have always responded, "piss on us first and then do the rest of it." They want talk, evidently, but the essence of the ritual is not merely talk. Whatever else the joke may be about, its real subject is itself (will the routine stay within the bounds of the joke?)—but what would joke analysts find funny in that?

I have not yet revealed, by way of evidence, whether anyone ever laughed at Bruce's threat. For the sake of misdirection, let me mention that when Bruce told the joke, if that is what it is, in Australia, no one laughed. But the fact is that Bruce did not tell quite the same joke in Australia. Here is what he told the Australians, as reported by his biographer, Albert Goldman: "I'm going to do something that's never been done in a nightclub—I'm going to piss on you." To note that the Australian audience did not laugh at this is to underestimate the severity of its verdict. "The audience cowered. A few masochistic giggles were the only response. Some people thought Lenny was mad. Some thought he needed a fix. Some thought he was being deliberately outrageous because he wanted the engagement canceled."[8]

The Australian audience did not, in short, think the joke a good one, which does not mean that they thought it a bad one; they did not attribute to the bit a humorous intention in the first place. They were certainly within their rights as a comedy audience not to find the comedian funny—the first axiom of standup theory is that there is no gainsaying an audience's judgment. The contretemps was more primitive than that, so primitive that we may wonder, along with the anthropologist Mary Douglas: "When people throw excrement at one another whenever they meet, either verbally or actually, can this be interpreted as a case of wit, or merely written down as a case of throwing excrement?"[9]

It was a case of throwing excrement in Australia: Mary Douglas's way of phrasing the matter obscures the distinction between talk and action for the sake of putting into relief the distinction between aggression and seduction. It was wit in America: the audience's assurance that Bruce was only talking turns aggression into a mode of seduction. I have timed one American audience's laughter in response to this routine, and it lasts seventeen seconds; I have never heard laughter that prolonged. Two seconds of laughter may greet a standard joke from the *Tonight Show* monologue. The response to the best joke of the night—usually one that reflects back on the joking itself, so that laughter comes in two cognitive waves—might last six seconds. An oddity of the laughter at Bruce's urination threat is that it does not, on the contrary, wane and wax. There is a half second of rumbling followed by seventeen seconds of uncontrolled laughing, accompanied by one or two people clapping though not applauding, adding the percussion to their laughter, as if it were not possible to laugh sharply enough. It takes, evidently, a half second for the joke to work, which more or less automatically sets off two seconds of laughter, leaving a full quarter of a minute to be puzzled over.

I quoted Mary Douglas as wondering whether it is witty or not "when people throw excrement at one another whenever they meet." The intriguing phrase is "whenever they meet." It could not be a case of ritual joking if it only happened once; if it keeps happening, it seems a fair question how it could be anything but a ritual. Whatever the behavior means, the participants in it seem to want to keep meaning it. In this light, we notice that Bruce's urination threat in Australia had no ritual tradition to be invoked: urinating on an audience is merely a "nightclub novelty." How would that be funny? Maybe we could eke a little humor out of the jovial, showbiz tinniness of this characterization of offensive micturition. But there is no surprise in referring to the act as a surprise. On the other hand, Bruce in America seems to be unsure how often his audience would want to see the bit (he assumes only once, though he has experience to the contrary), but it seems never to have crossed his mind that they might find the offering a shock. And they laugh when they realize themselves how appropriate the offering is.

The audience's laughter is extended because the oscillation between its two functions (one—"It's a joke, right?"; two—"This makes unexpected sense") is uncalmable, and both functions are self-prolonging because self-reflexive ("We're laughing to find ourselves laughing"). Still undetermined is what sort of sense their masochism makes, which would require a full analysis of what it meant to be a Jewish comedian (in this case, a suburban kid who came to the city to learn what it meant to be a Jewish comedian) in and around 1955, and what it meant then to be an audience. It will have to be sufficient here to say that Freud may or may not be right that jokes are almost entirely fueled by displaced aggression and sex, but the supposition perfectly fits the suburban convergence of American and Jewish humor in 1955, if suburbs exist on the energy of the same displacements. Jokes and suburbanization have the same commuting structure.

My focus here must be on the quality of the talk (as measured by its distance from the quality of jokes)—and the important point under this heading is that, in Bruce's quatrain, two styles of talking cross: suburban talk (considerate, worried, familiar, redundant) and urban (trash) talk, which is always on the verge of not being talk at all, ambiguously diffusing and exacerbating all prior physical tensions. That is the intersection at which the American conversation—but not the Australian—takes place: witness the format of the late night "talk" show, wherein Jack Paar from Ohio, Johnny Carson from Iowa and Nebraska, Dick Cavett from Nebraska, and David Letterman from Indiana interview, depending on the era, Jackie Mason or Don Rickles or Eddie Murphy. The relevant trope is chiasmus: the suburban kid is the city host, and the city kid is his guest even in the city. This is the essence of the American talk show, and standup talk as well (Lenny Bruce himself assumes the role of host along with that of unmannered guest), and their mode is the performance of abjection, which is the liquidification of the boundary between what does and does not belong.

I mean by abjection what everyone means by it: debasement, groveling prostration. I also mean what Julia Kristeva means: the abject is what cannot be subject or object to you—for example, nails, hair, urine, feces, the corpse itself—and abjection is worrying the abject's inalienability, as if it were a perpetually loose tooth."[10] The abject cannot be you, but you cannot rid yourself of it, either. What the two senses of abjection have in common is the sufferer's sense of being mired.

Up until this moment, I have considered the Lenny Bruce ur-gesture (or ur-jest) as if it were based on the threat of exposure of the penis and the phallus. But it has occurred to me that only one person has ever, in physical fact, urinated on me, and that person is my daughter when she was a baby (that she is my daughter and not my son is irrelevant except that its irrelevance is revealing). My reaction to the offense was to laugh at it. If my expertise is pertinent, then Lenny Bruce is abject in the sense that he is preoccupied with urine, or excrement in general, as that which dissolves his own boundaries, brings him back into fluid relation with the parental body. This is exactly the sort of fluidity that Bruce's mentor, Joe Ancis, was after in his comedy:

> Doing his famous Spritz with the absolute freedom and self-indulgence and private craziness that you can only get into when you have a listener who is practically another part of your own head, Joe paced the room as nervously as der Führer in his bunker. Interior monologue, free association, stream of consciousness—these are the fancy words for the Spritz.[11]

The spritz is a particular form of abject talk in which privacy is shared, and bunkers are freedom, and hatred is beloved. Inclusion repels; repression liberates; aggression bonds. "Stream of consciousness" is accurate, if interiors are exterior, because a spritz is a Yiddish spray. It is by spraying his audience, apparently, that Bruce wants to merge with it; or rather, in the process of assaulting them, he is ritually surprised that they take it as a particular intimacy. The spritz is a kind of indiscreet talk posing as a kind of prelinguistic (literally, infantile) indiscreteness. It is a revelation of talk as what is neither yours nor theirs (the listener is "practically another part of your own head"), neither subject nor object to you.

On stage, Bruce alternated between playing the father who must be feared and the son whose naughtiness must be indulged. The brilliance of the spritz is that both positions are conjured inseparably. Meanwhile, the audience oscillates between abused (terrorized, obedient) child and unflappable parent. There are child actors, child singers, child dancers, but not child comedians.[12] An actual child would prevent this vacillating infantilism, the essence, I think, of standup talk. If the best jokes, the ones that earn laughter lasting, say, up to six seconds, are metajokes, Bruce's urination threat is the meta-ur-joke, the joke on what standup humor, as a non-joke-based but rather talk-based form, is doing.

I am not arguing that standup humor is merely abject talk. The standup comedian is elevated and standing, he lectures down at his audience, he holds and controls the detachable mike. The odd thing is how phallic he makes his abjection, how publicly and proudly he displays his private shame, how erect he makes his prostration. Napoleon said that a heroic orator would create laughter by sitting down.[13] I am arguing that an abject monologist creates laughter by standing up. A one-sentence summary of standup theory is that what is stood up in standup is abjection. "Standing up" abjection is both to perform it vertically and to miss one's date with it; standup displays abjection and attempts to shed it, by living it as an act. (Is the standup comedian in costume or not? Is he talking or performing?) Thus purification—as in the case of American Puritans—is the natural complement of excremental abjection, and infantilism implies not only indulgence in the abject but freedom from all worldly encumbrances.

If fetishism is the standing up, in this sense, of castration (avowing it and disavowing it), then standup comedy is the standing up of abjection. Fetishism is preoccupation with the fact that what is essential to one's subjectivity cannot be possessed; standup is preoccupation with the fact that what is alien to one's subjectivity cannot be dispossessed. Standup in the 1950s was primarily a Jewish announcement that the suburbs could not be your exclusive address, that you would have to maintain a commuting relation with the sacred and profane city, city of sacred origins and also filth.

Lenny Bruce emphasized the city, though humor cannot help but commute, so to speak, sex and aggression and dirt; the New York City talk show was about the bridge between city and suburb, itself; Ellen DeGeneres posed (when she was doing standup) as the suburban girl-next-door, though her own standup would find a way to express and erect abjection in what appears to be pointless chat and chatter. The investigation of standup comedy is always into how much can be detached. The horror of standup is the horror of abjection: that everything always returns. The fantasy ideal of standup is the absolutely unencumbered life.

I want to introduce, accordingly, two philosophers of being (of what, if anything, exists beneath encumbrances) and having (of what, if anything, can be detached). First Lacan, for whom, in some relations of desire, a person x (weaker) may want to be what person y (stronger) does not have.[14] X cannot simply have it and offer it, because insofar as it is disposable, it is precisely not what y requires. But x cannot be it, either, because what y wants is generic and complementary, and x is specific and discrete. Thus Lacan forms a trinity of having/being/seeming: x wants to seem to be what y wants to seem to have. The thing in question, *ça va sans dire*, is the phallus.

On the other hand are the being/having dialectics of the Christian existentialist, Gabriel Marcel. If for Lacan detachability is the source of a thing's importance, for Marcel nothing vital is finally disposable. The body, for example, is not disposable, even by suicide. My body is mine, but it is also me; there is no I that can get rid of it. Beginning at the level of flesh, the world fails to split into subjects and objects. Corporeity is the "frontier district" between being and having, and pain, which drives my body into me, is the frontier guide for conducting having into being.[15]

Marjorie Garber argues that the Lacanian space of "seeming" is the home of the transvestite, who plays phallic hide-and-seek;[16] and Ellen DeGeneres was a mild transvestite in her later standup performances. But insofar as the dream of standup is of the unencumbered life, the penis or the phallus is just one more abject—one more thing to try to be free of. Thus we can begin with at least a symmetry of DeGeneres and Bruce—one promotes the abject to the position of the phallus, one demotes the phallus to the position of the abject—that, it must be the case, will bring them from different origins to one way of making a living. That way of making a living, furthermore, will be in both cases antithetical to Marcel's Christian existentialism, in which pain makes possible the conversion of having into being in what Kristeva would call abject space. Laughter is the antithesis of pain insofar as it closes the borders of having and being. And it may be, in more talk-centered terms, the antithesis of the promise in Marcel, by which one makes an objective truth out of a subjective intention. Everything in standup—this is the ideal—can be laughed off.

I want the being/having/seeming trinity to work out, partly, because the title and mantra of DeGeneres's best-selling book is *My Point . . . And I Do Have One*. Does she have one? It depends on what one, exactly, is. She hardly ever has a statement—political or ethical, say—to make. But her apparently aimless talk conceals something she always has in mind: the imminent punchline. DeGeneres is involved in two kinds of seeming: seeming not to have a point, which she brings to our attention by the joke of asserting that she has one; and seeming to have a point, which we register in the form of the punchline, even if the punchline has pointlessness as its content. These are the paradoxes of adding a masculine necessity (talking as punching) to the harmless diffusions of female blather, female chat, female chatter.

The title phrase appears twice in the book. In the first instance, DeGeneres is discussing "ridiculous fears" (e.g., "Fear of combing your hair so hard your head bleeds while your date is waiting in the front room"), an unexpected abjection that takes her to the subject of the "boogey man"; boogey men remind her of K.C. and the Sunshine Band, which DeGeneres "danced to as much as the rest of you in 1975." Then: "But I digress. My point . . . and I do have one, is that I still get scared at night. Every tiny creak, every little noise, I open my eyes wide and listen with them."[17]

The iteration of the phrase comes in the middle of a discourse on Maine, which DeGeneres momentarily confuses with Montana. DeGeneres is camping when she hears "some kind of noise": "Since I'm alone in the middle of the woods, I'm a little bit scared." It is, however, only a family of deer—"mother, father, and two little baby deer"—drinking from a brook. Their cuteness causes DeGeneres to think, "I wish I had a gun." No: she did not have that wish or fantasy, but she did go camping in Maine. No: she never went camping in Maine, but she did spend some nights at the Hilton on Maui. Finally: "My point . . . and I do have one, is that I was being sarcastic. I don't understand hunting at all."[18]

It is evident what causes DeGeneres to digress: fear. In the first story, the digression is away from the fear, and fear is the point. In the second story, fear begins the digression (that she is scared in the woods is a baroque way to introduce her antihunting message). In both cases, the fear is of being alone in uncertainty; in both cases, DeGeneres hears a noise whose origin she cannot see. I hope it is not illicit to force the content of DeGeneres's standup onto the form: she blathers, she digresses, she chatters to get the alien noise out of her head and her own noise substituted for it. Her need to digress is so strong that it turns her book into an oral performance; that the book reads like transcriptions of her standup seems at first an ineptitude, second like a necessity of her comic psyche. The book does not work unless you add the blithe quaver of her voice to her words.

Terrors, by the time DeGeneres is, according to calendar measure, an adult, have not been transcended but they have been transformed. Once the terror has been redefined, not as natural or supernatural but as human—for example, the date sitting in the parlor—aloneness becomes not the source of DeGeneres's terror but the best defense against it. The best defense is to avoid the ones with rifles (DeGeneres is profoundly identified with animals). This is a self-destructive syndrome for most performance, but good breeding ground for what increasingly comes to seem a form of escapist art, though it is not the audience that is escaping. It is as if DeGeneres chatters to an audience to palliate fears whose origin is also the audience.

> Someone recently wrote a letter recently to a magazine recently (and you know it must really be recently since I've mentioned it so many times) asking, "Why does Ellen DeGeneres always wear pants and never skirts?"

> I'm guessing that the person who wrote that letter meant skirt, a noun signifying an article of clothing, and not skirt, a verb defined as, "to evade or elude (as a topic of conversation) by circumlocution." Because, if they mean the verb skirt, well, they're dead wrong. I'm always skirting.[19]

She is skirting even in this passage, with violent decisiveness ("they're dead wrong"): to skirt is to digress is to escape is not to explain wearing pants. By this formulation, the ingenuous chat is concealing (skirting), and pants (not the skirt) are what it conceals: ingenuousness is evasion. Then

DeGeneres returns to the point. She wears pants because at summer camp she was "tattooed with designs of bougainvillea," which provoked an attack of bees; this "point" has the look of another skirting, unless you remember that DeGeneres had recommended explaining sex to children in terms of male bees buzzing around the queen.[20] Is DeGeneres approaching a confession? For a millisecond, she seems to want to:

> All kidding aside—actually, I change my mind. I don't want to put all kidding aside. I want the kidding right there in front where all can see it. The main point of this book is kidding. If I put all kidding aside, there would be nothing left but nonkidding, and believe me, that wouldn't make a very interesting book.[21]

In sum: DeGeneres wants to get to her "main point." She wants to put her main point, exhibitionistically, in front and not aside. Except kidding is her point. Which is to say that digression itself is the point. What she does not want to put aside is the aside. The physical presence she is after is absent-minded and disembodied talk. In place of an inchoate promise that almost has no temporal or spatial extension ("All kidding aside"), DeGeneres turns to kidding as a way of making talk usurp the visibility of the body ("in front where all can see it") but none of its inalienability.

The talk DeGeneres refuses to give up is called either skirting or kidding. One engages in skirting to evade the significance of panting. One kids to evade responsibility for what DeGeneres calls "nonkidding."

Nonkidding means, of course, authenticity, but it also implies a peculiar relationship with kids. We know that DeGeneres does not herself have kids because she keeps informing us so, though never directly. Near the beginning of her recent CD, *Taste This*,[22] DeGeneres shares some personal feelings with the audience. The hard thing about the job of comedian is the traveling: three-and-a-half weeks are too long to be on the road. She is forced to ask friends to water the plants, turn on the lights, and "make sure that the mobile over the crib isn't tangled or the baby's gonna get bored. [laugh] So that's, you know, hard to impose on people. [pause] I don't have a baby; I have a mobile and a crib. [laugh] I just have 'em. I enjoy those things; I don't know why." DeGeneres continues: "I want to have a baby. I don't want to have the baby. I just wanna [very fast] have-a-baby." She concedes that "it's a beautiful thing you end up with—I'm aware of that. But I want to have a new washer and dryer but I don't think I'd go through that for that." She does have a goddaughter, who is "the light of my life. She's three [pause] or five, or something. She lives clear across town—I don't have that kind of time."

It is a fine routine, but it begins to seem more than a routine, less than routine, when DeGeneres repeats it in the book, then returns to the preterition in a variant form, when she describes a typical day. "Okay, that brings me to around six o'clock when I go to pick up the kids from day care. Not my kids; I drive a van for the neighborhood moms who are busy."²³ This is almost not humorous at all, but it is like a reduction of the ideal of standup, which is the replacement of supposing by ruthless disposing. I have a baby; I don't have a baby. My goddaughter lights my life; I don't see her. I have kids; I don't have kids. DeGeneres has invented a new relationship to children: unhaving them; nonkidding.

If the inevitably problematic form of having for a standup is having the phallus, the inevitably problematic form of having for a woman is having a baby. In Freudian terms, of course, penis envy ought to be redirected in the latter direction and not the former. (Joking is an all-male sport in Freud.) This would not be worth mentioning if it were not the sort of judgment a comedy audience is conventionally as ready to make as Freud. The illusion of the comedian, phallic or not, is that he (*sic*) is unencumbered, but the peculiar difficulty of female standup is the necessity of making explicit the lack of desire to have something or other.

What could the solution be except a repudiation of either the paternal or the maternal possessions? In the case of Lenny Bruce, it takes a moment to intuit that his vulgar threat is, in another aspect, infantile helplessness. In DeGeneres's case, the threat is displaced from audience to baby to non-baby, which allows her to make explicit her own move from mother to infant, forcing the audience from child to parent. We expect the abandoned baby routine to end with the admission that DeGeneres does not have one—so we are slightly confused when she adds that she nevertheless owns the crib and mobile. They are, she tells us on the CD, for her own enjoyment. In the book version, she also wants to be prepared. She has a nurse, and "in case I decide to have a baby, it's nice to know that Bok Choy is there."²⁴ Even Bok Choy's function, however, gets submitted to DeGeneres's own regressive pleasure: "To keep him in practice, I have him read me a bedtime story every night and occasionally I let him burp me."

It is safe to say that self-babying is never far removed among DeGeneres's temptations; being burped by Bok Choy is as sensual a pleasure as she ever, in her standup, reports. It is as if the correct outcome of penis envy for her is the subversion of Freudian/Lacanian wisdom: the phallus becomes the baby, all right, but the baby and not the phallus becomes her. It may be worth noting that on her TV show *Ellen*, in a season devoted to the coy delay of "Ellen's" coming out as a lesbian, the only people who came out early in the season were her parents, who came out as heterosexuals, against the horror of which DeGeneres literally started babbling baby talk.

Babbling is where standup talk always risks ending. Comic abjection manifests itself in public talk of public urination or professional burping; but both are preverbal pleasures, and the pleasure is in what is shamelessly discharged. The genius of Bruce, DeGeneres, and all standup talk is to transmute abject miring itself into the sign of freedom.

The purpose of discharging anything, of course, is painlessness; freedom to a standup primarily means freedom from pain. If the cost of disencumbering is infantilism, the benefit of infantilism is that you avoid the miseries of adulthood and, if you are a woman, the pain of childbirth. DeGeneres's routine on the unhaving of children returns, in the book version, to the washer and dryer analogy: "Giving birth is just so much pain. . . . [I]f I want a new washer and dryer, I wouldn't necessarily want to have a new washer and dryer. . . . I don't think I could go through that pain (having the child—let's just forget the washer and dryer now, okay?)"[25]

Having a baby in this sense, of course, means parturition, separating from it, though having a baby, in DeGeneres's imaginary sense, means possessing it. But possessing it means possessing it as a consumer good, like a washer and dryer, which means possessing it as a disposable item. That is how, in the standup ethos, anything at all is possessed, so possession turns out just to mean constant separation, whenever the tour schedule demands it. Everything is always left behind, detachable, alienable. If pain, according to a Christian existentialist, forces having into being, then DeGeneres uses comic talk, as the antithesis of pain, to detach being from having altogether. The end, for Marcel, is universal being, being that finds the universe increasingly indisposable to infinity. The end, for DeGeneres, is evacuated being, which finds the universe disposable down and into the body itself, as if the body were a baby one chooses not to have. The body of the standup is conjured by talk and can be returned to it.

How far can the process go? Once she begins throwing off encumbrances—once she begins to renounce having of any kind—DeGeneres cannot stop before she repudiates talking itself, which always invites unwanted intimacies with the audience to be skirted. That is to say that standup talk stands up abjection: it re-creates it by disavowing it. I am not unmindful of the fact that on television and in real life, DeGeneres (or Morgan) exited the closet, unleashing a fury of talk, some of it by the Ellens themselves. But if I am right about American abjection and its relation to American jokes, then as a standup comedian, what DeGeneres can only pursue is absolute laughing off—absolute skirting and kidding.

In the picture on the back of *My Point . . . And I Do Have One,* DeGeneres is sitting in a corner of a room. She is pulling her legs in tight against her body. One hand is around one ankle; the other hand is against the other. One knee is pulled up to the level of Ellen's bowing head; the other knee is lower. The reason one knee is higher is that DeGeneres has one foot up on a low parallelepiped of some kind, which she is sitting on in the corner, and the other foot off it.

We do not see DeGeneres's face: she is looking straight down into the narrow gap behind her knees. We are faced only by her cropped hair. What on earth is she doing? First of all, she is hiding, in a childish way: by folding her body into as small a space as she can in the restricting corner of a room. She is attempting to make herself minuscule.

Second, she is hiding by a less common stratagem. The wall behind her and to her side is white. The floor and box beneath her, either naturally or as the result of shadows, are white too but almost gray. The color scheme is mimicked by Ellen's clothing: whiter shirt, white but grayer pants. Her socks are white. She wears white sneakers with whitish laces. Her arms seem to be tan, probably inadvertently, and she has on rings and a bracelet, but she has her arms exposed for a purpose, and what they do is exhibit the body that is trying to furl toward the wall. Also, her head, shoulders, and the curve of her arms form a kind of zero. Her circle of hair is another zero, like a dumb blond stone on the ring of curving shoulders and arms. She is trying not to hide in the room but to be the room, a chameleon who works not by color but by colorlessness.

DeGeneres is doing a third thing: bowing. She bows her head in shame, perhaps. She has been banished to the corner for committing some indecency. But she is also taking her bow, at the end of her performance. The moment of her pride is exactly the moment of her shame; the inverse of Lenny Bruce, who performed shame proudly, DeGeneres exhibits her pride shamefully. Or, rather, we seem to witness DeGeneres's desire to transcend those categories, to precede or preempt shame and pride, the phallic and the abject, in a posture the most obvious term for which is "fetal"—the posture of all her unhad children. At the end of kidding is nonkidding.

Standup is the talking up of abjection, so DeGeneres sits down to take her bow. Comic abjection has finally assumed an abject posture, which is not good enough: American abjection always works by silence, camouflage, and cunning. Spritzing and skirting may be regarded as the extremes of infantilism that foreshadow a single, presexual, literally infantile outcome. This is the end of standup talk.

Notes

1. That the term dates from 1966 I have from Robert A. Stebbins, *The Laugh-Makers: Standup Comedy as Art, Business, and Life-Style* (Montreal: McGill–Queen's University Press, 1990). Stebbins has it on the authority of *Webster's Collegiate Dictionary*. The first

reference in the *O.E.D.* is also from 1966.

2. See Samuel S. Janus, "The Great Comedians: Personality and Other Factors," *American Journal of Psychoanalysis* 35 (1975): 173. Janus interviewed fifty-five nationally known comedians. He indicates (but does not document) that the great majority were Jewish, even though the percentage by 1975 was in decline; I heard Steve Allen (I cannot footnote the occasion) make the 80 percent estimate. Fifty-one were male; none of the fifty-five identified himself or herself as homosexual.

3. Mark 7:20.

4. From the record *To Is a Preposition, Come Is a Verb* (Pip Records/Pickwick, 1964). I borrow the convention of dividing the "joke" into breath-lines from *Breaking It Up! The Best Routines of the Stand-up Comics,* ed. Ross Firestone (New York: Bantam, 1975).

5. Jerry M. Suls, "Cognitive Processes in Humor Appreciation," in *Basic Issues,* vol. 1 of *Handbook of Humor Research,* ed. Paul E. McGhee and Jeffrey H. Goldstein (New York: Springer-Verlag, 1983), 39–57.

6. Sigmund Freud, *Jokes and Their Relation to the Unconscious,* vol. 8 of *The Standard Edition of the Complete Psychological Works of Sigmund Freud,* trans. James Strachey (London: Hogarth Press), passim.

7. Mahadev L. Apte, "Humor Research, Methodology, and Theory in Anthropology," in *Basic Issues,* op. cit., 183–212, 189–92.

8. Albert Goldman, *Ladies and Gentlemen—Lenny Bruce!!* (New York: Random House, 1974), 373.

9. Mary Douglas, *Implicit Meanings: Essays in Anthropology* (London: Routledge and Kegan Paul, 1975), 92.

10. Julia Kristeva, *Powers of Horror: An Essay in Abjection,* trans. Leon S. Roudiez (New York: Columbia University Press, 1982), passim.

11. Goldman, *Lenny Bruce,* 109.

12. Many of his comedians felt that being young was a comic handicap. See Samuel S. Janus, "The Great Comedians: Personality and Other Factors," *American Journal of Psychoanalysis* 35 (1975): 169–74. Janus looked for child comedians, found none.

13. Henri Bergson, *Laughter: An Essay in the Meaning of the Comic,* trans. Cloudesley Brereton and Fred Rothwell (New York: MacMillan, 1911), 52.

14. Jacques Lacan, "The Signification of the Phallus," in *Écrits: A Selection,* trans. Alan Sheridan (New York: Norton, 1977), 289–90. A child wishes to be the phallus in order to satisfy the mother; a woman wishes to be the phallus to serve as the signifier of the other.

15. Gabriel Marcel, *Being and Having: An Existentialist Diary,* trans. Katherine Farrer (New York: Harper and Row, 1965), 82–83, 85, 86, 115, 144.

16. Marjorie Garber, *Vested Interests: Cross-Dressing and Cultural Anxiety* (New York: HarperCollins, 1993), 121.

17. Ellen DeGeneres, *My Point . . . And I Do Have One* (New York: Bantam 1996), 109–10.

18. Ibid., 145–46.

19. Ibid., 93.

20. Ibid., 77.

21. Ibid., 94.

22. Ellen DeGeneres, *Taste This* (Atlantic Records, 1996).

23. DeGeneres, *My Point,* 171.

24. Ibid., 73.

25. Ibid.

Chat three
Culture Klatch

"10" (Quotation Marks)

Marjorie Garber

When Representative Henry Hyde addressed the Senate on the solemn occasion of the Clinton impeachment hearings, he gave his remarks the requisite element of gravity by salting them with familiar quotations—or quotations that seemed as if they ought to be familiar. For example, he cited Sir Thomas More, whose conscience would not permit him to acquiesce in the tricky business of Henry VIII's divorce and remarriage. But Hyde's quotation from this Tudor statesman had an oddly contemporary ring. "As he told his daughter Margaret," the congressman from Illinois informed the Senate, "'When a man takes an oath, Meg, he's holding his own self in his own hands. Like water. And if he opens his fingers *then*, he needn't hope to find himself again.'" Here the voice of Thomas More comes through slightly muffled; it is in fact the character of More from Robert Bolt's 1960 play *A Man for All Seasons* that is talking.[1]

The staffer who found this quotation apposite might have been inspired by Bolt's ardent preface, which explained the playwright's choice of hero: "A

man takes an oath only when he wants to commit himself quite exception-
ally to the statement, when he wants to make an identity between the truth
of it and his own virtue; he offers himself as a guarantee. And it works. There
is a special kind of shrug for a perjurer; we feel that the man has no self to
commit, no guarantee to offer."[2] But quoting Robert Bolt lacks the force—
historical, religious, canonical—of quoting Sir, later Saint, Thomas More.
Perhaps mindful of Robert Burton's famous declaration about quoting from
the classics, "A dwarf standing on the shoulders of a giant may see farther
than a giant himself,"[3] the tall, stooped Hyde craned across the ages, speaking to the future through a voice from the "past."

That I elect to stress the spuriousness of this "past" by enclosing the
word in quotation marks will indicate, at the outset, one of the curious prop-
erties of these typographical signifiers. For in their present condition of use,
they may indicate either authenticity or doubt. Make that "authenticity" or
"doubt." This is a property to which we shall want to return. But let us continue, for a moment, with the impeachment hearings.

In quest of authority, Congressman Hyde also, it is almost needless to
say, quoted Shakespeare in his opening remarks. And here the author was so
familiar that he did not need to be named. "Our cherished system of justice
will never be the same after this," Hyde intoned. "Depending on what you
decide, it will either be strengthened in its power to achieve justice, or it will
go the way of so much of our moral infrastructure and become a mere convention full of sound and fury, signifying nothing."[4]

It's probably unsportsmanlike to fault Representative Hyde for wrench-
ing this quotation out of context; both "sound and fury" and "signifying
nothing" have long ago passed into the general wordhoard, having been bor-
rowed by everyone from William Faulkner to Malcolm Evans.[5] But
Macbeth's famous cry of despair on the meaninglessness of (his) life, uttered
in response to the news of his wife's death, seems in a way singularly inappropriate for a political speech the entire point of which is to mark the
meaningfulness of the moment. "Life," in Macbeth's formulation, is:

> A poor player
> That struts and frets his hour upon the stage
> And then is heard no more: it is a tale
> Told by an idiot, full of sound and fury,
> Signifying nothing.
> *Macbeth* 5.5.24–28

The point of Hyde's citation was to rouse the Senate to greatness, by urging
them to *avoid* reducing justice to "sound and fury, signifying nothing."
Nonetheless, the proximity of "poor player" (a bad, unskilled, or hammy

actor) and "idiot" seem slightly risky in the context of an address to a group of U.S. senators. The New York *Daily News* found some amusement in the omission: "Hyde said a violated oath was 'full of sound and fury, signifying nothing.' But he left out the preceding line that life 'is a tale told by an idiot.'⁶ Identifying these as "Shakespeare's words from *Macbeth*," the paper implied that this view of "life" was somehow "Shakespeare's" rather than his character's. But at least the *Daily News* got the play right. An article in *Newsday* written by "an attorney specializing in intellectual property law" blithely described Hyde as beginning his remarks with "a quote from *Hamlet*—'full of sound and fury, signifying nothing.'"⁷

A scholar once wrote of Shakespeare that "to cite him in a lecture or an essay was to give lustre and prestige to the words and ideas that surrounded his magic name."⁸ But does that luster attach itself to the speaker as readily as to the writer? Or does the "poor player" syndrome kick in, reminding the audience all too clearly that the speaker is *not* Shakespeare, or, to cite another once-canonical text, "not Prince Hamlet," but rather:

> an attendant lord, one that will do
> To swell a progress, start a scene or two,
> Advise the prince; no doubt, an easy tool,
> Deferential, glad to be of use,
> Politic, cautious, and meticulous;
> Full of high sentence, but a bit obtuse;
> At time, indeed, almost ridiculous—
> Almost, at times, the Fool.⁹

By the end of the impeachment process even the *New York Times* had grown slightly restive. "Mr. Hyde," the *Times* reported, "mustered a veritable Bartlett's in offering his last impassioned plea for conviction. 'We happy few,' he said, turning in Shakespearean tribute to his fellow House Republicans." And, "Quoting Gibbon, Mr. Hyde acidly denounced the president by comparing him to a corupt Roman emperor, Septimius Severus: "'Severus promised, only to betray; he flattered, only to rule; and however he might occasionally bind himself by oath and treaty, his conscience, obsequious to his interest, always released him from the inconvenient obligation.'""¹⁰ A journalist writing for another newspaper had earlier dismissed the impeachment debate in the House as "blue suits quoting from Bartlett's."¹¹ The implication was that they were doubly out of fashion; they weren't, in any way, saying something new. Under these circumstances, was the quotation *more* authoritative and convincing than the speaker's own voice? Or *less*?

Who is speaking when we speak in quotation? In the case of Henry

Hyde's address to the Senate, was it Hyde, More, or Robert Bolt? Hyde, Macbeth, Shakespeare—or J. Alfred Prufrock?

"Quotation is a constant reminder that writing is a form of displacement," suggests Edward Said. "As a rhetorical device, quotation can serve to accommodate, to incorporate, to falsify (when wrongly or even rightly paraphrased), to accumulate, to defend, or to conquer—but always, even when in the form of a passing allusion, it is a reminder that other writing serves to displace present writing."[12]

Quotation reminds us that *writing* is displacement. What does it tell us about speech?

How does one indicate that one is speaking in quotation? Or "in quotation"? At scholarly conferences it has become conventional for the speaker to raise his or her hands above the shoulders and rapidly flex the first two fingers of each hand, miming the look of (American-style, double) quotation marks on the page. The effect is rather retro Rogers and Hammerstein; as one friend commented, this gesture always makes him think the speaker is auditioning for "Happy Talk." Do speakers from the British Isles, or others whose primary publication venue is Britain, gesture with single-finger quotation marks? (Nursery habitués might then be reminded not of *South Pacific* but of "The Itsy-Bitsy Spider.") But in fact the two-finger flex has become conventional rather than strictly mimetic, a sign of quoting rather than a quote sign. For some divas of the podium the gesture involves the shoulders as well as the hands and offers an opportunity to express, not only the activity of quotation, but also a certain attitude—often of wry skepticism—about the authority of both the quotation and the quotee. Some users call these protestation marks, indicating that they are the performed equivalent of what Derrida, following Heidegger, has termed being "under erasure"—a word with a horizontal line drawn through it, to indicate that it demarcates a nodal idea for which the present word is inappropriate or insufficient: *man*; *freedom*; *justice*. Others who employ the finger-waggling gesture refer to these airy points as "scare quotes"—both the word being framed, and the witchy gesture, contributing presumably to the currency of the term.

It was not always thus. Conference-goers with longer memories or grayer hair may recall the days when a sotto voce "quote . . . unquote" demarcated the boundaries of a cited phrase. (Without these oral punctuation marks the quoted passage often melted into the speaker's own text with no perceptible boundary, especially when the quotation was lengthy and unmemorable.) On the other hand, the necessity could itself invite dramatic improvisation. The rabbi of the temple of my youth, a Russian emigré with a grandiloquent flair for performance, used to wind up to a sonorous "and I am *qvoting*" before delivering whatever words of wisdom he had quarried for his sermon. Senators and other public figures, as we've seen in the case of Congressman Henry Hyde, often footnote their learned quotations in the text, lest the audience fail to register either the quotation or the erudition: "As Abraham Lincoln so wisely said"; "In the immortal words of John F. Kennedy"; "The Book of Isaiah tells us."

This practice works well when the figure being quoted is eminent, recognizable, and honored; in fact all three attributes then seem to attach themselves, in a rather ghostly fashion, to the present speaker, who appears in the act of quoting to have virtually incorporated the predecessor and to speak from the vantage point of the ages, as if the speaker were a Russian doll who had somehow swallowed up these articulate authorities and was therefore able to ventriloquize them from within. When the figure being quoted is *less* eminent or reputable, however, the old-style quote-unquote is deployed, but with a lawyerly edge, casting doubt on the veracity of the person quoted or underscoring the suspicious significance of the utterance. The effect is one of distancing rather than incorporation.

Thus, to return yet again to the House managers' presentation to the Senate, the words of principals in the case against President Clinton were cited in deliberate, and exaggerated, oral quotation marks: "Ms. Lewinsky testified quote, 'No one ever told me to lie,' unquote. When considered alone, this statement would seem exculpatory. In the context of other evidence, however, we see that this one statement gives a misleading inference. Of course, no one said, 'Now, Monica, you go down there and lie.' They didn't have to. Based on their previous spoken and even unspoken words, Ms. Lewinsky knew what was expected of her."[13] Or, again: "According to Ms. Lewinsky, Mr. Jordan told her that he has spoken with the president, that she came highly recommended, and that quote, 'We're in business,' unquote. However, the evidence reflects that Mr. Jordan took no steps to help Ms. Lewinsky until early December of that year, after she appeared on the witness list in the Jones case."

"Quote-unquote" often functions in this manner; thus a character in crime fiction can report of another that "he did have quote, a jolly good reason for bumping off one special person, unquote,"[14] while in Peter Ustinov's *Loser* we are told that someone "expressed the personal opinion that the picture was quote great for America unquote."[15] And "quote-unquote" when spoken together before the word in question indicates the greatest possible degree of skepticism. "The mayor's quote-unquote dedication to duty" means the speaker doesn't think the mayor is very dedicated.

Monica Lewinsky herself took note of the slippery problem posed by unmarked oral quotation when she was deposed by House managers in the impeachment hearing. "Sometimes in the, in my grand jury testimony, they've put quotations around things when I'm attributing statements to other people, and I didn't necessarily mean that those were direct quotes," she said, and several times in her deposition she cautioned "this is not a direct quote."[16] This lawyerly caution, however belatedly introduced, throws some doubt on the whole question of transcription and its authority. When "he said–she said" becomes "he said something like this" and "she said something like that," the effect of authenticity and evidence produced by direct quotation becomes blurred and etiolated.

For paradoxically, as we've already noted, quotation marks, when either written or spoken, can convey both absolute authenticity and veracity, on the one hand, and suspected inauthenticity, irony or doubt, on the other ("this 'leader' we elected";[17] or, from an article in an 1897 article in *Century* magazine, "I must put play in quotation-marks to express the sarcasm of it").[18] Either "This is exactly what was said" or "Can you imagine saying or believing this?"

The House managers, of course, did not waggle their fingers at the Senate as they quoted, either from the literary classics or from Monica Lewinsky. (It would have been far more entertaining had they done so.) And sonorous quoters of the classics do not, in general, do the "Happy Talk" finger-dance; it's virtually impossible to imagine citers of "Ask not what your country can do for you" or of "I have a dream" pausing to clench and unclench their fingertips before launching into the rhetorical stratosphere. In fact, this practice is pretty much limited to professors and graduate students, and even they do not usually perform it when quoting purple passages. "To be or not to be" has seldom, in my experience, been prefaced by a gesture of digital "quotation."

Consider for a moment how curious it is that we should pronounce any punctuation marks aloud. "Period!" is sometimes used as an intensifier ("No ice cream before dinner. Period!") that marks the closure of the conversation. No reply is invited or welcomed; the matter is closed. The Danish-born comedian Victor Borge often performed in the 1950s, to the delight of audiences, a routine called "Phonetic Punctuation," in which he gave appropriate popping and whirring noises to commas, question marks, and exclamation points, reading a passage aloud with its full oral complement of punctuation and accompanying these sounds with gestures. Borge's quotation marks were two commas (squeaky-pop; squeaky-pop) and a mimed scare-quote gesture. Apart from the sheer energy and inventiveness of his comic routine, Borge succeeded in defamiliarizing the role of punctuation in imparting meaning. Like Molière's gentleman who was astonished to find himself speaking prose, Borge's audiences often discovered, three centuries after the shift from rhetorical to syntactical punctuation practice, that these little squiggles were part of how they listened, and spoke.

Early printed quotations appeared not in the run-in text but in the margins, as glosses or evidence of what was being claimed; sometimes they looked more like modern footnotes than like quotations. As R. B. McKerrow notes, "Inverted commas were, until late in the seventeenth century, frequently used at the beginnings of lines to call attention to sententious remarks. . . . They were not especially associated with quotations until the eighteenth century."[19] But almost from the beginning, there was a real question about the relationship of quotation marks, and indeed all punctuation, to speech.

In English typography the *comma,* a word originally traceable to Greek rhetoric and prosody and meaning a short phrase or group of words, became a punctuation mark used to separate the smallest members of a sentence. Renaissance grammarians, reasoning from the fact that the comma makes clear the grammatical structure and thus the sense of a written passage, as does a short pause in speech, sometimes tended to describe the comma as the mark of such a spoken pause. Thus Puttenham's *English Poesie* says, "A little pause or comma is geuen to euery word," and Ben Jonson's *English Grammar* says, "A comma is a mean breathing."[20] But there is a difference between Puttenham's emphasis and Jonson's: Puttenham's notion of the purpose of punctuation is elocutionary, while Jonson's is syntactical. That is, Puttenham follows the largely medieval practice of treating points or stops as indications to the reader, especially one reading aloud to an audience, while Jonson is among the first writers in English to consider punctuation as a necessary guide to the grammatical construction of sentences. In this period quotations in the text were not marked by quotation marks, but by a word like *quoth* followed by a comma in run-in text (in Puttenham, for example, *ye may see, quoth the king, what it is to runne away and looke backwards).*[21] In other words, the mark of quotation was an oral, and aural, cue. It was the ear and not the eye that still predominated.

In the seventeenth century in England this began to change. The comma began to appear above the line as a quotation mark. The mark at the beginning of the quotation or line was inverted, and in later years these began to be called *inverted commas.* The commentary accompanying quotations in learned texts indicates both the use of, and some textual anxiety about, such designations. "To authenticate the date of the author's ideas, the parts of it which are contained in the present letter are marked with double commas," wrote one scholar.[22] "The reader must not take it for granted, even where inverted commas denote a closer attention to the text, that nothing is omitted," cautioned another.[23] A third drew the reader's attention to "turned commas, which designate extracts."[24] One nineteenth-century account of *Modern English Literature: Its Blemishes and Defects* took a passage to task for appearing "without inverted commas, or any other marks to show that the writer intended it as a quotation."[25]

If such anxieties—was it a quotation? was it authentic? was it complete?—could attend upon the *written* text, what were the implications and ramifications for speech? How was the *hearer* now to be sure when what was spoken was "in quotation"?

A similar history attends the onset of "quotation marks" on the continent of Europe. The French mark of quotation, the *guillemet,* was first used in 1546, according to the *Grande Encyclopédie.*[26] In the earliest printing in France, as in other European countries, the marks of quotation are absent. French typographical style differs from that of other languages in that dialogue is generally set without quotation marks. The words of each successive or alternate speaker are marked, instead, by an em dash. This is sometimes done in Italian, as well. (In French, passages of quotation can be prefaced or, more frequently, followed by the information that this is the beginning or the end: *fin de citation.*) German-language quotations are marked either by pairs of commas or by reversed *guillemets.* As with the English punctuation, these typographical practices all have consequences, not only for how passages are read with the eye, but also for how they are read aloud. And this in turn will effect their cultural currency, the way in which they are valued. Are these pearls of wisdom, gems of language—or clichés and curiosities? Snobbery, or common talk? Better, or worse, than "plain language"?

Some of the most quoted men and women in history have expressed themselves, quotably, on the question of quotation. Doctor Johnson roundly countered the criticism that quotation was pedantry: "No, sir, it is a good thing; there is a community of mind in it. Classical quotation is the *parole* of literary men all over the world."[27] Johnson's *parole* is a password, an open sesame, a code of belonging. Literary men recognize one another by the classical tags that ornament their language. This guild recognition system was still in effect two hundred years later among what naysayers like to describe disparagingly as the "cultural elite" (please note my quotation marks). As Justin Kaplan wrote in his preface to the sixteenth edition of *Bartlett's,* "We use quotations, like the Biblical Shibboleth, as passwords and secret handshakes, social strategic signals that say, 'I understand you. We speak the same language.'"[28] But we could associate Johnson's term also with the modern linguistic sense of *parole,* meaning "(spoken) word" or "utterance," the speech event, as contrasted with the linguistic system, or *langue.*

We might call to mind a well-known instance from the popular film *Ghost,* when Whoopi Goldberg, playing a supposedly spurious medium, is inhabited by the spirit of the murdered character played by Patrick Swayze.

Swayze's character speaks through Goldberg: her voice speaks his words. Commentators have noted the *frisson* that attaches to this cross-gender and cross-race haunting, as Goldberg (should I call her Goldberg or Swayze here? In any case she's clearly "in quotation," like all ghosts) moves to kiss the bemused widow (Demi Moore). The director and the camera chicken out, it's been said, by dissolving Goldberg into Swayze, so that the kiss is "correctly" sexed and raced: white woman kisses white man, not black woman. But we can read the Goldberg/Swayze pairing here also as an incarnate allegory of quotation: Who is speaking when Swayze's (or "Swayze's") words come out of Goldberg's mouth?

Henry James's Verena Tarrant of *The Bostonians*, a "high-class speaker" who is "the daughter of Doctor Tarrant, the mesmeric healer," may offer another (and "higher-class") model of speaking *through*. Verena is a hit on the Boston social circuit, an eloquent orator on behalf of women's rights whose facility for public speaking depends on her father's art. "I heard her last spring," reports a young man. "They call it inspirational. I don't know what it is—only it's exquisite, so fresh and poetical. She has to have her father to start her up. It seems to pass into her." Verena's freshness and poetical speech are hers and not hers. Once "started up" by her father, who strokes and smoothes her head, "She proceeded slowly, cautiously, as if she were listening for the prompter, catching, one by one, certain phrases that were whispered to her a great distance off, behind the scenes of the world. Then memory, or inspiration, returned to her, and presently she was in possession of her part."[29]

In some ways quotation is a kind of cultural ventriloquism, a throwing of the voice that is also an appropriation of authority. "He wrapped himself in quotations—as a beggar would enfold himself in the purple of Emperors," wrote Kipling of an ambitious young writer who "rhymed 'dove' with 'love' and 'moon' with 'June' and devoutly believed that they had never so been rhymed before."[30] The English poet and diplomat Matthew Prior had made the same point, more satirically, almost two hundred years earlier:

> He rang'd his tropes, and preach'd up patience;
> Back'd his opinion with quotations.[31]

Here, as you can see, we have entered the murky *mise en abîme* world of the quotation about quotations. Books of quotations, whether intended for inspiration, spiritual comfort, instant edification, or self-aggrandizement, have been around at least since John Bartlett's first edition of *Familiar Quotations* in 1855. (Current avatars, all published in the 1990s, include *Bartlett's Book of Business Quotation*, the *Executive's Quotation Book*, *The Golf Quotation Book*, *The Mother's Quotation Book*, *The Military Quotation Book*, *The*

Eccentric's Quotation Book, and *The Culture-Vulture's Quotation Book,* to
name just a few.) The young Winston Churchill, in later years the source of
obsessive quotation by politicians across the spectrum (for one of the slippery qualities of a quotable quote is that it can be used to point almost any
moral) delivered himself of an encomium to Bartlett's work that could readily serve as a dust jacket blurb:

> It is a good thing for an uneducated man to read books of quotations.
> Bartlett's *Familiar Quotations* is an admirable work, and I studied it intently.
> The quotations when engraved upon the memory give you good thoughts.
> They also make you anxious to read the authors and look for more.[32]

But clearly there's a difference between quoting an apposite phrase and
knowing what you're really saying. So widespread had become the habit of
quoting for *parole* or entry into an exclusive club by the beginning of the
twentieth century that Fowler felt impelled to warn against it in *A
Dictionary of Modern English Usage* (1926):

> QUOTATION . . . A writer expresses himself in words that have been used
> before because they give his meaning better than he can give it himself, or
> because they are beautiful or witty, or because he expects them to touch a
> chord of association in his reader, or because he wishes to show that he is
> learned and well read. Quotations due to the last motive are invariably ill-
> advised; the discerning reader detects it and is contemptuous, the undis-
> cerning perhaps is impressed, but even then is at the same time repelled,
> pretentious quotations being the surest road to tedium.[33]

When Henry Hyde quotes Gibbon on Severus a political cartoonist can
lampoon him as beating a literal dead horse. But Hyde, a man in his seventies reared and educated in the same state that produced the Lincoln-
Douglas debates, came of age at a time when rhetoric and oratory were
requisite parts of the education of a citizen in the liberal arts. It was only in
the 1960s that the Harvard University department of English discontinued
its offerings in public speaking, rhetorical theory, and the oral interpretation
of dramatic literature (English N, P, and Q). The advanced course in principles and practice of public speaking promised study of "speech composition
and rhetoric; logic; the psychology of audiences; persuasive presentation. A
large proportion of the speech practice will consist of public appearances on
selected occasions before various audiences."[34] English Q (for Quotation?)
and its fellow public speaking courses did not count toward the concentra-
tion (Harvard jargon for major) in English. Presumably their ranks were
filled, not with the aspiring young John Updikes, but with the aspiring

young John Kennedys—or Henry Hydes. With the demise of public speaking as an academic subject at the elite universities came a shift in the value, and valuation, of oral quotation from the classics. It would not be too long before Walter Mondale, in an attempt to connect with the electorate, would find himself quoting instead from a hamburger commercial: "Where's the beef?" Here the exclusive club was the highest office in the land, and the *parole* was, supposedly, in lingua franca.

In his *Essay Concerning Human Understanding* John Locke recorded the pitfalls of quotation "where the originals are wanting":

> Passion, interest, inadvertency, mistake of his meaning, and a thousand odd reasons, or capricios, men's minds are acted by, (impossible to be discovered,) may make one man quote another man's words or meanings wrong. He that has but ever so little examined the citations of writers, cannot doubt how little credit the quotations deserve, where the originals are wanting; and consequently how much less quotations of quotations can be relied on.[35]

Being "quoted out of context" is one of the most frequent complaints of politicians, so it might seem surprising that they give themselves permission to make so free with the literary classics. The Bartlett version of a famous quote often omits not only the context but also, in the case of fiction, drama, or poetry, the speaker, with the result that such profoundly ambiguous utterances as Iago's on reputation, Polonius's "this, above all: to thine own self be true," and Pope's "hope springs eternal in the human breast" appear regularly in political speeches without a trace of irony as the ringing "philosophy" of the (often uncited) author—and, by implication, of all good men. I do not mean to attribute this practice only to the collection called *Bartlett's*—as we've seen, there have been hundreds of books of quotations, "beauties," and "household words," and most follow the same schema, excerpting passages with the minimum of context and explanation. The result is, again paradoxically, the elevation of a local observation to the status of oracular truth.

Quotations—especially disembodied quotations—can serve an educative function, providing (or counterfeiting) wisdom. Detached from their contexts, they seem not only "true" but iconic, monumental. But as we noticed in the analogy to *Ghost*, a quotation does not remain disembodied for long. Once it is reincarnated in a new speaker, it takes on a new set of meanings, and often sheds or alters the "original" meaning it may be thought to have possessed.

Ralph Waldo Emerson remarks in his essay "Quotation and Originality" that "a writer appears to more advantage in the pages of another's book than in his own. In his own he waits as a candidate for your approbation; in another's he is a lawgiver."[36] This seems almost depressingly true these days, when the iteration of theoretical catchphrases (for example, Foucault's definition of the homosexual, or Judith Butler on gender as a repetition of stylized acts) seems all too often to replace systemic thought or argumentation. Such quotations are inserted into a borrower-text as precisely what its author did not claim: a ground of fact. In her fine study of quotation in Emerson and Dickinson, Debra Fried notes "the equivocal stance of American writers to quotations—are they truly the voice of one's genius, or are they unreliable promptings from tired ghosts?"[37]

When a quotation becomes so familiar that it slides, almost imperceptibly, into aphorism or maxim, the cautionary quotation marks will disappear entirely, leaving the cultural residue: doxa, or "wisdom." Locke insists that quotations never become truer over time ("This is certain, that what in one age was affirmed upon slight grounds, can never after come to be more valid in future ages by being oft repeated. But the further still it is from the original, the less valid it is, and has always less force in the mouth or writing of him that last made use of it than in his from whom he received it").[38] Yet the doxa effect of quotation, especially, I would contend, in an oral context and in an increasingly less classically educated society, has today a strong free-floating force. Eliot's smugly complacent view of the ancients—"they are what we know"—has been replaced by a suspiciousness of too much learning that is oddly gratified by "familiar quotations" that function as sound bites. Not, they are what we know, but, they are what we quote. Old authors are regarded as having written, not books, but quotes. Classical tags have turned into "tagging," a practice done by graffiti artists. "Capping" quotations is an arcane activity largely engaged in by the louche heroes of twenties drama and detective fiction.

Even more problematic than this practice of misquotation by quoting out of context, however, is what might be described as quotation by free indirect discourse: the invention of phrases that famous speakers *should* have said. These *bon mots* often show up in books of quotations under the hazy label "Attributed," the equivalent in the world of quotation of the phrase "school of" in art history. Thus Voltaire's famous, and frequently cited, "I disapprove of what you say, but I will defend to the death your right to say it" is found nowhere in the works of Voltaire, but is offered instead in a 1906 volume entitled *The Friends of Voltaire* as a paraphrase of something Voltaire wrote in his *Essay on Tolerance*. At issue was a current literary contretemps that ended in a book burning. What the volume's editor, S. G. Tallentyre (the pen name of Evelyn Beatrice Hall) wrote was this—in double quotation marks: "'I disapprove of what you say, but I will defend to the death your right to say it,' was his attitude now."[39] Asked about the quotation many years after her book was published, Hall explained that she had not intended to imply that Voltaire used those words verbatim, and would be very surprised if they were to be found in any of his works.

To give just one more example from a legion of possibilities: Alice Roosevelt Longworth, credited with wittily remarking, "I do wish [Calvin Coolidge] did not look as if he had been weaned on a pickle," was in fact, as she acknowledged, quoting someone else, a patient of her doctor's. After the doctor had passed on the quip, Longworth gleefully reported, "Of course, I repeated it to everyone I saw." She *became* its speaker, though she was not its originator.

A well-known passage from Derrida sets out the stakes of iterability in terms that specifically engage the question of marking a quotation as a quotation, either in writing or in speech:

> Every sign, linguistic or nonlinguistic, spoken or written (in the current sense of this opposition), in a small or large unit, can be *cited*, put between quotation marks; in so doing it can break with every given context, engendering an infinity of new contexts in a manner which is absolutely illimitable. This does not imply that the mark is valid outside of a context, but on the contrary that there are only contexts without any center of absolute anchoring [*ancrage*]. This citation, this duplication or duplicity, this iterability of the mark is neither an accident nor an anomaly, it is that (normal/abnormal) without which a mark could not even have a function called "normal." What would a mark be that could not be cited? Or one whose origins would not get lost along the way?[40]

Signs, linguistic and nonlinguistic, can be put in quotation marks. In order to be recognized *as* signs, they have to be able to be repeated—to be iterable and citational. (In French the word *citation* means "quotation.") And since every repetition is a repetition with a difference, duplication becomes "duplicity." The "same" spoken again will always be "different." Derrida's "quotation marks" are here, so to speak, uttered in quotation marks. (With genial rhetorical ingenuousness he would inquire, fifteen years after the appearance of this influential essay, "Why does deconstruction have the reputation, justified or not, of treating things obliquely, indirectly, with 'quotation marks,' and of always asking whether things arrive at the indicated address?")[41] To what extent, if at all, can these figurative quotation marks be understood as speaking to the question of quotation?

By extension, we might say that *every* quotation is a quotation out of context, inevitably both a duplication and a duplicity. Emerson, famously ambivalent about quotation as a practice—"I hate quotation," he wrote in his journal. "Tell me what you know"[42]—noted both that "all minds quote. . . . the originals are not original." (Even this observation is of course not "original"; compare it to Burton's *Anatomy of Melancholy*: "We can say nothing but what has been said. Our poets steal from Homer. . . . Our story-dressers do as much; he that comes last is commonly best.")[43] And Emerson also saw that citation changes meaning: "We are as much informed of a writer's genius by what he selects as by what he originates. We read the quotation with his eyes, and find a new and fervent sense; as a passage from one of the poets, well recited, borrows new interest from the rendering. As the journals say, 'the italics are ours.'"[44] In fact Emerson goes so far as to endorse, though again ambivalently, the made-up quotation: "It is a familiar expedient of brilliant writers, and not less of witty talkers, the device of ascribing their own sentence to an imaginary person, in order to give it weight,—as Cicero, Cowley, Swift, Landor and Carlyle have done."[45]

"Ascribing their own sentence to an imaginary person." This gesture of othering or displacement pairs oddly but pertinently with the converse practice of appropriation, described by Kaplan as "converting other people's words to our own use" and thereby giving them "meanings quite different from what their authors may have intended."[46] Both are authority moves. And both depend upon the floating power of the quotation *as* quotation. "Attributed" is a powerful author, in the sense that the phrase marked by this sign of a missing signature is manifestly familiar enough to demand recognition.

J. L. Austin's *How to Do Things with Words* offers two ways for the performer of a performative utterance to refer to the fact that he or she is "doing the uttering, and so the acting": (a) in verbal utterances, by *his being the person who does* the uttering—what we may call the utterance-*origin*," and (b) in written utterances (or "inscriptions") *by his appending his signature.*[47]

Austin, we may note, is very much the kind of educated reader-writer who does communicate in unmarked quotations, tags, and allusions: "To feel the firm ground of prejudice slipping away is exhilarating, but brings in its revenges" (*Twelfth Night*); "there are many transitional stages between suiting the action to the word and the pure performative" (*Hamlet*).[48] Indeed, and perhaps unsurprisingly given his subject, "suiting the action to the word" is for Austin a favorite phrase, one that returns (bringing in its revenges?) when he finally, at the very end of his series of lectures, comes around to discussing the verb "I quote."

"I quote" is for Austin one of a group of words he calls expositives, words "used in acts of exposition involving the expounding of views, the conducting of arguments, and the clarifying of usages and references." We may dispute, he acknowledges, "whether they are not straight descriptions of our feelings, practice, &c., especially sometimes over matters of suiting the action to the word, as when I say 'I turn next to,' 'I quote,' 'I cite,' 'I recapitulate.'"[49] Those who have followed the fortunes and felicities of Austin's *Words* over the last thirty years or so may find themselves wondering whether quotation and allusion might fall under his doctrine of etiolations: performative utterances that are, as he claims, "*in a peculiar way* hollow and void if said by an actor on a stage, or if introduced in a poem, or spoken in soliloquy."[50] But a quotation, at least if marked by quotation marks, seems clearly voiced *as* an act of quotation. It would seem to be performatively valid, at least in terms of its quoting function, if not in terms of its truth content. What about an allusion? A modern critic has nicely described the difference between quotation and allusion as "a difference signaled by the formal signs of an alien texture," locating the two practices at different points along a continuum of textual appropriation. "Most allusions have some textural fringes which lead to effects which pure quotations more fully exploit."[51]

Much has been said about the category of etiolated or "hollow" utterances, and I will not attempt to recapitulate it here. But let me cite one key passage from Derrida's rather spirited riposte to Austin, a passage, a quotation, that is itself, of course, also by now familiar:

> given [the] structure of iteration, the intention animating the utterance will never be through and through present to itself and to its content. The iteration structuring it a priori introduces into it a dehiscence and a cleft [*brisure*] which are essential . . . this essential absence of intending the actuality of utterance, this structural unconscious, if you like, prohibits any saturation of the context.[52]

In the case of a quotation the absence of the primary intending subject is itself a normative structuring element (phrases like "as Emerson says," "to quote Hamlet," "in the words of the immortal Bard" all imply that the first speaker is not present but is being invoked by the quoter). And, as we have seen, the juxtaposition of contexts between the two utterances (the "original" quotation and its iteration or reuse) can indeed function much like a structural unconscious. Henry Hyde's invocation of the "sound and fury" line from *Macbeth* was not "intended" to label his colleagues in the House of Representatives as idiots, any more than, in the Clarence Thomas hearings, Senator Alan Simpson's quotation of Iago's famous speech on reputation was "meant" to cast doubt on Thomas's veracity. But the quoted line does work very much like an "unconscious," bringing unwelcome and unvoiced associations to light.

What Derrida calls "saturation," full presence, is by his argument never possible in any citation. But in the special kind of citation known as quotation, a citation of a citation, the dehiscence and the cleft are particularly manifest. This may be the case of a letter *never* returning to its sender. Both the addressee and the "author" are, in the parlance of the post office stamp, unknown.

I want now to turn to two famous quotations in literary studies where the intention of the speaker has always seemed enigmatic and where the utterance is apparently a nonce utterance, with no other words from the same speaker against which to test it. The first of these quotations can be found in Keats's "Ode on a Grecian Urn," and the speaker, it would appear, is the urn itself.

Here is Helen Vendler's account of the last lines of the poem:

> The poet himself utters the closing words in which the urn's motto and commentary are encapsulated as a quotation:
>
> When old age shall this generation waste,
>   Thou shalt remain, in midst of other woe,
> Than ours, a friend to man, to whom thou say'st,
>   "Beauty is Truth, truth beauty"—that is all
>   Ye know on earth, and all ye need to know.
>
> The last two lines are spoken by the urn, which places special emphasis on the mottolike epigram before going on to comment on its unique worth. But the whole last sentence of the poem is the sentence of the speaker who, in his prophecy, recounts what the urn will say to succeeding generations.[53]

Vendler explains, in a footnote after the phrase "spoken by the urn," that "This crux now seems settled," and refers the reader to a discussion in Jack Stillinger's *Twentieth-Century Interpretations of Keats' Odes* "where the *consensus gentium* seems to be that the last two lines are spoken by the urn to men."[54]

Let us leave aside for a moment the question of whether a crux settled is, in literary studies, a happy or an unhappy development. In the phrase "the *consensus gentium*" the wisdom of wise men seems redoubled by the Latin phrase (he who can understand it is part of the insider group, part, indeed, of the *consensus gentium*). And despite the fact that the poet-speaker says "say'st," one could perhaps argue that he is reading the motto on the urn, or rather (since there is no implication that the urn is in fact inscribed with words, and if it were the words would presumably be in a language that antedates even that of the native speakers of *consensus gentium*) that he reads the motto *into* the urn's "message."

Who is speaking, here? What do the quotation marks mean? And where, indeed, do they or should they end? I remember lively classroom discussions about this poem that included the termination of the quote marks as part of the—then not-yet-settled—"crux." Here is Earl Wasserman on the question, writing in 1953:

> If man is to "know" that beauty is truth, he must learn it, not by direct experience, but indirectly; it must be told him by the urn ("to whom thou say'st"), for otherwise he could not know it, since it is not true of the sphere of his direct experience. . . .
>
> *[O]n* implies a commentary, and it is Keats who must make the commentary on the drama that he has been observing and experiencing within the urn. It is the poet, therefore, who speaks the words, "that is all / Ye know on earth, and all ye need to know," and he is addressing himself to man, the reader. Hence the shift of reference from "thou" (urn) to "ye" (man).[55]

And here is Walter Jackson Bate's authoritative account, in his 1964 biography of the poet:

> The perennially disputed close of the poem then follows. The focus of the dispute is the final two lines, discussion of which already fills a small book of critical essays. . . . [Keats] was probably too ill to oversee the publication of the 1820 volume, where the lines were printed:
>   "Beauty is truth, truth beauty"—that is all
>   Ye know on earth, and all ye need to know.
> Hence it was long assumed that the final remark is the poet's own personal comment on the aphorism, either as a consoling admonition to his fellow human beings (addressed as "ye" though he has been speaking in terms of "us" and "other woe/than ours") or else as a congratulatory bow to the figures on the urn (though the whole burden of the stanza is what the urn, as a "friend," is offering to man). The texts of the transcripts make it plain that the entire two lines are meant as the message or reassurance to man from the urn, without intrusion by the poet.

Here Bate includes a footnote that directs the reader to fuller discussions of the transcribed text, adding, "all four transcripts (those of George Keats, Brown, Woodhouse and Dilke) lack a full stop after 'truth beauty,' lack quotation marks, and by dashes break the final lines not into two parts but into three. That of Dilke is typical: 'Beauty is truth,—truth beauty,—that is all.'"[56]

So the "originals," or rather the period transcriptions of Keats's "original," all lack quotation marks. Bate (at least the Bate of the 1964 biography) insists that these texts "make it plain" that the entire two lines are the message from the urn. Vendler appears to agree ("are spoken by the urn") but goes on to declare that "the whole last sentence of the poem is the sentence of the speaker who, in his prophecy, recounts what the urn will say to succeeding generations." The speaker thus imagines what the urn will say and translates it for posterity. Vendler encloses only the words from "beauty" to "beauty" in quotation marks. Bate, printing the lines as he thinks they should be printed, has:

> "Beauty is truth, truth beauty, —that is all
> Ye know on earth, and all ye need to know."

He explains, "the final two lines are in the vein of the inscriptions on Greek monuments addressed to the passing stranger. The elusive message is meant to be that of the urn, not of the poet speaking for himself." And he adds this deduction from the life of the poet: "Keats never comes close to anything as bald as the simple equation of these two abstractions, 'beauty' and 'truth,' that he permits the urn to make here (least of all does he advance anything seriously comparable to the words that follow)."[57]

The sentiment "Beauty is truth, truth beauty—that is all / Ye know on earth, and all ye need to know" is, we are thus told, *out of character* for John Keats. Bate deftly associates this kind of bromide with the "pseudo-statements" criticized by I. A. Richards, and emphasizes the distortion that comes with phrases taken out of context. Let us look once more at Bate's own reading of the problem:

> [P]artly because of the aphoristic nature of the final lines, they are constantly being separated not only from the context of the poem but even from the sentence in which they occur, and the efforts to put them back into the context only increase the concentrated focus on these innocent words. Perhaps the modern critical irritability with the phrasing would be less sharp if the Victorians themselves had not so frequently isolated the lines from their context and quoted them enthusiastically as what I.A. Richards calls a "pseudo-statement."[58]

So: in the case of the "Ode on a Grecian Urn," the final, aphoristic lines are often quoted out of context, as a pseudostatement, and placed in quotation marks. The quotation marks, apparently absent in the earliest transcripts of the poem, are inserted as intended clarifications: the encapsulated speaker, the urn, starts speaking *here* and stops *there*. Where *here* and *there* are depends upon whether the critic thinks Keats believes the sentiments of the last two lines of the ode, and also upon whether he or she thinks the diction in which they are expressed is appropriate to the poet's (or the poem's "speaker's") voice. The itinerant and shifting nature of the lines, their "quota-bility," the very quality that seems to further banalize them (Eliot calls them a "serious blemish," and faults them for being "grammatically meaning-less")[59] is in fact exacerbated by those "Victorian" quotation marks that, per-haps as a mark of emphasis, seem to translate the last two lines from the realm of free indirect discourse to that of direct (if slightly obliquely attrib-uted) speech.

In this most canonical of examples, the presence and absence of quota-tion marks indicates the presence and absence of an origin, and the presence and absence of a truth. Much earlier we noted the paradox that quotation marks can be signs of both authenticity and suspicion: the real thing and the "pseudo." In the "Ode on a Grecian Urn" one of the most famous sound bites in all of romantic literature is framed by quotation marks and then dis-avowed. It is the urn that speaks, not the poet. Or if the poet-speaker is speaking, he is paraphrasing "what the urn will say to succeeding genera-tions." The absence of quotation marks in the transcripts of Keats's contem-poraries is characteristic of early-nineteenth-century punctuation. Subsequent attempts to fix and clarify meaning, by enclosing either the first half-line or the entire two lines in quotation marks, introduce authenticity, authority, and voice as effects of interpretation masquerading as originary fact: what the poet meant, or meant to do. And because quotation marks are themselves by convention marks of origin—indicating that this is the real thing, not a paraphrase—the "crux" can be finally "settled," if we don't mind mixing our metaphors, by the imposition of anachronistic punctuation that is clearly spurious.

So determined is a certain faction of the poetic establishment to protect Keats from the claim that he speaks (and espouses) this sentiment that even *Bartlett's* goes to the extraordinary length of appending a literary-critical footnote. After the phrase "beauty is truth, truth beauty" (enclosed, as in Vendler's text, by quotation marks) there is the following footnote from W. H. Auden:

> If asked who said, "Beauty is truth, truth beauty!" a great many readers would answer, "Keats." But Keats said nothing of the sort. It is what he said the Grecian Urn said, his description and criticism of a certain kind of work of art, the kind from which the evils and problems of this life, the "heart high sorrowful and cloyed," are deliberately excluded. The Urn, for example, depicts, among other beautiful sights, the citadel of a hill town; it does not depict warfare, the evil which makes the citadel necessary.[60]

But time, to paraphrase Austin's felicitous paraphrase, will bring in its re-venges. The crux will not stay settled in the popular imagination. Urn, schmurn—the public knows who is speaking, and it is not the pot but the poet. Here are some media allusions to this famous passage:

From a scientific report about waist-to-hip ratio (WHR) in the human species: "Beauty is truth and truth beauty, to quote John Keats. But what is the truth about beauty? A scientific investigation of what men find beautiful in a woman's shape suggests that concepts of beauty are more to do with Western influences than what comes as an inbuilt, or innate desire."[61]

From an article about fall foliage in New England:

> "'Beauty is truth—truth beauty—that is all Ye know on earth,
> and all ye need to know.'
> —John Keats

"By now, anyone who has passed more than a few autumns in New Hampshire knows why the state's fall foliage is colored so flagrantly. . . . 'Beauty (or ugliness) is not out there in a man's environment but here, within a man's brain,' wrote Faber Birren . . . a craftsman, [and] pioneer in the study of the psychology of color."[62]

Lead sentence in an Arts and Leisure article about the merits of live-performance recording: "According to John Keats, beauty is truth and vice versa. Some recording artists disagree."[63]

Headline in the New York Times, *drawing attention to "a new Israeli esthetic along the Mediterranean"*: "THE SECULAR JEWS: Beauty Is Truth. That Is All the Stylish Need to Know."[64]

Headline of an editorial on the National Endowment for the Arts: "BEAUTY IS TRUTH: Government Has a Role in Nurturing the Arts."[65]

Headline for a Los Angeles Times *column*: "If 'Beauty Is Truth, Truth Beauty,' That's Not All We Need to Know Today: What's 'Telegenic'?"[66]

And, somewhat ironically in view of subsequent developments, this opening paragraph from a 1983 piece in the *New York Times*: "John Keats wrote that 'beauty is truth, truth beauty—that is all ye know on earth, and all ye need to know.' But is that all we need to know about Vanessa Williams, the new Miss America?"[67]

In none of these citations does the "famous crux" figure at all, nor does anyone seem to wish to credit the urn. Exactly what Eliot seems to have feared, that Keats will be blamed (or praised) for the bathetic sentiment behind the aphorism, comes resoundingly true. No one is interested in the views of an Attic shape, however fair or unfair its attitude. The canonical figure of the poet guarantees the "beauty is truth" line as a touchstone, unironized, unqualified—except for the vicissitudes of fallen modern life.

It is tempting to end this discussion of quotation marks and the quotation as floating signifier on this note. But I would like to interject one more famous utterance into the equation—one that has been, in the history of modern literature, as problematic and teasing as that of the urn. The speaker in this case is not a vase but an *avis*: specifically, Edgar Allan Poe's enigmatical raven. And what it speaks, of course, is the single word "Nevermore."

What is fascinating about the raven (and "The Raven") is the mixture of pertinence and impertinence generated by its steadfast iteration. Once it arrives and perches on the pallid bust of Pallas (and here I do in fact suspect a little intertextual allusion to Keats's Grecian urn) the raven has only one word for the increasingly importunate narrator. No matter what the query— "Tell me what thy lordly name is"; will you leave me, as have my other friends?; "is there balm in Gilead?"; will my soul clasp Lenore's in heaven?— the all-purpose answer, superbly overdetermined and always infuriatingly apt, is "Nevermore."

"Much I marvelled this ungainly fowl to hear discourse so plainly," says the narrator, "though its answer little meaning—little relevancy bore." But perhaps the problem was not that the single word "Nevermore" had little meaning and relevancy, but rather that it had too much. To call this "reply so aptly spoken" a floating (or to use Poe's own word for the bird, "flitting") signifier seems an understatement:

> "Doubtless," said I, "what it utters is its only stock and store
> Caught from some unhappy master whom unmerciful Disaster
> Followed fast and followed faster till his songs one burden bore—"

In stanza after stanza the word "Nevermore," sometimes in quotation marks and sometimes not, is repeated with a difference, gaining "meaning" both from the act of repetition and from the uncanniness of the too-aptly spoken reply. "Nevermore" is an empty signifier that becomes, precisely, saturated, or even supersaturated. It has no "origin," no intending subject; it is from the beginning a quotation, and a quotation out of context, since no one— not the narrator, not the reader—presumes that the raven is actually hearing and responding to the questions hurled at it by the increasingly agitated narrator, often called a student, and clearly suffering from an etiolating ("weak and weary") excess of learnedness ("many a quaint and curious volume of forgotten lore"). (Perhaps this "quaint and curious volume" is the same "very rare and very remarkable volume" that was the occasion for the first meeting between C. Augustus Dupin and his unnamed colleague and friend.[68] But this may be to consider too curiously.)

Explaining his choice of language and his cast of characters in the fascinating little piece called "Philosophy of Composition," Poe himself insists that the word "Nevermore" was the key to the whole: it answered fully the needs for sonority, melancholy, and the *o* and *r* sounds required by the refrain. "In such a search it would have been absolutely impossible to overlook the word 'nevermore.' In fact, it was the very first which presented itself."

> The next *desideratum* was a pretext for the continuous use of the one word "nevermore." In observing the difficulty which I at once found in inventing a sufficiently plausible reason for its continuous repetition, I did not fail to perceive that this difficulty arose solely from the pre-assumption that the word was to be so continuously or monotonously spoken by *a human* being—I did not fail to perceive, in short, that the difficulty lay in the reconciliation of this monotony with the exercise of reason on the part of the creature repeating the word. Here, then, immediately arose the idea of a *non*-reasoning creature capable of speech; and, very naturally, a parrot, in the first instance, suggested itself, but was superseded forthwith by a Raven, as equally capable of speech, and infinitely more in keeping with the intended *tone*.[69]

Now, whatever the "intended *tone*" of Poe's own enigmatical text here, the phenomenon he produces is instructive: a specifically *non*reasoning creature capable of speech carries the burden of meaning or, more accurately, is the occasion for wild interpretation. (That ravens were imagined to speak may be attested to in literary terms by another famous speaker—one well known to Henry Hyde: "The raven himself is hoarse, / That croaks the fatal entrance of Duncan / Under our battlements.") "Nevermore" migrates from stanza to stanza, sometimes marked as something the raven "quoth" and sometimes appropriated by the narrator. The progression from "nothing more" (the refrain word of the first stanza) to "nevermore" (the refrain word of the last), neither enclosed in quotation marks, is made possible by the intervention of an authoritative speaker whose word is taken *as* authoritative partly because it is repeated with a difference and partly because it is "in quotation." That the origin of the word is *elsewhere*, and is *lost*, does not undercut its authority. The raven, we could say, quotes (or "quoth") "out of context"—and this becomes part of the force of his free-standing, and free-ranging, utterance.

When the Cleveland Browns football team moved from Cleveland to Baltimore in 1996 the new owners had a contest to rename the team. The winner, to the amusement of many and the pleasure of some, was the Ravens—a tribute to Poe, who died and was buried in Baltimore. Sportwriters had predictable fun imagining a "Nevermore Defense" and a team that, if it failed, could be labeled "a pallid bust."[70] One prophecied a change of fortunes for the club: "Why a raven? To make the 'Nevermore!' believable."[71] Headline writers could not resist quoting perhaps the most notorious of all lines about quoting: "Quoth the Ravens, Play Everymore,

Kelly"; "Quoth the Ravens fans, Nevermore, after Pizza Hut Promotion"; "Quoth the Former Raven Everitt, Evermore"; "Quoth You on the Ravens; Nevermore!"[72] But perhaps the most striking if inadvertent effect was that these Ravens, too, began to be quotable, and enigmatic: "The Ravens are involved in preliminary talks that might lead to acquiring [a new quarterback]," read one account. "Neither Ravens owner Art Modell nor team vice president of player personnel Ozzie Newsome would comment."[73]

The choice of Ravens may have been overdetermined by the existence, in another sport, of a longstanding Baltimore team that bears the name of a bird: the Baltimore Orioles baseball club. Baltimore Orioles is felicitous in at least two senses: (1) there is an American songbird called the Baltimore oriole, and (2) both the double-dactyl scansion and the repetition of the *o* or *or* sounds (Baltim*ore* O*ri*oles) seem to make the name sound right. Baltimore Ravens lacks both ornithological and metrical inevitability. But we should not entirely forget the unarticulated but latent mantra of Poe's oft-quoted talking bird: behind the same open *o*s and *or*s of Balti*more*, and concealed by the aural brightness of Raven, may lurk the same ghostly word, in context more a spondee than a dactyl, "Never*more*."

I want to offer this kind of poetic event as a model, sign, or epitome of the fate of spoken quotation. Always "in quotation," whether its quotation marks are showing or not, the quotation often blends, apparently seamlessly but with its seams and its semes showing, into the parent text of the quoter. As in the philosophical brainteaser "'This statement is false' is true," the location and comprehension of a quotation's limits, and the degree to which *its* voice is marked as different from the speaker's, can radically alter both our sense of its truth value and our interpretation of its meaning.

Notes

1. Robert Bolt, *A Man for All Seasons* (1960; New York: Random House, 1962), 140. Here is how the event was recorded by More's son-in-law and biographer, William Roper: "[W]hereas the oath confirming the Supremacy and matrimony was by the first statute in few words comprised, the Lord Chancellor and Master Secretary did of their own heads add more words to it, to make it appear unto the King's ears more pleasant and plausible. And that oath, so amplified, caused they to be ministered to Sir Thomas More and to all other throughout the realm. Which Sir Thomas More perceiving, said unto my wife: 'I may tell thee, Meg, they that have committed me hither for refusing of this oath not agreeable with the stature, are not by their own law able to justify my imprisonment. And surely, daughter, it is great pity that any Christian prince shold by a flexible council ready to follow his affections, and by a weak clergy lacking grace constantly to stand to their learning, with flattery be so shamefully abused.'" William Roper, *The Life of Sir Thomas More* in *Two Early Tudor Lives*, ed. Richard S. Sylvester and Davis P. Harding (New Haven, CT, and London: Yale University Press, 1962), 240.
2. Bolt, *A Man for All Seasons*, xiii–xiv.

3. Robert Burton, "Democritus to the Reader," in *The Anatomy of Melancholy*.
4. "Front and Center, Five Accusers: The Excerpts; Henry J. Hyde," *The Boston Globe*, January 25, 1999, A26.
5. Malcolm Evans, *Signifying Nothing* (Athens: University of Georgia Press, 1986).
6. Thomas M. DeFrank, with Richard Sisk, Kenneth R. Bazinet, and Timothy J. Burger, "A Legacy from Era of Nixon," *Daily News* (New York), January 15, 1999, 38.
7. Jonathan Kirsch, "Droning Does Not a Good Case Make," *Newsday*, January 18, 1999, A31.
8. Esther Cloudman Dunn, *Shakespeare in America* (New York: Macmillan, 1939), 250.
9. T. S. Eliot, "The Love Song of J. Alfred Prufrock," in *Complete Poems and Plays 1909–1950* (New York: Harcourt, Brace & World, 1952), 7.
10. Francis X. Clines, "Slouching toward Deliverance," *The New York Times*, February 9, 1999, A16.
11. Richard Roeper, "In Senate, We Haven't Witnessed Nothing Yet," *Chicago Sun-Times*, January 20, 1999, 11.
12. Edward Said, *Beginnings: Intention and Method* (1975; New York: Columbia University Press, 1985), 22.
13. Representative Ed Bryant, Tennessee. In "Front and Center . . . ," *The Boston Globe*, January 25, 1999, A26.
14. Bruce Hamilton, *Too Much of Water* (1958; New York: Garland, 1983), 245.
15. Peter Ustinov, *Loser* (London: Michael O'Mara, 1989), 140.
16. Monica S. Lewinsky, excerpts from her deposition in the impeachment trial of President Clinton. In "From Monica Lewinsky: 'I Feel Very Uncomfortable Making Judgments,'" *The New York Times*, February 6, 1999, A11.
17. *The American Heritage Dictionary* (Boston: Houghton Mifflin, 1973), s.v. "quotation mark."
18. *Century* magazine 563/1 (1897).
19. R. B. McKerrow, *An Introduction to Bibliography for Literary Students* (Oxford: Clarendon Press, and London: Oxford University Press, 1927), 316.
20. George Puttenham, *The Arte of English Poesie 1589*, ed. Edward Arber (London: A. Constable, 1906; rpt. Kent, OH: Kent State University Press, 1970), 3: 29, 222. Ben Jonson, *English Grammar* (1637).
21. Puttenham, *Arte of English Poesie*, 3: 18, 199.
22. Watt, *Philosophical Transactions of the Royal Society* (1784), 74: 330 note.
23. Henry Hallam, *Introduction to the Literature of the Fifteenth, Sixteenth, and Seventeeth Centuries* (London: J. Murray, 1837), 3: 3, 99.
24. Andrew Ure, *Dictionary of Arts, Manufactures, and Mines* (New York: Appleton, 1858), 3: 647.
25. Henry Breen, *Modern English Literature: Its Blemishes and Defects* (London: Longman, Brown, Green and Longmans, 1857), 272.
26. *La Grande Encyclopédie* (Paris: 1885–1903), cited in Douglas C. McMurtrie, *Typographical Style Governing the Use of the Guillemet—The French Mark of Quotation* (Greenwich, CT: Condé Nast Press, 1922), 3.
27. James Boswell, *Life of Johnson* (London: Oxford University Press, 1965), 1143 (May 8, 1781).
28. Justin Kaplan, preface to the sixteenth edition of John Bartlett, *Familiar Quotations* (Boston: Little, Brown, 1992), ix.
29. Henry James, *The Bostonians* (1886; London: Penguin Books, 1986), 78, 84.

30. Rudyard Kipling, "'The Finest Story in the World,'" in *Many Inventions* (New York: D. Appleton and Company, 1899), 114.

31. Matthew Prior, *Paulo Purganti and His Wife* (1708).

32. Winston Churchill, *My Early Life: A Roving Commission* (London: T. Butterworth, 1930), 116.

33. Henry Watson Fowler and Francis George Fowler, *A Dictionary of Modern English Usage* (London: H. Milford, 1927), s.v. "Quotation."

34. Courses of Instruction, Harvard University, 1958–59: 162.

35. John Locke, *An Essay Concerning Human Understanding*, collated and annotated by Alexander Campbell Fraser (New York: Dover Publications, 1959), II: 379.

36. Ralph Waldo Emerson, "Quotation and Originality," in *The Portable Emerson*, ed. Mark Van Doren (New York: Viking Press, 1946), 296.

37. Debra Fried, *Valves of Attention: Quotation and Context in the Age of Emerson* (Ph.D. dissertation, Yale University, 1983; Ann Arbor: University Microfilms International, 1990), 5.

38. Ibid.

39. Another scholar claims that a closer source—still far from the famous quote—is a letter Voltaire wrote to M. le Riche. Norman Guterman, *A Book of French Quotations* (New York: Anchor, 1990), 189. ("Monsieur l'abbé, I detest what you write, but I would give my life to make it possible for you to continue to write" [letter of February 6, 1770]).

40. Jacques Derrida, "Signature Event Context," trans. Samuel Weber and Jeffrey Mehlman, in *Limited Inc* (Evanston, IL: Northwestern University Press, 1988), 12.

41. Jacques Derrida, "Force of Law: The Mystical Foundation of Authority," in *Deconstruction and the Possibility of Justice*, ed. Drucilla Cornell, Michael Rosenfeld, and David Gray Carlson (New York and London: Routledge, 1992), 15–16.

42. Ralph Waldo Emerson, journal entry, May 1849. In *Emerson in His Journals*, ed. Joel Porte (Cambridge, MA, and London: Harvard University Press, 1982), 401.

43. Burton, op. cit.

44. Ralph Waldo Emerson, "Quotation and Originality," in *Letters and Social Aims* (Boston and New York: Houghton Mifflin, 1875), 194.

45. Emerson, "Quotation and Originality," 196.

46. Kaplan, preface to *Familiar Quotations*, ix.

47. J. L. Austin, *How to Do Things with Words* (1962; Cambridge, MA: Harvard University Press, 1975), 60–61.

48. Ibid., 61, 81.

49. Ibid., 161.

50. Ibid., 22.

51. Leonard Diepeveen, *Changing Voices: The Modern Quoting Poem* (Ann Arbor: University of Michigan Press, 1993), 4, 7.

52. Derrida, "Signature Event Context," 18.

53. Helen Vendler, *The Odes of John Keats* (Cambridge, MA: Harvard University Press, 1983), 134.

54. Ibid., 312.

55. Earl Wasserman, "The Ode on a Grecian Urn," in *Keats: A Collection of Critical Essays*, ed. Walter Jackson Bate (Englewood Cliffs, NJ: Prentice-Hall, 1964), 138–39. Reprinted from Wasserman, *The Finer Tone: Keats' Major Poems* (Baltimore: Johns Hopkins University Press, 1953).

56. Walter Jackson Bate, *John Keats* (Cambridge, MA: Harvard University Press, 1964), 516.

57. Ibid., 517.

58. Ibid., 516.

59. T. S. Eliot, "Dante," in *Selected Essays* (New York: Harcourt, Brace, 1932), 230–31. Cited in Bate, 517.

60. W. H. Auden, *The Dyer's Hand* [1962], in *Familiar Quotations*, op. cit., 416 (and previous editions).

61. Steve Connor, "Science: The Truth about . . . Beauty," *The Independent* (London), November 27, 1998.

62. Ralph Jimenez, "Variety Is as Important as Color to Make Landscape Intriguing," *The Boston Globe*, October 4, 1998, 10.

63. Hans Fantel, "Is Truth Also Beauty?" *The New York Times*, November 26, 1989, 2: 8.

64. Joel Greenberg, "The Secular Jews: Beauty Is Truth: That Is All the Stylish Need to Know," *The New York Times*, April 6, 1998, A12.

65. "Beauty Is Truth: Government Has a Role in Nurturing the Arts," *The Houston Chronicle*, July 5, 1997, 34.

66. Jack Smith, "If Beauty Is Truth . . . ," *Los Angeles Times*, May 18, 1987, 5: 1.

67. "Larger Triumph, Larger Loss: American Beauty," *The New York Times*, September 20, 1983, A28.

68. Edgar Allan Poe, "The Murder in the Rue Morgue," in *Great Short Works of Edgar Allan Poe*, ed. G. R. Thompson (New York: Harper and Row, 1970), 276.

69. Edgar Allan Poe, "Philosophy of Composition," in *Great Short Works*, op. cit., 534.

70. Michael Dresser, "Tintinnabulation," *The Baltimore Sun*, March 29, 1996, 19A.

71. Gwinn Owens, "Why a Raven?" *The Baltimore Sun*, May 1, 1996, 13A.

72. *Houston Chronicle*, January 11, 1998, 2: 21; *San Diego Union-Tribune*, November 18, 1997, D2; *The Los Angeles Times*, July 5, 1997, 2; *St. Louis Post-Dispatch*, September 17, 1997, 25.

73. "Ravens Aim for Mitchell or Johnson," *The Baltimore Sun*, February 5, 1999, 1D.

Talking to the Animals

11

Alec Irwin

Talk traces a boundary between the human and nonhuman worlds. Trees don't talk. Nor (pace Annie Dillard) do stones. Nor do clouds and rainbows. Nor do dogs. Talk stops where human culture stops, and conversely, where there is no more talk, we have reached the limit beyond which culture's codes of rights and responsibilities (response-abilities) no longer apply.

The master concept of Western civilization, the Greek *logos*, telescopes reason and speech (and insinuates the problematic possibility of talk). Reason is not reducible to talk, may even be threatened by talk. Yet a rational being must be one you can talk to, and who can talk back. A being that can't talk is a being to which moral responsibility can't be reliably imputed, and whose interests we are not in any obvious sense obligated to consider when we weigh our own moral choices. Only beings with the capacity to deliberate, argue, and explain themselves—beings that can, if they choose, indulge in talk—belong to the realm of freedom, thus of moral choice, thus of accountability and rights.

The qualitative distinction between the rational, verbal human world and the rest of the planet has served *Homo sapiens* well. In recent centuries, this separation has permitted beings who claim the status of "ends in themselves" to exercise a frank, systematic, and unapologetic domination over the mere "things of nature."[1] Such things, including nonhuman living beings, have no membership in the moral Kingdom of Ends. When it's expedient, they can safely be regarded as expendable tools for the furtherance of human aims.

Under these circumstances, a desire to extend talk beyond the boundaries of the human species would seem to be a doubtful, even a dangerous impulse. Talk already causes enough problems within human society, even as it confirms our species' privileged status. If talk were to slip out of our control and begin to impart its ambiguous power to other parts of nature, the results could be catastrophic. *Homo sapiens* ought to be vigilant in preventing the *pharmakon* of talk from circulating (even imaginatively) outside our own kind.[2] Yet a glance at history (not to mention our embarrassing behavior with our pets) shows that human beings aren't—and never have been—content just to talk to each other. We yearn, in Dr. Dolittle's words, to "converse in Polar Bear and Python, to curse in fluent Kangaroo."

The dream of talking to animals has been one of the most persistent features of human culture. The oldest myths and folktales of the Bantu, the Celts, the Inuit converge in their obsession with talking animals, in their dream of a Golden Age when animals and humans shared a common language. Similar notions resurface in Native American legends, in Hindu mythology and Chinese folklore, in the *Roman de renart*. And far from capitulating before the assaults of modern science, the dream thrives today. Taco Bell commercials, visitor totals at Disneyworld, and the box office earnings of *Babe* bear eloquent and lucrative witness to the undiminished fascination of the loquacious quadruped. Not only has science not eradicated our dreams of chatting with beasts, but science itself sparks new hopes for interspecies talk: analyzing the "languages" of whales and dolphins, beaming radio messages into outer space, and teaching ASL to apes. Far from withering in the disenchanted world of modernity, our Dolittlean dream appears more robust than ever.

Why is this? Why should we want so much to talk to animals (or to imagine animals as already talking behind our backs)? What are we really dreaming when we dream (write, film, sing) about talking animals? And how should we react when science steps in and seeks to give reality to our collective reverie of interspecies chat? I believe it's important to look at the outer edges of the phenomenon of talk and ask what is at stake in our efforts to talk to the animals, to extend the boundaries of talk out into the silent, mysterious realm of the nonhuman. "Talk" as a mode of communication connotes the familiar, the reassuringly everyday; yet at the same time, talk hints at undisciplined impulses, a dangerous volatility, the undermining of estab-lished orders.[3] I want to suggest that the ambiguity inherent in the notion of talk matches deep ambivalences in our attitudes toward animals. To illumi-nate these ambivalences I will examine some odd and rather disparate cul-tural items, from Disney movies to 1980s scientific literature on ape-language experimentation. Though diverse in form and outlook, these items all emerged in or after the mid-1970s, a historical hinge-point in de-bates on "animal liberation."[4] My aim is to explore ways in which conflicted feelings about the liberation and/or domination of animals intertwine with ongoing cultural interrogations of talk.

The Beauty of the Beast: Defanging Talk

Talk is, among other things, a primary catalyst of human intimacy. We can't genuinely feel close to someone unless we have talked to her or him. Conversely, the way to get to know people is through talk, even if at the start this takes the form of an exchange of formulaic banalities. Relationships that involve nothing but polite chat or superficial banter may feel unsatisfying and insubstantial; yet it's hard to imagine any kind of peaceable human co-existence, much less sustained friendship, that wouldn't involve talk as a cen-tral component.

Humans have persistently longed for integration and closeness not only with each other, but with some (real or imagined) "larger whole": the natu-ral world, the cosmos, the vast otherness that lies outside us, yet with which we feel an obscure link (or at least its possibility). Animals stand as em-blematic representatives of this exteriority that inspires both longing and fear. The animal is the other par excellence. Thus it seems at once odd and understandable that we should reach toward this radical, animal alterity with the instrument of everydayness: talk. Just as logical is that our association of talk with animals should bring into the foreground some of our anxieties about talk itself. The suspicion haunts us that, if talk is the catalyst of inti-macy, it can also destroy intimacy. To function properly, talk requires selec-tive breeding and training, a dressage comparable to that we impose on animals to fit them usefully into the human order.

The Beauty and the Beast legend is one of the classic templates through which Western people have rehearsed our conflicted relation to the natural world and especially to animals. The story stages talk as a means whereby an-imals can be made to reveal a hidden humanity, but suggests at the same time that talk itself needs to undergo purifying transformation. The Beast has been the object of innumerable adaptations and appropriations, from Mme Leprince de Beaumont's eighteenth-century *conte* (itself based on ear-lier popular sources) to Kierkegaard, Cocteau, Split Britches, and beyond. But it's the animated film version from the Disney studios that most clearly

expresses the truths our culture wants to draw out of this parable of the re-
demptive, humanizing powers of love and language.

The general plot is familiar. A handsome prince has been changed by
magic into a fanged, hairy Beast who lives reclusively in his enchanted castle, surrounded by servants who have themselves been metamorphosed into
objects (clock, candlestick, teapot, etc.) that move and talk. The spell can be
broken only if the Beast learns to love and be loved by a human being. The
Beast imprisons an eccentric old inventor (Maurice) in his dungeon, but the
inventor's plucky daughter (Belle) offers herself as a hostage in her father's
place, and the Beast accepts the bargain. At first repulsed by the Beast's violent temper and horrifying appearance, Belle slowly senses a deeper nobility
and gentleness within him, which she nurtures through a period of shy
courtship. The Beast proves he has learned to love Belle by setting her free
from her captivity. Enraged villagers besiege his castle a short time later, but
the Beast offers no resistance; he spares the life of even the most brutish of
the attackers (Belle's frustrated would-be suitor Gaston), who responds by
stabbing the Beast treacherously from behind. As Belle, flinging herself on
the dying body, cries "I love you," the Beast is lifted up magically into the
air and transfigured; rays of light project from his limbs and he glides to the
earth again, restored to life in his former beautiful human shape.[5] The success
of the original film inspired the inevitable sequels, including *Belle's Magical
World*, which jumps backward chronologically to dwell on the poignant early
phases of the lovers' relationship (when the Beast was still a beast).

What retains our attention here is that Disney's *Beauty and the Beast* is a
story that both honors and disciplines talk. Talk—spontaneous, free-flowing
verbal communication between human and hairy animal—is at the center of
Beauty and the Beast, propelling the film's action and furnishing the medium
that unites its two central characters. Yet talk also leads to misunderstandings and raises anxieties. The Disney tale acknowledges talk's creative importance yet attempts to purify talk, to set limits to its unchecked
proliferation and to move it in the direction of proper speech.

On the one hand, it is by talking with the Beast that Belle initiates and
sustains the relationship that leads ultimately to the restoration of his humanity. Throughout its early phases, the relation between Belle and her cap-
tor relies on verbal sparring and repartee that gradually bridge the gulf
between the two characters and reveal deeper commonalities. The comically
uncontrolled patter of the household servants transformed into household
objects—Lumière the candelabra, Cogsworth the clock, Mrs. Potts the
teapot—also plays a catalyzing role at this stage of the protagonists' rap-
prochement. Belle's delight in the servants' overflowing (and grotesquely accented) talk is crucial in helping her begin to feel at home in the Beast's
castle. But comic chatter, even from enchanted teapots, has its limits, and

Belle quickly longs for more authentic modes of communication. "There are times I think that no one seems to listen / There are times I think they listen but don't hear," she sings in *Belle's Magical World* (the "they" referring, as the accompanying images suggest, both to herself and the Beast). "There are times I think they hear, but something's missing / The thoughts behind the words aren't clear."[6] A problem has been identified: a structural unreliability in beastly talk, "something missing" at talk's very core, which Belle is going to make it her business to restore. A new form of communication must be shaped, one that can allow genuine thoughts and feelings—and *only* genuine thoughts and feelings—to find expression. Belle's subsequent relationship with the Beast will take the form of a progressive disciplining of their (but in fact above all *his*) initially rough, uncontrolled, unstable, and insufficiently "clear" talk.

For an animal to talk at all may be an achievement, but it's far from good enough if the ultimate goal is to bring human and beast together. If the Beast intends to win Belle's love, he can't just rattle on any old way. The Beast must give up violent, unreflective, emotional talk and learn proper speaking. The process is dramatized in scenes in which the Beast, under the coaching of his servants and of Belle herself, painfully and reluctantly modulates his utterances step by step from the register of explosive rage to that of studied, submissive politeness. From "*You come out or I'll break the door down!*" to "It would give me great pleasure if you would join me for dinner . . . please."[7] The Beast and talk itself are both being disciplined in these passages: molded, purified, educated, stripped of their too-spontaneous and disorderly elements. Significantly, as things really start to get serious between Belle and the Beast, their conversations center increasingly around books; talk passes into the orbit and order of the printed word. A crucial symbolic threshold is crossed when the Beast leads the bibliophilic Belle into the library of his castle and tells her the riches it contains are now all hers. Subsequent sequences show the pair reading together by the fireside and amiably discussing literature. The change in talk mirrors and completes a change of heart. The spontaneity, spark, and occasional violence of the pair's early talk are reined in. The unpredictable, chaotic energy of talk is gently but firmly disciplined under the symbolic guidance of the Book.

Belle aims ultimately at a form of communication that conserves talk's unforced spontaneity but hems in talk's menacing and unpredictable elements. In a song from *Belle's Magical World*, she evokes this nobler talk as one through which she and the Beast would be able to "speak our minds and listen with our hearts":

I can hear you, you can hear me
When we listen with our hearts.

> I understand you, you understand me,
> That's the place that we can start.
> Words of kindness and forgiveness
> Bring us closer, not apart,
> When we speak our minds and listen with our hearts.[8]

This new, more authentic mode of communication retains traces of the spontaneity and directness of plain talk ("speaking our minds"), but removes the shadows and ambiguities, the double-entendre tendency of talk to be "heard" in different registers, and thus to lead to misunderstandings, or indeed to become the instrument of conscious trickery and deception (exemplified in the film by the "big talk" of the vain, fatuous Gaston and the "fast talk" of his conniving comic sidekick Le Fou). Uncontrolled talk can separate people (or people and beasts), make them feel more isolated and "apart" from each other. Talk smoothed, domesticated, and brought under moral rules (the benevolent law of "kindness and forgiveness") can and must "bring us closer," healing gaps and separations, allowing the radically and menacingly other to be "heard" and fully "understood." "Listening with our hearts," we move toward a mode of talk that approximates pure speech, a pure communication of essence without ambiguity or distortion, yet which arises naturally from the depths of our being. Our hearts (like Irigarayan lips) talk/speak to each other in a secret intimacy in which there is no possibility of lies or deception.

The power that accompanies purified, tamed talk is triumphantly confirmed in the scene of the Beast's resurrection and transfiguration. It is Belle's articulation of the magical phrase "I love you" that catalyzes the Beast's metamorphosis, releasing the human form concealed beneath the frightening animal husk. This phrase crowns the pure language Belle has labored to bring forth. It partakes of positive qualities that can be linked with talk: intimacy, honesty, emotive force, uncalculating spontaneity. Yet it has been stripped of the negative or troubling aspects that make talk untrustworthy (irony and staginess, multiple meanings, lack of depth). The phrase mobilizes talk's ability to catalyze closeness, but restrains talk's disturbing, protean proliferation, concentrating the full scope of authentic communication in a single, self-sufficient, supremely economical, and supremely significant declaration. Belle's "I love you" is performative language in a sense ironically closer to J. L. Austin's notion of "words that do things"—that is, that enact real changes in the world of human relationships and commitments—than to the unruly performativity of decadent Wildean discourse, let alone contemporary performance art.[9]

What we learn from Belle and the Beast is that there is something animal about talk itself, and that the unruly animal always requires discipline—strict but benevolent—so that its inner sweetness can be released. To catalyze intimacy, talk must be housebroken, defanged and declawed. In the world of the film, Belle's pure and purifying words perform this transformation. When the process culminates, the Beast is literally talked into becoming a man, into giving up his frightening, violent, ugly aspect (in particular his intimidating incisors) and revealing his hidden humanity. Talk has thus bridged and healed the most dramatic gap of all: that between humans and the silent, mysterious otherness of the natural world. But in the process talk itself has been talked into giving something up: its own multivalence, mobility, and scariness. Not only the Beast, but talk itself emerges from the Disneyean alembic transmuted: less likely to sharpen its claws on the furniture (or on human flesh), but also considerably less interesting.

Day of the Dolphin: The Pointing Flipper of Accusation

Part of our desire to talk to animals is a yearning to enter into intimacy with them (and with the natural world they represent). Yet we fear this closeness, too, for many reasons. On the one hand, intimacy with animals (could it genuinely be achieved) might challenge certain human prerogatives (like the right to eat our friends for dinner); on the other it might change animals themselves. Our imaginative efforts to "get close" to animals through talk might compromise the very otherness that makes animals fascinating in the first place: that mysterious alterity in which romantic souls have sensed a mode of being not simply different from but better than our own. If it's true that there is something suspiciously, dangerously "animal" about talk, it's also the case that the animal is beyond talk, perhaps above talk. Thus the natural purity of the animal may judge and condemn the impure artifices of human loquaciousness. Even if animals had language, they might be too wise, too "natural," to "talk."

Mike Nichols's 1973 film *The Day of the Dolphin* stages the desire to communicate with animals and the simultaneous conflicted concern that our talk might corrupt them (as we fear it has corrupted us). In contrast to the lineage of sly, deceptive, "fast-talking" animal heroes archetypally represented in the *Roman de renart* and the "Brer Fox" stories, Nichols offers us a fable in which human beings know only dishonest talk, while animals possess pure, authentic speech. This recoding allows Nichols to present his dolphins as moral judges pointing an accusing flipper at human cruelty.

Nichols's film is something of a milestone in the movie history of talking to animals, in that it removes talking beasts from any sort of whimsical or fairytale frame and presents them as key players in a plot that claims both naturalistic credibility and political relevance. The film goes to considerable lengths to appear more "realistic"—scientifically believable—than the bestselling Robert Merle novel on which it is based, particularly with respect to the linguistic performance of its cetacean protagonists (Merle's dolphins talk to their human mentors in supple and idiomatic English, with a vocabulary including words like "submarine," "harness," and "betray").[10]

Scientific investigation of the communicational aptitudes of large sea mammals was a hot topic at the time *Day of the Dolphin* was made. So were the Watergate scandal, the Cold War, Vietnam, and the general corruption of our social and political institutions. Nichols's film concerns marine biologist Dr. Jake Terrell (George C. Scott), who dreams of teaching dolphins to talk, but fears (rightly) the possible abusive exploitation of such a breakthrough. At a remote laboratory in the Caribbean, using the funds of a mysterious group known as the Foundation, whose officials he tries to keep in the dark about the real nature of his work, Terrell succeeds in teaching the rudiments of human speech to a dolphin named Alpha (or "Fa") and Fa's female companion Beta ("Bi"). Fa is able to understand Terrell's verbal commands and to formulate short sentences himself (though his grammar isn't too great). He refers to Terrell as "Pa." Thrusting his head out of the water of his pool, Fa voices practical requests: "Pa give fish now." But Fa's thinking, feeling, and language skills actually reach much more sophisticated levels, as the film progressively reveals. We learn that in addition to English, the dolphins already possess their own highly sophisticated language of underwater clicks and whistles ("Dolphinese"). The cetacean idiom allows for the expression of complex ideas and the communication of tender feelings. But Terrell's analyses lead him to the realization that Dolphinese is a language *in which it is impossible to lie.* The dolphin tongue is the archetype of pure speech: a language in which there can be no deception, but only statements of material fact and expressions of genuine emotion.

Fa and Bi share a pure love that the film celebrates through exultant sequences of their watery frolicking. Their affection also extends to their human family: "Pa" and his wife and research associate Maggie ("Ma"). The dolphins frequently verbalize their devotion to their trusted human friends: "Fa love Pa," the dolphin declares, raising his upper body out of the water and laying his snout on the scientist's feet. The animals make clear that it is only their love for Pa and Ma that motivates them to go along with the fatiguing process of acquiring human language. The dolphins themselves gain nothing meaningful from this undertaking (their own language is already fully sufficient for their needs); they accept the process and the sacrifices it involves for them out of unselfish love for their human partners.

Unfortunately, in the human world very different motives guide behavior. The sinister leaders of the Foundation plant a spy among Terrell's assistants and manage to get wind of the real nature of his experiments. Hooked in with rogue forces in the U.S. government planning to assassinate the president, the Foundation's chiefs scheme to train the intelligent dolphins to attach an underwater bomb to the hull of the presidential yacht. They invade Terrell's compound and kidnap Alpha and Beta, killing an expendable human being or two in the process. The conspirators transfer the dolphins to a boat waiting in a secret location off shore, where they teach them how to transport and attach the explosive device, calling the bomb a "ball" and telling Fa and Bi the whole process is only a game.

Unable to track the plotters, Terrell and his team wait in anguish, agonizingly aware of the trusting dolphins' vulnerability. Before coming in contact with men, the innocent creatures "have never been lied to," Terrell realizes. They are completely unprepared for the deceitful ways of the would-be assassins. Once the president has been eliminated, moreover, it's clear the killers will destroy Fa and Bi, as well. The dolphins will be eyewitnesses, indeed unintentional accessories to the crime: witnesses endowed on the one hand with human speech, but on the other with an utterly unhuman reluctance to lie. The assassins know that, if questioned, Fa and Bi will undoubtedly "talk," in the most dangerous sense of the term: that is, they will tell the truth. Deceitful humans, threatened by the animal's candor, must kill the beast to conceal their own murderous machinations.

In the end, the intelligence and moral discernment of the dolphins allow them to foil the assassins' plot (they plant the mine on the hull of the killers' own boat instead of the presidential vessel). Yet the audience, along with Terrell, is left wondering if the animals' innocence has not been irreparably compromised by their contact with human talk and their apprenticeship in the sordid ways of human society. In the film's climactic scenes, realizing that Fa and Bi will never be safe as long as they are in contact with humans, Terrell orders the dolphins to turn their backs forever on dry land, the wicked species that rules it, and the talk that gives *Homo sapiens* our manipulative power. "Fa and Bi go to water," Terrell commands (meaning, out to the open ocean). "Fa not talk to men." "Not talk?" Fa asks doubtfully. Terrell confirms his order: "Swim, eat, play. Not talk."[11] Talk is the primary instrument, if not itself the root, of human evil. For their own good, the dolphins must reject talk and return to their own natural elements: the ocean's depths and the purity of a nonhuman speech untainted by violence and deceit.

The film hammers home the oppositions dolphin innocence versus human corruption, healthy animal nature versus depraved society, linking these contrasts to the tension between pure dolphin speech and humans' untrustworthy talk. The animals' world is simple, limpid as the crystalline waters through which they glide, just like dolphin language. Human society, meanwhile, grimly mirroring human talk, reveals itself as a murky, violent, Piranesian universe of plots, counterplots, corruption, and murder. The essential point is that dolphins *use* language, but they are not trapped in it. They combine communication in Dolphinese with a purity and intensity of sensation humans can only dream of. Terrell explains dolphins' moment-by-moment experience in these terms to a lecture audience: "Imagine that your life is spent in an environment of total physical sensation. That *every one of your* senses is heightened to a level that in humans could only be described as ecstatic. That you're able to see, to perceive with every part of your being, . . . [that] every inch of your surface, your skin, is a receptor, a perfectly accurate source of information about the world for miles around." Whereas human talk envelopes and entraps, seems to cling to us with a kind of gluey, viscous quality, threatening to dull our awareness of the real, dolphin speech is pure, transparent, leaves its users free and open for joyful, sensuous participation in nature's all-embracing flow.

Moreover, the film tells us, the relative simplicity of Dolphinese and its subservience to "ecstatic" physical sensation are not signs of lower cetacean intelligence, but the reflection of a choice made by these animals to orient their collective existence to a particular pattern of values. The dolphin's "brain is as big as a man's," Terrell stresses, but cetacean brain power is put to very different uses. Dolphins "decided" several million years ago to leave land and return to the ocean.[12] Thus their life of gentleness and sensuous, playful innocence is the result of a moral decision. At some decisive moment in the species' history, dolphins chose the sea over the land, and true speech over false, unruly, artificial talk.

This leads to a surprising role reversal between human and beast, a turnaround in the knowledge flow between the scientists who ostensibly impart language and knowledge and the beasts who receive them. "You taught them our language," Terrell's wife says of Fa and Bi. "Why? So they would become like you?" On the contrary, a chastened Terrell affirms, "We should become like them." We presume to teach the dolphins, but it's *they* who ought to instruct us. What are the tarnished glories of our human language and culture in comparison with what these beasts possess: moral purity, true love, ecstatic participatory joy in existence? We enmesh ourselves in lies and violence; these animals enjoy authentic, integral participation in being. Rather than forcing our corrupt/corrupting talk and our instrumental rationality on dolphins, Terrell concludes, we should be trying to learn from them how to reconnect pure speech with "instinct and energy," making human lives more like dolphins' lives.[13]

Thus, if in *Beauty and the Beast* the human is the teacher who corrects the animal's rough talk and so initiates the beast into humanity, in Nichols's film, animals are the moral teachers, possessors of an authentic speech that shames humans' impure chatter. In Disney, the wild animal is tamed and transformed through a disciplining of talk. In *The Day of the Dolphin*, already tamed animals are sent back to the wild to flee talk's contagion and the violence it summons.

Talking Apes, Human Truth, and the Slave Revolt in Morals

While *The Day of the Dolphin* may not win any prizes for believability, the film's basic premise found support in the serious science of its day. In the

1970s and 1980s, a celebrated series of animal-language experiments involving cetaceans and above all apes brought talking animals out of the realm of fairytale and into the scientific journals. Anthropologists, biologists, and linguists joined Cocteau and Disney in trying to bring forth talking beasts, only this time in the real world. The subject of vehement (and still ongoing) debates, ape-language research provides both confirmation of the enduring power of our dream of extending talk beyond our own species, and an indication of the anxieties that are stirred when we begin to think animals might really start talking back. When ape-language research first attracted public attention, some looked to science's talking apes to reveal truth—human truth, *our* truth—at last. Yet it is unclear whether we were or are, in Nietzsche's words, equipped to "withstand a truth concerning man" when that truth—our "true biography"—is told to us by a monkey.[14]

Having begun with isolated, sporadic efforts in the early twentieth century, experiments aimed at teaching apes to talk surged into public consciousness in the 1970s, with the publication of data from Project Washoe, led by primate researchers R. Allen Gardner and Beatrice Gardner. The Gardners' claimed successes in teaching American Sign Language (ASL) to Washoe, a female chimpanzee, shook the scientific community, and gripped the imagination of the lay public. One giddy commentator declared: "It is unlikely that any of us will in our lifetimes see again a scientific breakthrough as profound in its implications as the moment when Washoe, the baby chimpanzee, raised her hand and signed 'come-gimme' to a comprehending human."[15] In the years that followed the Gardners' pioneering work, other major research campaigns explored the nature and limits of apes' language skills. Probably the most famous of these projects was Francine Patterson's work with Koko the signing gorilla. Koko generated not only articles in specialized scholarly journals, but a wave of media reports, books aimed at mainstream audiences and/or children, and publications in popular middle-brow magazines like *National Geographic*.[16]

Different experimenters and critics ultimately came to sharply different conclusions on the question of whether any of the apes involved in these programs actually learned to "talk." For researchers like the Gardners, Patterson, and Roger and Deborah Fouts, the answer was and remains an unequivocal yes. "We have shown . . . that chimpanzees can pass this language [ASL] on to the next generation, that they use it spontaneously to converse with each other as well as with humans, [and] that they can use their signs to think with."[17] For others the response is a just as resolute no. "None of the ape-language projects succeeded . . . in implanting in an ape a capacity for language equal to that of a young child, let alone of an adult."[18]

What interests us is less whether Washoe or Koko really talked than the passion with which the matter was (and continues to be) talked *about* by humans. The exactitude of the experimental results is of less concern than the hopes and terrors the *idea* of these experiments brought to the surface. As Joel Wallman has rightly stressed, the fierceness of the intellectual controversy mirrors the crucial importance of language itself, and the unique place of language in humans' self-understanding:

> For articulate language is not just one among other capacities thought to be exclusively human abilities. No one would get excited, it has been observed, if it were shown that an ape could mix a dry martini (Atherton and Schwartz 1983). Rather, language, at least in the European intellectual tradition, is the quintessential human attribute, at once evidence and source of most that is transcendent in us, distinguishing ours from the merely mechanical nature of the beast. Language is regarded as the sine qua non of culture, and . . . with the relinquishing of tool use and more recently tool making . . . as uniquely human capabilities, the significance of language as a separator has grown.[19]

If the ability to talk is the most important "separator" between human beings and other creatures' merely "mechanical nature," we can see the profound significance for understandings of our relation to the natural world if this barrier were to crumble. And this collapse of boundaries is precisely what experiments like Project Washoe and Patterson's work with Koko appeared to announce. Using data from the ape-language experiments purporting to show that chimpanzees and gorillas were capable of talking (in ASL) at a level close to that of young humans, "ape partisans" advocated nothing less than a profound reconfiguration of our human "self-definition as a species."[20] This challenge provoked complex and divergent reactions, sometimes in the same people: on the one hand an almost euphoric sense that "we are not alone" in a speechless and inscrutable universe; on the other, disquiet at the thought that "human" is no longer a privileged "special classification," but "merely an adjective" qualifying our own essentially "animal nature."[21]

Perhaps the most intriguing cultural response to the threatened collapse of barriers between humans and beasts came from science fiction, in the form of the *Planet of the Apes* movies. The production and popularity of these films coincided, not surprisingly, with the heyday of ape-language research. The five *Apes* films staged a densely interwoven complex of American (and more broadly Western) cultural anxieties, including worries about race, the environment, and nuclear war, and of course the question of humans' relationship to animals. Presenting a dystopian world in which warlike talking apes rule over a slave caste of miserable, congenitally mute humans, the *Apes* series forcefully suggested just how dangerous talk could be if it fell into the wrong paws. *Planet of the Apes* telescoped anxieties about human uniqueness, animals' status, and global political instability, fusing these themes with subterranean worries about the nature of talk itself. The films drew viewers into a world in which the most familiar and seemingly fundamental hierarchies had been destabilized, in which a conferral of the privilege of talk on apes had led to the ultimate Nietzschean "slave revolt in morals," an uprising of subjugated nonhuman species against their human masters.

The original *Planet of the Apes* begins when a spaceship from Earth veers off course and crash-lands on an unknown world, leaving the vessel's captain, astronaut Taylor (Charlton Heston), and the two surviving members of his crew stranded. The space travelers find their way to a settlement of mute human barbarians just in time to be caught up in a slaving raid conducted by rifle-wielding, jackbooted simians on horseback. One of the astronauts is killed; Taylor and his single remaining companion are transported back to the Ape City.

In the ape capital, Taylor and the audience plunge into a linguistic-zoological-political nightmare that suggests how far things might go if *Homo sapiens* were to lose our exclusive grip on the evolutionary scepter/weapon that is language. Ape City systematically inverts all "normal" relations between human and beast. Here, apes talk, while humans are incapable of speech. Apes wear clothes and engage in elaborate social and religious rituals; naked humans are kept in cages, squatting in their own filth, or are harnessed as draft animals. In a particularly piquant reversal, ape medical researchers use humans as lab specimens; they carry out a lobotomy on Taylor's final remaining crew member. "How the hell did this upside down civilization get started?" Taylor demands of the ape minister of science, the sinister Dr. Zaius. "You may well call it upside down," Zaius replies frostily, "since you occupy its lowest rank. And deservedly so." In the film's famous final sequence, in which Charlton Heston kneels weeping on the beach before a half-buried, calcinated Statue of Liberty, the terrible truth comes out. The Planet of the Apes is not an alien world halfway across the universe, as Taylor had continued to believe (that simians in another galaxy should coincidentally converse in English seems not to have awakened his suspicions), but our Earth itself a couple of millennia in the future.[22]

The subsequent *Apes* movies drive home the point that humans ourselves forged—through scientific hubris and greed—the shattered, inverted world in which Taylor must endure his bitter exile. The sequels (some set chronologically prior to the action of the original film) reveal that the race of talking simians was created as a slave caste by human science in the days before nuclear war. In a rebellion depicted in *Conquest of the Planet of the Apes*, the enslaved simians rise up against their tyrannical human masters and overthrow them. We learn that humans engineered and made inevitable our own downfall: on the one hand by oppressing "lower" creatures; but on the other (and more fatally) by imparting to those lower beings the ability to talk.

The *Apes* films condensed anxieties about animals and about talk itself simmering in an era that saw not only ape-language research and the beginning of the animal rights movement, but a series of political and cultural crises that provoked widespread disillusionment, extending to language itself. The 1960s and 1970s saw a new suspicion of language, fueled by the surfeit of hysterical Cold War propaganda, the debacle of Vietnam, the incendiary talk of radical groups like the Black Panthers and the Weathermen, the Watergate affair. In this period the uses and abuses of talk in the public realm—talk's elusiveness, corrupting doubleness, and manipulative, performative aspects—weighed on the minds of large numbers of Americans. Citizens who listened to the solemn lies of government military spokespeople attempting to explain Vietnam, then to Richard Nixon trying to talk his way out of Watergate, were simultaneously being told that scientists had taught nonhuman life forms to talk: that is, potentially, to become liars and manipulators in their turn. Indeed, some researchers trumpeted apes' capacity to lie as one of the most important proofs of their linguistic competence. Koko's ability to "lie to escape the consequences of her own misbehavior" could be taken as the most convincing demonstration that she had *really* learned to talk, that she was *really* a "person."[23]

The *Apes* movies crystallized and capitalized upon the resulting ambivalence. They reminded viewers that talk—so familiar, ubiquitous, and apparently harmless—is also a weapon. Like animals themselves in the world of modern technology, talk initially seems furtive, feeble, picturesque but essentially insignificant. Yet talk can be charged with subversive power. If talk and animals, these two strangers, were to join forces, the result might be a shakeup of our worldviews and political structures more far-reaching than anything we can imagine. The human truth the *Apes* movies proclaim is that our mastery of nature is fragile. We rule the globe thanks to forces/capacities/entities we have learned to exploit but can never fully control. Both animals and talk belong to this category of abused but fundamentally untamed entities. Animals and talk alike serve us as slaves, on whose toil and submission our survival depends. Yet animals and talk are faithless servants waiting for the first chance to revolt. Separately or (worse) together, these slaves could at any moment elude our surveillance, rise up, and destroy us. In the *Apes* series, simians informed and transformed by talk stage a revolution that hurls humans from our evolutionary throne.

The movies' other piece of bad news (though of course it's not really new) is that the brutal animal and the insidious force of talk are enemies we carry perpetually inside us. As the ape minister Dr. Zaius warns Taylor, the most threatening talking beast is the animal we humans are. Zaius takes leave of Taylor by citing a passage from the ape civilization's sacred scriptures: "Beware the beast Man. . . . Alone among God's primates, he kills for sport, or lust, or greed. . . . Let him not breed in great numbers, for he will make a desert of his home, and yours."[24] Simply for us to leave God's *other* primates in peace will not solve our problems (though it might be a place to start). And even if humans decide not to create signifying monkeys by scientific means (or prove unable to do so), we must still face the garrulous— and dangerous—beast within.

"Of ourselves we are not 'knowers.'"[25] Are we "knowers" of animals? Must we know animals in order, at last, to know ourselves, to find our place in the house of being? Yet how can we know the animal, compel it to tell the truth—our truth—unless we can make it talk? This question must give us pause (paws?). For when the animal talks, will we like what we hear? And once it starts talking, will we ever be able to shut it up again?

Looking into the depthless eyes of an animal we see the terribly familiar and the infinitely remote. The brother toward whom we reach out; the alien from whom we shrink back in instinctive fear. We will always dream the animal as the talking animal, and the talking animal will always simultaneously threaten and fascinate. Today just as at the dawn of civilization, the talking animal remains the oracle we long to interrogate (if necessary, create), and the monster we cannot permit to exist. This monster would complete us, yet could also destroy us (and might, we fear, be morally justified in doing so).

Animals are the other we cannot elude, because it has its site within ourselves. We perceive, then, the connection between animals and our talk, and why the promises and fears associated with talk and animals are intertwined. Like the animal, talk both nourishes and gnaws at us (parasitically sucks our substance). At the same time, talk worries (and thrills) us with its tendency to run wild, its irrational excess. Like the household pets we patronize and envy, talk seems at once superficial and profound, naive and gifted with an immemorial wisdom. Talk is elusive, only partially predictable, therefore always disquieting even as it reassures. Like the beast, talk is familiar, yet unseizable; manipulable, yet savage; powerless, yet threatening; indispensable to us, yet subject to impulses we can't understand. We rely upon talk and animals, but can we, dare we, trust them?

Like Disney's Belle, we want to tame animals through talk, and domesticate talk itself. Yet perhaps Terrell's conclusion in *The Day of the Dolphin* is the right one: it is humans and our corrupt chatter that require discipline and punishment, while animals point beyond parasitic, violent talk toward a pure speech suffusing radiant bodies. But short of this horizon of transparent language that can never lie, animals and talk remain dangerous, as astronaut Taylor discovered, and our guilty love for them perpetually crash-lands us on a ravaged planet that is both *unheimlich* and the only home we'll ever know.

Notes

1. Immanuel Kant, *Grounding for the Metaphysics of Morals*, trans. James Ellington (1785; Indianapolis, IN: Hackett, 1993), 43.
2. See Shelley Salamensky, "'Dangerous' Talk: Phenomenology, Performativity, Cultural Crisis," in this volume.
3. Ibid.
4. See Peter Singer, *Animal Liberation: A New Ethics for the Treatment of Animals* (New York: Random House, 1975).
5. *Beauty and the Beast*, dir. Gary Trousdale and Kirk Wise (United States: Walt Disney Company, 1991).
6. *Belle's Magical World*, dir. Cullen Blaine et al. (United States: Walt Disney Company, 1993). Original video release.
7. *Beauty and the Beast*.
8. *Belle's Magical World*.
9. J. L. Austin, *How to Do Things with Words* (Cambridge, MA: Harvard University Press, 1962).
10. Robert Merle, *The Day of the Dolphin*, trans. Helen Weaver (New York: Simon and Schuster, 1969).
11. *The Day of the Dolphin*, dir. Mike Nichols (United States: Avco Embassy Pictures, 1973).
12. Ibid.
13. Ibid.
14. Friedrich Nietzsche, *The Genealogy of Morals*, trans. Francis Golffing (1887; Garden City, NY: Anchor, 1956), 275.
15. Jane Hill, "Apes and Language," *Annual Review of Anthropology* 7 (1978): 89–112. Cited in Joel Wallman, *Aping Language* (Cambridge and New York: Cambridge University Press, 1992), 5.
16. See, for example, Francine Patterson, "Conversations with a Gorilla," *National Geographic* 154 (1978): 438–65; Francine Patterson, *The Education of Koko* (New York: Holt, Rinehart, and Winston, 1981); Francine Patterson, *Koko's Kitten* (New York: Scholastic Books, 1985).
17. Roger S. Fouts and Deborah H. Fouts, "Chimpanzees' Use of Sign Language," in *The Great Ape Project: Equality beyond Humanity*, ed. Paola Cavalieri and Peter Singer (New York: St. Martin's Press, 1993), 39.
18. Joel Wallman, *Aping Language* (Cambridge and New York: Cambridge University Press, 1992), 4.
19. Ibid., 5. The parenthetical reference is to Margaret Atherton and Robert Schwartz, "Talk to the Animals," in *Language in Primates: Perspectives and Implications*, ed. Judith de Luce and Hugh T. Wilder (New York: Springer-Verlag, 1983).
20. Wallman, *Aping Language*, 5, 7.
21. Fouts and Fouts, "Chimpanzees' Use of Sign Language," 31.
22. *Planet of the Apes*, dir. Franklin J. Schaffner (United States: Twentieth Century–Fox Films, 1968).
23. Francine Patterson and Wendy Gordon, "The Case for the Personhood of Gorillas," in *The Great Ape Project*, 58.
24. *Planet of the Apes*.
25. Nietzsche, *The Genealogy of Morals*, 149.

Satan and Sybil

12

Talk, Possession, and Dissociation

Steven Connor

Clov: What is there to
keep me here?
Hamm: The dialogue.
—*Samuel Beckett,*
Waiting for Godot

Speaking and Talking

English maintains a subtle but sustained set of distinctions between talking and speaking. Speaking implies in English a freely chosen act of expression. Why else does the interrogator demand of his victim, "Talk!" Were the interrogator to demand, "Speak!" he would be according to his subject more capacity for self-determination than the situation permits. The interrogator who demands that his subject *talk* is acknowledging the coerced nature of what will be delivered up to her. The one who *talks* tells me what I want to know, or what I think he knows; the one who *speaks* tells me what he thinks he knows. Talking is therefore associated with unwilling, or unconscious, utterance. Because human beings experience their humanity in terms of their capacity for voluntary utterance, talking can seem less human than speaking; to "talk" under interrogation is also sometimes to "squeal" or to "blab." When animals are accorded speech, they are more often said to "talk" rather than to "speak." Talking also has in it a hint of the mechanical, or automatic, a fact borne out in the preference for the word "talking" when we are crediting dolls, machines, and objects with the power of speech. The jeer contained in the phrase "talking head" would be absent from the phrase "speaking head." The exceptions to this rule assigning talking to inhuman or less-than-human entities—the "speaking clock," the "speak-your-weight" machine—exist presumably because these are meant to be machines that have the exactitude and reliability we associate with purposeful rather than casual or unconscious speech.

When we want to suggest the vacuity of somebody's language, we tend to avoid references to speech: you "talk" rather than "speak," "through your hat," or "out of your arse." We "talk in our sleep": we do not "speak in our sleep." That talking often implies a language over which we do not have complete control accounts for the fact that we refer to people who speak too much as "talkative" rather than "speakative." Because talk is less rational, less determinate than speech, there is always a hint of the superfluous or the gratuitous in it. Because we use the word "speaking" when we mean that someone is speaking as themselves, we also use it when they are deliberately speaking as somebody else, or using another's language or mode of discourse. We are more likely to use the phrase "she speaks French" of someone whose first language is not French, but who can consciously shift to the use of it; "talking French" is something that French people are likely to be said to be doing.

Speaking is therefore oriented toward the conscious act of utterance, the determinate use of language for particular purposes. Speech often involves expressive declaration rather than the delivery of opinion or information; hence the impossibility of a phrase such as "the love that dare not talk its name." Talking is oriented toward the process and themes of speech, whether free or constrained. Speech thus appears self-conscious and autonomic, while talking is unconscious and heteronomic. This can also mean that the term "talking" is preferred in contexts where the emphasis is upon the theme of a discourse rather than its action: we speak of the need to "speak out," but of the action of "talking it over" or "talking things through."

It is for this reason that we tend to use the word "talking" when referring to habitual or casual social process rather than individual "speech." Even when an individual is not speaking as himself, but subsuming his individuality in an identification with a particular group, the emphasis on the who of the utterance may often prescribe the use of the word "speech": thus, "speaking as a Londoner/only child/working parent," not "talking as. . . ." We have "speech act" theory, but, asked what a "talk act" might be, most of us would probably imagine some kind of performance, either involving the staging or simulation of social discourse, or the display of vocal virtuosity. It may be that the same distinction between individual and social forms of speech governs the nominal forms of the verbs. In contemporary English, two or more persons can have "a talk," but not "a speak" (the phrase to "have speech" with someone being now obsolescent). A "speech" is always attributable to an individual. "Speech," without a definite or indefinite article, is our generic term for oral language, conceived, we might say, in terms of individual utterance, rather than "talk." In the phrase "the talking cure," as opposed to the "speaking cure," the intended associations are with the undogmatic, exploratory, copersonal aspects of language. A "speaking cure" would presumably imply something too rigidly directive. Finally, and most significantly for my purposes in this essay, one is said to "speak in tongues," but to "talk to oneself." Glossolalia may result in unintelligible utterance, but "speaking" seems the appropriate word given the fact that the glossolalic is felt to empty himself or herself into the act of giving voice. No response is possible to glossolalic utterance on the same level, other than the acknowledgment of the act and fact of the utterance itself. In talking to oneself, by contrast, one abdicates from control over, or coincidence with one's own voice. Talk is the abeyance of voice, or the "who is speaking?" of voice.

A way of summarizing these differences would be to say that speech is of the I, whereas talk is of the it. Speech is the voice of the self, whereas talk is the voice of the other, whether the otherness be that of other individual speakers, or that of impersonal language use. This distinction is a result of the long and uneven process whereby Western culture has developed the idea of the definingly human nature of language and the definingly personal nature of "voice." This essay reflects on the meanings of speaking and talking in cases of possession and dissociation, cases in which, it appears, an imperative arises to secure speech and voice against talk. My emphasis will not be on the psychopathology of these conditions, but on the ways in which they are staged and set forth, in spectacle and narrative. Such representations often have as their aim the clarification of the distinction between speaking and talking, even as they themselves proliferate some of the impalpabilities and approximations of talk against the unreproachable solidity and self-sameness of speech. The possibility of being drawn into dialogue with the other, which is always part of the stagings of possession, suggests that subjects might not always fully and exactly coincide with what they say, or with the act of saying it, and that other subjects, and other-than-subjects might come to be implicated in the act of talking. For the I to take the place of the it means encountering the I in the midst of itself, of its it-selves.

Name and Number

Michel de Certeau asks, "Is there a 'discourse of the other' in cases of possession?" Meaning: Is there an authentic language of the hysteric, the madwoman, the victim of possession, the mystic, that might be retrieved from the mass of historical documentation that mediates these voices?[1] De

Certeau's answer is given from the beginning. In cases of possession, the discourse of the other is always muffled, channeled, covered over, by the official discourses that stand in for the one possessed, and speak on her behalf. In order to expel the invading presence from discourse, it is necessary, first of all, to take it into discourse. For de Certeau, the means by which the other in possession is allowed to speak is the same as that which authorizes human beings as speaking subjects, the giving of a name. It is being named that allows the other to speak, to come into its own as an autonomous agency. The speech of the hysteric or the one possessed is both raised into discourse and held at a distance from it. "Whether in Africa or South America, therapy in cases of possession essentially consists of naming, of ascribing a term to what manifests itself as speech, but as an uncertain speech inseparable from fits, gestures and cries."[2] To give a name to the possessing agency is to give it a certain power of its own, allowing its barking, howling, and mewing to count as discourse. But it is also to assign a place for that discourse, a place that is not its own:

> the treatise of demonology assigns in advance to the possessed woman the condition and place of her speech. From psychiatric discourse the "mentally ill" or the "madwoman" gains the possibility of uttering statements; in the same fashion, the "possessed woman" can speak only thanks to the demonological interrogation or knowledge—although her locus is not that of the discourse of knowledge being held about her. The possessed woman's speech is established relative to the discourse that awaits her in *that* place, on the demonological stage, just as the language of the crazed woman in the hospital is only what has been prepared for her on the psychiatric stage.[3]

De Certeau rightly emphazises the importance of supplying a name for the possessing devil(s). Of equal importance to the exorcistic process was the necessity of numbering them. The accounts given in Mark 5 and Luke 8 of Christ's exorcism of the Gadarene man with an unclean spirit famously conflate naming and numeration. Slightly different versions are given by the two evangelists of the spirit's reply to Christ's enquiry as to his name. Mark writes: "And he asked him, What is thy name? And he saith unto him, My name is Legion; for we are many." Luke offers a less puzzling version of the exchange, himself supplying the words attributed to the demoniac by Mark: "And Jesus asked him, saying, What is thy name? And he said, Legion: because many devils were entered into him." It is not clear whether Legion, a word that metonymically signifies a multitude or host, is indeed the collective name of the demons, or a metaname signifying the refusal to be accommodated by a single name. Nevertheless, the mere expedient of requiring a name from the innominate multitude (the herd of swine into which they are sent numbers over two thousand) seems to force them into name and number.

Early accounts of possession and exorcism were indeed much concerned with establishing the number of devils resident in the bodies of the possessed, and resisting what we might call the demoniality of the plural. In some Catholic possession cases, the very attempt to pin down the identity of the possessing agency seems to produce multiplication. Late in 1565, a young girl of fifteen or sixteen named Nicole Obry had a vision of her grandfather while she was at prayer in the town of Vervins, near Laon, in a Huguenot area of Picardy. The vision declared that his spirit had entered the girl and demanded that she and her family perform various penances for the repose of his soul, since he had died unconfessed. A Dominican friar named Pierre de la Motte forced the possessing entity to confess that it was in fact Beelzebub, not a spirit or angel. The devil was exorcised several times a day, resuming residence in Nicole's body as often as he was driven away. Indeed, he started inviting his friends round, in the form of twenty-eight other, minor devils. Pierre la Motte succeeded in driving out twenty-six of the twenty-nine, but Beelzebub and two associates (Astaroth and Cerberus) stubbornly stayed put, announcing that they would leave only if adjured to do so by the Bishop of Laon, who duly arrived on the scene in January 1566. Nicole was carried to the church, and a climactic series of exorcisms, watched by large crowds of people, was performed on a public scaffold set up inside the choir of the cathedral of Laon. Finally, on February 8, 1566, Beelzebub was driven out.[4]

De Certeau's reflections are provoked by his study of the famous possessions and exorcisms at the Ursuline convent of Loudun nearly seventy years later. The elaborately documented judicial proceedings provoked by the Loudun events of 1634 provide evidence of even more intricate discursive negotiations between investigators and possessed than at Laon. De Certeau describes a process in which an official dialogue is used to keep a looser, more casual kind of dialogue at bay. The official dialogue is concerned to establish a truth about the dialogue itself; it takes, and attempts to keep, as its subject, the questions "Who is speaking here?" and "What kind of speech is this?" (Interrogators were made suspicious that the devil's grasp of Latin declensions was as weak as that of the uneducated prioress whose body he was occupying.) In possession discourses, the subject of possession is made to speak demonstratively, in order to prove and instance its own condition. "Listen to this: you surely couldn't ask for anything viler, darker, more devilish than this?"

De Certeau wants to try to hear whether there is any other voice to be heard in the disturbance of discourse evident in possession. His question is: "Who is speaking when the possessed woman speaks as the devil?" This means, in fact, that he asks the same question of the discourse that is asked by the exorcist, the doctor, and the civil authorities. De Certeau sees the provocation and excitement of possessed speech as consisting in the limit, transgression, or "exterritoriality" that it represents with respect to ordinary discourse. But the real danger of engaging the devil in public conversation lies not in its transgression of dialogue, but rather the threat that it offers to the power of controlling dialogue within dialogue. This is a much more ordinary, intimate jeopardy than the transgression, or alterity evoked by de Certeau; it is the average hazard of dialogue itself. In talking with, as opposed to speaking to, the one who takes the place of the demon, the question "Who is speaking?" can always fall unnoticed into abeyance.

Is It Not Ours to Talk against Him?

In Protestant England, the assumption that the way to treat possession was to draw the devil into speech, as a way of publically identifying its discourse, and subordinating it to the powers of the exorcising authorities, was regularly contested. Around the turn of the seventeenth century, there was great concern in England about the tendency of exorcism to multiply and perpetuate demonic discourse rather than to silence it. Some of the most emphatic denunciations of possession and exorcism in this period are to be found in the writings of Samuel Harsnett, bishop of London. Harsnett became embroiled in bitter controversy with a Puritan minister named John Darrell, who had achieved some notoriety during the late 1590s with his apparent cures of cases of possession. Darrell's procedures were very different from those practiced across the English Channel, where it was customary to force the possessing devil into elaborate and repeated displays and declarations. Although he was insistent that the devil himself was present in the bodies of those he treated, Darrell relied not upon spectacular public exorcisms, but upon private fasting and prayer. However, Harsnett sought to associate Darrell's exorcisms with Catholic excesses, most notably in his *Declaration of Egregious Popish Impostures* of 1603. This was not a direct assault upon Darrell, but a lengthy and passionate revival of an exorcism scandal of some seventeen years previously, when in 1585 and 1586 a number of Catholic priests had conducted public exorcisms of six demoniacs in the houses of a number of recusant Catholics. Harsnett's purpose seems to have been to smear Darrell by association with the illegal, idolatrous, and politically subversive actions of the Catholics.

Harsnett is appalled by what he sees as the cruel, absurd, and obscene mummeries of the exorcistic procedures as set forth in the testimonies of the alleged victims of possession, but plays the dangerous game of denouncing the excesses of exorcism through imitative travesty. His own discourse therefore risks being drawn into the very theatricality and obsessiveness that fuel his disgust. Harsnett reserves some of his most vicious invective for what he

calls "dialoguizing with the devil," the detailed and prolonged exchanges between the exorcists and the various possessing devils, which allowed and even
gloried in the vilest and most unrelieved blasphemy:

> We do not assever, that the devil cannot say a troth, or that he hath not
> some-time proclaimed the truth: we know he cried, and said to our Saviour
> Christ, *We know thee, who thou art, the holy one of God*: wherein he sayd,
> and cried truly: but this was upon coaction, from the mighty hand of God,
> and not uppon questioning, and dialoguizing with the devil, which we
> never read that eyther our Saviour or his holy disciples did. Nay, wee see
> that our Saviour checked the devil, so saying truly of him, and commaun-
> ded him to hold his peace, as not accepting of any witnes, or testimony
> from the devils.[5]

As possession cases became more and more elaborate, the question of
whether or not to allow the devil to speak became ever more sharply posed.
On the one hand, there were strong psychological, political, theological, and
dramaturgical pressures for the devil to identify himself, if only to prove that
the case in question was one of real possession and not of hysteria or coun-
terfeit. The Bible attested that the devil was forced to acknowledge the divine power of Christ; getting the devil to speak to you as a Catholic or
Protestant exorcist was a way of getting the devil to speak for one's authority as a true inheritor of Christ's ministry and power. However, it was also
well known that the devil was the father of lies, and thus could only be
trusted to be untrustworthy. Catholic exorcists tended to assume the subordination of words to objects—the host, holy water, and sanctified relics and
other powerful substances—and ritual actions, and to try to reduce the
words of the devil to the condition of an object; in Laon the devil's name was
written on a piece of paper and burned before his eyes. A Protestant sensibility such as Harsnett's, convinced as it was of the authority of the divine
Word over that of magical objects, was also deeply suspicious of the idolatrous powers of the human word.

A century or so later, in a climate of much increased scepticism about
the powers of the devil or the reality of possession, dialoguizing with the
devil could be seen as a means not of exercising divine power over him, but
of making him open to the powers of reason. Richard Dugdale was a
Lancashire gardener who, after imprudently offering himself to the devil if
he would make him a good dancer, experienced a series of terrifying appari-
tions and became possessed. Among his symptoms were maniacal dancing,
trances, clairvoyance, sudden and unaccountable changes in body weight,
and the vomiting of stones and other objects. Along with these bodily enactments, the devil began to speak through Dugdale, in Latin and Greek,

and in voices that issued from his body rather than his lips; a striking feature of this case was the fact that the devil spoke from a lump that formed in his chest. He was attended by a number of ministers who employed the approved Protestant means of fasting and prayer, but combined unusually, and controversially, with extended public wrangling and remonstrance with the devil. The author of a pamphlet describing Dugdale's case defends this practice on grounds that would have seemed much less plausible a century earlier, and still seemed foolhardy to some:

> some Professors questioned the lawfulness of talking to Satan, but found Reasons . . . it seem'd lawful and useful when manag'd in a right manner for removing Satan, or impairing his interest; since Satan can understand Men's talk, it must needs make some impression on him; and if any impressions, Then why not such as may disadvantage, or remove him? And being on Men's bad talk to Satan, he may get advantage and prevail against them. Why may not good talk to him prevail against him, since things that are contrary produce contrary effects or consequences? And can it be Satan's interest, to use such talk against us, as is praeternatural to him? Why then is it not ours to talk against him, as is our natural Talent and Province, or to oppose him with our own Weapons, when he challenges us at them? . . . and Man's word being one of Christ's great Ordinances, and Weapons of our Warfare, mighty through God against Satan, Why may it not as our Saviours—*It is written*—remove Satan from man's body.[6]

Sceptics like Zachary Taylor, who joined the controversy about the Surrey demoniac, were less impressed by the "Frothy Speeches" attributed to devil and minister alike.[7] Taylor simultaneously piles up evidence of inconsistencies that ought to make one doubt the authentic presence of the devil in Richard Dugdale, and warns of the dangers of the dialogue with the entity assumed to be present: "by the Speeches that pass between Mr. *Carrington* [the exorcising minister] and the Devil, one would be tempted to think they were Familiar enough, and understand one another pretty well."[8] Taylor, like Harsnett, does not believe that the devil is responsible for what is believed to be his side of the dialogue; but he fears the devilish power of dialogue itself, as it "passes between" speakers, to conjure up devilish attribution.

The Protestant suspicion of the word would be comprehensively dismissed in the medicalization of the experiences previously categorized as possession that took place during the course of the nineteenth century. Since that time, psychoanalytically and psychologically inflected accounts of the experience of possession have been dominant. For these accounts, dialogue with the hysteric's or demoniac's other has come to be seen as a necessary and constitutive part of the treatment. The essential difference between theories of spirit possession and theories of psychological fragmentation concerns the question of the origin and destination of the possessing agent. In a discourse of possession, the devil, or other tenant entity, is believed to be exogenous, and to have emanated from outside its victim. In psychological disorders, by contrast, the other, or others, are assumed to originate in the self. Exorcism requires a dissociation of what has become intermingled with the self, an expulsion of the other into the inane from which it has come. Cure, in the case of a psychological disorder, requires the reintegration of the split-off elements of the self.

Stephen Braude has pointed to one of the difficulties attending the integration hypothesis in the fallacy of what he calls the "principle of compositional reversibility." By this he means the belief that the structure of dissociations at the time of treatment testifies to the fundamental organization of the being prior to dissociation, such that the split person may be able to be put back together along the same lines. But trauma, and especially that of childhood abuse, which seems to feature so regularly in cases of multiple personality disorder, does not necessarily bring about a splitting of the victim along their essential, preexisting faultlines; rather it initiates the habit or strategy of dissociation as a way of coping with intolerable suffering. I find Braude's argument that "it is far more reasonable to maintain that a multiple's array of alters *at any time* represents merely one of many possible dissociative solutions to contingent problems in living"[9] very persuasive. What this means in discursive terms is that dissociation may be as much an effect of the talk involved in and around the treatment as it is a preexisting state of things that may be brought to declarative speech.

Showing and Telling

The spectacular stagings of exorcism in the sixteenth and seventeenth centuries are characterized by the locking or clotting of time: the display of the devils' expulsion is enacted over and over again. Certainly the theatrical spectacles of exorcism multiplied in narrative accounts across Britain, Germany, and the rest of Europe, but these narrative accounts climax in and center upon the moments of revelation and self-declaration by the possessing agency. One of the striking characteristics of the spectacle of possession is the suspension of duration in declaration; the coming to speech of the devil is held and repeated compulsively. Sixteenth- and seventeenth-century exorcisms were much concerned with the question of the localization of the speech of the possessing agency; the bypassing of the mouth in particular, with the various ventriloquial enactments common in these possessions, provoked a careful mapping of demonic speech. The devil could speak from the belly, from the throat, the nostrils, or even from strange vocal lumps, as in the case of Richard Dugdale.

One might almost say that this kind of speech strives toward, or is itself coerced, into a condition of visibility, in which the expressive body is read as a kind of speech, and speech receives a kind of simultaneous transcription on the surface of the body. The skin in particular comes to represent a spectacular compromise between speaking and writing, providing a kind of voice print. The role of the skin is particularly important in the dermographic manifestations and exhibitions of Charcot's patients at the Sâlpetrière and in the complex interchanges between automatic writing and entranced utterance in mediumistic performances. As the site of an inscription that both rises to visibility from below and within the person of the sufferer, but may also be written upon her from above and outside, the skin permits a kind of visual ventriloquism, in which the body is taken to have written on itself an endogenous truth that can nevertheless only be read from the outside. The relations between voice and bodily inscription have been explored in Janet Beizer's discussion of the interchange between medical displays and narrative representations of hysteria in the nineteenth century.[10] Voice and writing are also fused in the phenomena of spiritualism, for example in the automatic writing that met the demand for a kind of visible speech in the séance, before the widespread development of forms of auditory manifestation such as the "direct voice" from the 1890s onward.[11] Where the voice of the spirits cannot be heard, it often seems necessary for the voice that writes itself through the operations of the ouija board to be highly phoneticized. One of the most striking examples is perhaps that of "Patience Worth," a seventeenth-century Puritan woman, who spoke and composed poems in an elaborately particularized archaic dialect through the person of a contemporary medium, Pearl Curran.[12]

The most striking fact about dissociative identity disorder in our century has been its tendency both to proliferate narrative and to proliferate *in* narrative, as the focus upon the spectacular display of declaration has given way to a demand for story. Dissociative identity disorder has taken hold in the form of compelling popular narratives, in which the movement through and binding together of time is more important than the climactic bringing to presence and visibility of the devil. The narratives of divided identity evidence and themselves enforce a powerfully temporalized idea of the human person, rather than the demand for spatialization of the subject common in possession and exorcistic narratives. In narratives of divided identity, what matters is not the where but the when of the speech of the other in the self. The question to be asked is not where the other selves come from or reside, but when, in the history of the subject, they were formed. The therapeutic aim has been commonly not to bring the other to climactic presence in speech, but to get the fragments of the person to convene in a conversation of times, to allow the story of the person to be told.

The move from spectacle to narrative may be measured not just in the eager appropriation of themes of possession and divided identity by narrative writers from the mid-nineteenth-century onward—an abbreviated list would include Harry Cockton's *Sylvester Sound, the Somnambulist* (1844),[13] T. J. Arthur's *Agnes the Possessed* (1853),[14] Wilkie Collins's *The Moonstone* (1868), Dickens's *The Mystery of Edwin Drood* (1870), Robert Louis Stevenson's *The Strange Case of Dr. Jekyll and Mr. Hyde* (1886), Oscar Wilde's *The Picture of Dorian Gray* (1890), George du Maurier's *Trilby* (1894)—but also in the move from cultural spectacles like Charcot's demonstrations or the Victorian scene of the séance to the narrative case histories of Freud, Pierre Janet, and Morton Prince. Prince's account of his investigation of the four selves of Miss Beauchamp—he never decided whether the patient who presented herself to him was the real Miss Beauchamp or not—exerted a particularly strong influence over twentieth-century narratives of divided identity.[15] After a lull in the middle years of the century, the idea of dissociated identity has made a decided comeback in the years after the Second World War, and in particular from the 1970s onward, with the appearance of influential popular case histories like those of "Eve" and "Sybil."[16]

The process of the psychoanalytic talking cure, always shadowed by and increasingly itself shadowing the narrative form of the "case history" itself, appears to be a temporal process that involves a progressive exchange or reciprocity (not always benign) of voices. As Claire Kahane suggests, Freud's simultaneous uncovering and recovering of Dora's story is conducted through the voice, and has the voice as its secret core:

> In Dora's case . . . one story led to another; the ground kept shifting as Freud attempted to discover the "true" object of Dora's passion. Ultimately, Freud's narrative unveiled the voice itself as the passionate object of the hysteric and of psychoanalysis. Who has the voice? Who does what with it? To whom does it belong?[17]

Kahane's historical claim is that "It was no mere coincidence that at the same time that the woman orator became an increasingly audible and visible figure in the pulpit and on the podium, female hysteria, with its characteristic symptoms of aphonia and paralysis, swept across Europe and America in epidemic proportion."[18] Kahane accepts an orthodox view of hysteria as the displacement of voice into the mute appearances of the body. But the period about which she writes is not only the era of Charcot, Breuer, and Freud, but also of Gurney, Janet, Ribot, and Prince, who set themselves to investigate phenomena that were often confused with and associated with hysteria but are in reality very different from it—automatism, "split personality," and dissociation of identity.

Freudian psychoanalysis reads hysteria as the bursting out of repressed voice, and promises to treat hysteria by giving a voice to the body. Some early examples of dissociative disorder do seem to resemble this repudiation of speech in the form of a retreat from the vocal self into a more inchoate and more primitive avocality. Mary Reynolds, whose case was reported by Dr. Weir Mitchell and summarized in some detail by William James in his *Principles of Psychology* in 1890, woke after a long sleep in an amnesic, child-like condition, and had to learn to speak anew.[19] Peter Scott, whose case was reported by Dr. C. L. Dana in the *Psychological Review* in 1894, had a simi-lar experience of radically regressive dissociation, when, after nearly asphyx-iating after sleeping in a room with a leaking gas pipe, he woke unable to remember anything about his family or previous life, and in possession of only a few words. Like Mary Reynolds, he too, had to be taught to speak all over again. Another male example of this process is Thomas Hanna, whose case was reported by Boris Sidis and S. P. Goodhart in 1905: after having been rendered unconscious by a fall from a carriage, he awoke in the condi-tion of a newborn child, unable to make sense of anything in his environ-ment. He had to relearn language and the spatial and temporal concepts associated with it from scratch.[20] This coupling of dissociation with the wip-ing clean of language does indeed look like an intensified form of the hys-teric's abrogation of the voice, in which speech is not merely displaced, but vanishes altogether. (One must acknowledge an important difference be-tween these cases of amnesiac splitting and cases of hysteria, however: in the former, the infant personality is not locked in time, but in all cases begins to learn and grow.)

In any case, dissociation of identity had begun to take a form very dif-ferent from hysteria by the beginning of this century. Dissociated selves were neither muted, nor did they exhibit that hysterical excess or garrulity that is the counterpart to mutism, but talkative. What is more, their talkativeness had a peculiar feature that distinguished these cases not only from hysteria but also from earlier forms of possession or mediumship. In hysteria, the dis-tressed body stands as a substitute for the voiceless self: it speaks, imperfectly to be sure, but unignorably, on behalf of and in place of that self. The situ-ation is closely analogous to that of the victim of possession whose voice, body, and personality are surrendered to the devil that speaks through them. In such cases, as well as in mediumistic phenomena, there seems to be a rule barring all intrapsychic contact between the self and its alter. By contrast, in conditions of dissociated identity involving more than one alter, not only are the alters more confidently and conventionally talkative as individuals, they also have dynamic relations among themselves; they are aware to different degrees both of the "primary personality" and of each other, and often claim to be able to talk to each other. Kahane may be right in her judgement that, in hysteria, and its analogues, the question is "Who has the voice?" In dissociated identity states, the question is how to understand and resynchronize the relations of talk between the different components of the self. It is for this reason that Morton Prince preferred to speak not of the "unconscious," but of "co-conscious selves."[21] Oddly, the hypostatized notion of "the unconscious" promoted, despite Freud's precautions, by Freudian thought, resembles that Protestant mode of responding to possession that insists on hearing only "the devil" in possessed speech, rather than being drawn into complex negotiations with swarms of different entities, all capable not only of speaking through the person of the victim of possession, but also among themselves. A Freudian model centers therefore on the excavation, disposition, and reparation of the voice, rather than on the analysis of talk. It is perhaps not surprising that this model tends to throw up conceptions of the unconscious as a singular, hypostasized alterity, capable of being embodied in an idealized discourse or voice of the other: a subliminal transcendence of language within language itself. The importance of talk in possession and dissociation phenomena, and the ways in which they are engaged with, suggests that the other of discourse, or discourse of the other, is at once more diffuse, less determinately indeterminate, and more familiarly estranged than this.

Sybilline Leaves

One striking feature of the most characteristic and compelling accounts of dissociative identity is how ordinarily self-sufficient and competent many of the personalities appear to be for much of the time. Hysterics suffer, unignorably and pitiably, from extreme kinds of dysfunction: loss of sight, hearing, language, motor functions. The most developed separate personalities of the multiple tend to function tolerably well in various social circumstances. What causes suffering to the primary self in dissociative identity disorder is not being able to make sense of the blanks in their lives, and the fact of having no access to the other lives they nevertheless lead. The hysteric is deprived of the capacity to speak and live. The victim of dissociation is denied access to the lives and voices they nevertheless continue to have.

This may be to say that relations of talk are much more important in dissociative identity disorders than questions of voice. This is partly because the multiple is determined from the outside in, rather than from the inside out. Dissociative identity disorder has come to seem so much an expression of a late-twentieth-century sensibility because of the way in which it literalizes the idea of an externalized rather than an internalized unconscious, the creation of different selves and centers of consciousness for different purposes. Nevertheless, the most influential narratives of dissociative identity disorder still tend to work within a Freudian framework in which the engine of splitting is taken to be internal conflict leading to repression, rather than a generalized strategy of growing different selves to cope with different kinds of external demand. These narratives often center upon the inside-out process of giving voice, rather than the outside-in processes of talk, in ways that sometimes appear to be at odds with the condition they aim to describe. We may take as an example Flora Rheeta Schreiber's account of the treatment and cure of "Sybil." There is a striking contradiction in Schreiber's narrative between the complex, evolving and indeterminate relations between the alters uncovered in the long process of Sybil's therapy with her analyst Dr. Wilbur, and the demand, shared by patient, physician, and narrator, for clear and absolute distinctions between the selves. The book is prefaced by a cast list that gives details of these sixteen different constituent personalities, along with their "dates of birth." They include, alongside the primary self, described only as "Sybil Isabel Dorsett . . . a depleted person; the waking self," "Victoria Antoinette Scharleau (1926): nicknamed Vicky; a self-assured, sophisticated, attractive blonde; the memory trace of Sybil's selves . . . Peggy Lou Baldwin (1926): an assertive, enthusiastic, and often angry pixie with a pug nose, a Dutch haircut, and a mischievous smile" and "Sid Dorsett (1928): one of Sybil's two male selves; a carpenter and general handyman; he has fair skin, dark hair, and blue eyes."[22] Although switches between different personalities bring about changes in posture and general bodily appearance, amplified by the fact that these personalities have their own distinctive tastes in clothes, it is changes in voice that fundamentally signal and define these different personalities. Vicky, who knows most about Sybil and her alters, is identified decisively on her first appearance as "the woman of the world with the graceful movements, the mellifluous voice and the faultless diction."[23] The first appearance of an alter in Dr. Wilbur's presence, the impulsive, destructive Peggy Lou Baldwin, is signaled equally emphatically by a change of voice:

> The voice was . . . quite different, childlike, not like Sybil's voice. Yet that little girl had uttered a woman's words in its denunciation of men: "Men are all alike. You jist can't trust 'em." And the word *jist*. Sybil, perfectionist schoolteacher, strict grammarian, would never use a substandard word such as *jist*.[24]

The voice is more than just one sign among others of bodily difference: it seems to govern the production of a wholly new body. Sybil's alters, as represented in Schreiber's *Sybil*, are, so to speak, phonomorphic entities. Of course, when we are reading, we do not hear Peggy's characteristic voice any more than we actually see her hairstyle or posture. But the fact that we do see her speech on the page reinforces the process whereby discourse is fixed and polarized into distinct voices. It is a literary redoubling of the "visible

speech" of the séance. For the reader of *Sybil*, there is in fact nothing to prevent the attribution of a full personality to each of the alters as they speak,
especially when we are given transcriptions of conversations between the different alters, like this remarkable sequence, in which the alters decide to
commit themselves to treatment:

> As the car swung in front of Whittier Hall and Dr. Wilbur said good-bye
> to Sybil, Marcia Lynn turned to Vanessa Gail, her close friend, and said in
> an English accent: "She cares about us." Vanessa, who was a tall, slender
> girl with a willowy figure, dark chestnut-red hair, light brown eyes, and an
> expressive oval face, communicated to Mary that single, simple sentence:
> "She cares about us." Mary, a maternal little-old-lady type, plump,
> thoughtful and contemplative, repeated with a slight smile, as if it were a
> question: "She cares about us?" Then Marcia Lynn, Vanessa Gail, and
> Mary put into execution an internal grapevine through which the message
> rang loud and clear: *This Dr. Wilbur cares about us.*[25]

The clarity and distinctness of the personalities is guaranteed by the continuity of their voices; they are fully and self-consciously themselves in their
speech. Paradoxically, it is precisely this untroubled self-identity that makes
them seem at times so ludicrously artificial. Just as a soap opera or thriller
demands its standard types, so accounts of dissociation depend upon the
principle of absolute explicitness or self-declaration. In the story of Sybil, as
in Morton Prince's account of the Misses Beauchamp, the alleged personalities are convincing precisely to the degree that they are so unconvincingly
aware of and identical with the "selves" that they wear stamped on them like
captions: the Imp, the Sophisticate, the Virgin, the Whore. The secondary
personalities are most obviously unreal in the fact that they are incapable of
ambivalence, slippage, approximation; incapable, in short, of losing themselves in their speech (losing themselves into talk, perhaps), other than by
dropping out of existence altogether. Interestingly, the alter Vicky has a lineage of secondary and tertiary selves just like her host Sybil; unlike Sybil,
however, Vicky suffers no depletion of awareness or capacity as a result of
this delegation of selves, which thus reduplicate rather than replace her.[26]
(Obviously, in a case such as that of Sybil, where we are dealing with a self-
consciously novelized version of the case, this flatness can be laid at the door
of the writer; but we obviously cannot leave out of account the formative influence of popular narrative forms like the novel and film in the formation
and coordination of alters.)

These types and the voices that make them wholly distinct correspond
precisely to the demonic attributions demanded of the exorcist. In that it involves numbering, naming, and knowledge, voice is necessary to the process

of both dissolution and regathering. And yet, there are factors within the accounts of dissociative disorder that pull against this drive to give speech to these alters and to deliver them self-declaringly to speech. For Sybil to be able to speak with one voice, the demands of the "Who is speaking?" must actually be loosened, to accommodate the process of talking. The regathered self will always have had to be able to do more than speak with its own voice and bear its own name; it will need to have undergone and acknowledged a conversation with its-selves.

It is talking that discloses the stubborn, average, approximate, everyday worldliness of even such a terrifying and fascinating phenomenon as dissociative identity. Talk has no intrinsic value, not even the value of the unvalued. It can no more be seized on as an ideal—the ideal, say, of polyphonic speech, or of a discourse of the other—than it can reliably be excluded from the operations of voice. Talk is always both less and more than voice, not because it is a fuller, suppler, more multivoiced, more essentially social form of language (dissociated identities are not to divided identities as *Middlemarch* is to a lyric poem), but because talk is not a form of language qua language at all. Talking depends upon an entire range of skills and capacities that are not essentially linguistic: the ability to wait one's turn, to crack (and get) jokes, to imitate others' voices and turns of phrase, to detect (and ignore) insincerity, elation, and boredom, to integrate gesture and speech, to echo others' postures, and so forth. This moreness of talk is the reason for its denigration as something less than self-conscious, self-directing, and self-declaring utterance. The worldliness of talk comes from the fact that it is always a process of instantiating a world, which is nevertheless never the whole world. As Stephen Braude has maintained, the fact that the capacity for talk displays so many different features does not imply that it is best understood as an aggregation of more primary, and functionally distinguishable operations. In a similar way, it does not make sense to think of a multiple's array of alters as autonomously functioning centers of consciousness, or to base upon them a model of the mind as a system of parallel processing units. "There is no clear thing which each alter does, much less something isolable from things other alters do . . . an alter's 'thing' is really no more than an arrangement of dispositions overlapping and intimately linked to other such arrangements within a single system of dispositions."[27] Talk is not the promise of speaking with one voice, nor the ideal aggregation of lots of different acts of speech. It is the always shifting but itself unbudgeable horizon within which voices come to be heard and known. At one point, Vicky, who comes to act as a kind of confidante for Dr. Wilbur, offers some reflections on the reasons for Sybil's resistance to integrating treatment:

"She gets scared about words—all this talk here—making things better and then having the whole world to face." Vicky leaned her head on her hand thoughtfully. "Sybil's afraid that if she gets better, something terrible will happen. It's as if the serpent is about to get her once again even though the serpent is losing his name."[28]

Voice can be made known and audible. Voice is the ideal of being there in my words. Talk—"all this talk here"—is never in fact exactly here. But that is why the serpent loses his name in it, and why we can never be wholly strange either to ourselves or to our others.

Notes

1. Michel de Certeau, *The Writing of History*, trans. Tom Conley (New York: Columbia University Press, 1988), 246.
2. Ibid., 247.
3. Ibid., 248.
4. There are a number of accounts of the possession and dispossession of Nicole Obry, both contemporary and written in the centuries following the events. Most are heavily dependent upon the official record produced by the exorcising priest, Jean Boulaese, *Le Thrésor et entière histoire de la triomphante victoire du corps de Dieu sur l'esprit maling Beelzebub, obtenue à Laon l'an mil cinq cens soixante-dix* (Paris, 1578), 56–57. Boulaese had produced a small pamphlet immediately after the event, *Le Miracle de Laon en Lannoys, représenté au vif et escript en latin francoys, italien, espagnol, et allement* (Cambray: Chez Pierre Lombard, 1566), reprinted in *Guillaume Postel, "De Summopere" (1566) and Jean Boulaese, "Le Miracle de Laon" (1566)*, ed. and trans. Irena Backus (Genève: Librairie Droz S. A., 1995). Later accounts are heavily dependent upon that of Boulaese. They include J. Roger, *Histoire de Nicole de Vervins d'après les historiens contemporains* (Paris: Henri Plon, 1863), and Louise Langlet, *Une possession au XVIe siècle: étude medicale de la vie at de l'hystérie de Nicole Obry, dite Nicole de Vervins, 1566* (Reims, 1910). D. Walker synthesizes all the available accounts admirably in his in *Unclean Spirits: Possession and Exorcism in France and England in the Late Sixteenth and Early Seventeenth Centuries* (London: Scolar Press, 1981).
5. Samuel Harsnett, *A Declaration of egregious popish impostures, to with-draw the harts of her Majesties subjects from their alleagance and from the truth of Christian religion professed in England, under the pretence of casting out devils* (London: James Roberts, 1603), reprinted in F. W. Brownlow, *Shakespeare, Harsnett, and the Devils of Denham* (Newark: University of Delaware Press, and London and Toronto: Associated University Presses, 1996), 332.
6. *The Surrey Demoniack, or, an account of Satans strange and dreadful actings in and about the body of Richard Dugdale of Surey, near Whalley in Lancashire* (London: Jonathan Robinson, 1697), 23–24.
7. Zachary Taylor, *The Surey Impostor: being an answer to a late fanatical pamphlet, entituled the Surey Demoniack* (London: John Jones and Ephraim Johnson, 1697), 4.
8. Ibid., 5.
9. Stephen E. Braude, *First Person Plural: Multiple Personality and the Philosophy of Mind* (London: Routledge, 1991), 127.
10. Janet Beizer, *Ventriloquized Bodies: Narratives of Hysteria in Nineteenth-Century France*

(Ithaca, NY, and London: Cornell University Press, 1994), 20–29.

11. I discuss the importance of the "direct voice" in spiritualism in "The Machine in the Ghost: Spiritualism, Technology, and the 'Direct Voice,'" in *Ghosts: Psychoanalysis, History, Deconstruction*, ed. Peter Buse (Basingstoke: Macmillan, 1998), 203–25.

12. C. E. Cory, "Patience Worth," *Psychological Review* 26 (1919): 297–407; W. F. Prince, *The Case of Patience Worth: A Critical Study of Certain Unusual Phenomena* (Boston: Boston Society for Psychical Research, 1927).

13. Harry Cockton, *Sylvester Sound, the Somnambulist* (London: W. M. Clark, 1844).

14. T. S. Arthur, *Agnes the Possessed: A Revelation of Mesmerism* (London: J. S. Hudson, 1853).

15. Morton Prince, *The Dissociation of a Personality: The Hunt for the Real Miss Beauchamp* (1905; Oxford: Oxford University Press, 1978).

16. C. H. Thigpen and H. M. Cleckley, *The Three Faces of Eve* (New York: McGraw Hill, 1957); C. C. Sizemore and E. S. Pittillo, *I'm Eve* (New York: Doubleday, 1977); Flora Rheeta Schreiber, *Sybil: The True Story of a Woman Possessed by Sixteen Different Personalities* (1973; Harmondsworth: Penguin, 1975).

17. Claire Kahane, *Passions of the Voice: Hysteria, Narrative, and the Figure of the Speaking Woman, 1850–1915* (Baltimore and London: Johns Hopkins University Press, 1995), 12–13.

18. Ibid., 7.

19. Eric T. Carlson, "The History of Multiple Personality in the United States: Mary Reynolds and Her Subsequent Reputation," *Bulletin of the History of Medicine* 58 (1974): 72–82.

20. Boris Sidis and Simon Goodhart, *Multiple Personality: An Experimental Investigation into the Nature of Human Individuality* (1905; New York: Greenwood Press, 1968), 83–226.

21. Morton Prince, *The Dissociation of a Personality: A Study in Abnormal Psychology*, 2d ed. (London: Longmans, Green and Co., 1908), 530.

22. Schreiber, *Sybil*, 9.

23. Ibid., 94.

24. Ibid., 62–3.

25. Ibid., 115–16.

26. Ibid., 310.

27. Braude, *First Person Plural*, 186, 187.

28. Schreiber, *Sybil*, 267–68.

The Talking Cure

13

Origins of Psychoanalysis

Nicholas Rand

The Origins and General Aims of Talk Therapy

Psychoanalysis did not invent the concept of "talking cure," but did create our twentieth-century idea and practice of it. Well before Sigmund Freud used the term "psychoanalysis" for the first time in the early 1900s, therapy of or by the word had been foreshadowed in France, England, and Germany. The collective work of many doctors, alienists, and independent researchers concerning dreams, suggestion, hypnosis, mesmerism, somnambulism, hysteria, inorganic paralysis, and madness gradually led to the notion of moral or psychological afflictions that lent themselves to verbal forms of treatment.[1]

Verbal psychotherapy, however, made its most notable and also most explicit nineeenth-century appearance in the least likely realm: Greek philology. In 1857, Jacob Bernays, none other than the uncle to Freud's wife-to-be, Martha Bernays, published his highly regarded "Outlines of Aristotle's Lost Treatise on the Effect of Tragedy."[2] Bernays focused his investigation on the potential meaning of the central but enigmatic formula used by Aristotle in the *Poetics*: *katharsis ton pathematon* (purgation of emotions). In the opinion of most contemporary and subsequent thinkers, including Nietzsche, Bernays carried off a stunning resolution of the centuries-long controversy—stretching from the Italian and English Renaissance through Corneille, Lessing, Goethe, Schiller, and others—over the moral and/or aesthetic implications of catharsis or purification in drama. Bernays did this by rejecting all previous interpretations, anchoring catharsis in ancient medicine as well as curative practices related to orgiastic cults and the worship of Dionysus.

This shift in the understanding of catharsis did not go unnoticed. Surely it is no accident that, in their "Preliminary Communication" of 1893, Josef Breuer and Freud used the very term "catharsis" (defined as abreaction: to reactivate and throw off) to designate the curative effect they achieved through verbal therapy in their patients suffering from hysteria. It is also significant in this context that Freud's own persistent vacillation over the aims of psychoanalysis reached a climax when his closest friend, the Hungarian psychoanalyst Sandor Ferenczi, in 1929 revived, under the name of "neocatharsis," the systematic investigation and cure of psychological traumas. Originally introduced by Breuer and Freud, the treatment of traumas came to be soon and (apparently) definitively abandoned by Freud himself as the latter increasingly sought to see in psychoanalysis a universal anthropology, based on the vicissitudes of psychosexual drives, fantasies, and their repression.[3]

Let us return to 1857 for a moment. Bernays argues against all previous authorities that (1) the Aristotelian concept of catharsis has nothing to do with either purification of the passions or their transformation into virtue, and therefore (2) the corresponding meliorative function of theater—to serve as a moral derivative of the church or as her rival in the enterprise of bettering humankind—could not be traced to Aristotle. Instead, Bernays offers the following revolutionary medical—that is, psychologically oriented—definition of catharsis: "Transferred from the bodily to the psychological realm, [catharsis] designates a type of treatment—for something oppressive, inhibited or stifled—that does not seek to transform or repress the oppressive element, but rather to arouse and drive it into the open, thereby hoping to effect a soothing of that which had been inhibited or stifled."[4] In his reconstruction of the unadulterated conceptual substance of catharsis, Bernays sees the restoration of the "pathological point of view," noting that Aristotle was a physician himself as well as the son of a doctor.

The significance of Bernays's hitherto rarely noticed yet decisive contribution to twentieth-century talk therapy may be gleaned from Breuer's and Freud's "On the Psychical Mechanism of Hysterical Phenomena: Preliminary Communication" (1893):

> *each individual hysterical symptom disappeared when we had succeeded in*
> *bringing clearly to light the memory of the event by which it was provoked and*

> *in arousing its accompanying affect, and when the patient had described that*
> *event in the greatest possible detail and had put the affect into words. . . . The*
> psychical process must be repeated as vivdly as possible . . . and then given
> verbal utterance.[5]

> It will now be understood how it is that the psychotherapeutic procedure
> which we have described here has a curative effect. *It brings to an end the*
> *operative force of the idea which was not abreacted in the first instance, by al-*
> *lowing its strangulated affect to find a way out through speech; and . . . by in-*
> *troducing it into normal consciousness.*[6]

As is well known, the central concept of the so-called cathartic treatment—the emotional and verbal discharge of the stifled affect or emotion
associated with forgotten traumas—harkens back to Breuer's treatment of
Anna O (Bertha Pappenheim) in 1880. Whether or not Breuer had been influenced by reading or hearing about Bernays's treatise—which had been
hotly debated in intellectual circles far beyond obscure philological societies—is a matter for conjecture and ultimately immaterial. Far more important than the question of mere filiation is the commonality of thought
between Bernays, Breuer, and Freud concerning the existence and feasibility
of psychotherapy through the word.[7]

Striking similarities indeed unite Bernays's hermeneutic unearthing of
an ancient form of medical practice and the treatments described in the
pages of the *Studies on Hysteria* (1895). Bernays glosses Aristotle's enigmatic
formula *katharsis ton pathematon* and its context as follows: "Tragedy effects,
through (the arousal of) sorrowful compassion and fear, the soothing discharge of such (sorrowful and fearful) psychic affections."[8] Breuer says of
Anna O, "I have already described how completely her mind was relieved
when, shaking with fear and horror, she had reproduced these frightful images and given verbal utterance to them."[9] Further, Bernays uses a host of
psychomedical terms that seem to be lifted from Breuer and Freud, but are
actually extant in numerous ancient Greek texts: calming or soothing of the
emotions, affections, or diseased states of mind; cure through means that
provide affective relief; release of and coming to terms with psychological affections; elimination of pathogenic or illness-inducing material.

In support of his "pathological point of view" with respect to catharsis,
Bernays cites the Greek thinker Porphyry: "The forces attaching to the affections generally present in us human beings will be only the stronger if we
try to repress them completely. On the other hand, if these affects are elicited
in brief utterance and in the right proportion, they will experience joy in
moderation, [and the affections] will be stilled, discharged, and calmed in a
good-mannered way and without any violence. This is why, in comedy as
well as tragedy, we are used to soothing, mitigating, and discharging our own

emotions through the viewing of other people's affects."[10] Bernays calls this "the instigation (activation) theory" of psychological affections, validating the existence in ancient times of a theory that sees curative effect in the verbal and/or representative (dramatic) calling forth of hitherto suppressed, stifled, or inhibited and oppressive emotions.[11]

The potential conceptual relation between the ancient Aristotelian theory and the modern-day practical use of verbal psychotherapy is of paramount significance for two reasons at least. While no double-blind clinical studies existed in the nineteenth century and the practice of reproducing scientific experiments in independent laboratories did not become a widespread test for the reliability of results until after the Second World War, it would be wrong to assume that either Bernays, Breuer, or Freud ignored the necessity of independent validation of their work. For his interpretation of catharsis in the *Poetics*, Bernays marshals explicit evidence from Aristotle's other writings, just as he also draws on non-Aristotelian Greek sources for confirmation. Breuer and Freud ascribed their hypotheses chiefly to clinical discoveries, yet they also cited numerous other clinicians and theoreticians of the psyche, including Binet, Delboeuf, Janet, Moebius, Strümpell, and others, who—previously, simultaneously, or later—described similar phenomena and claimed comparable therapeutic results. Moreover, the very confluence between Bernays's philological and Breuer's and Freud's psychological investigations may be seen as an independent corroboration of the medical practice of the verbal release of inhibited, stifled, or strangulated affects. I leave open here the matter, often viciously belabored these last few years, of the historical worth of the therapeutic claims made by Breuer or Freud in connection with specific patients; I wish to shift the question to the conceptual plane. Under what conditions is talk therapy—described in 1857 by Bernays as Aristotelian and independently practiced by Breuer after 1880 and Freud from 1889 on—indeed desirable and effective?

While this question cannot be answered fully here, I can offer a few pointers as to how it might be approached. The development of Freudian theory is too complex to be reviewed hastily. Still, it is quite safe to say, because ample evidence exists, that Freud himself undermined the unequivocal recognition of his evolving discipline by adopting contradictory, even self-defeating methodologies of research. On the one hand, Freud fully subscribed to Breuer's original clinical discovery of the verbal discharge of traumatically stifled emotions—and devised ever more refined means for understanding and eliciting such emotions. At the same time, however, Freud shut the door tight, applying predetermined, universalizing conceptions of the psyche in the "treatment" of his patients, thus preventing them from gaining insight into the genuine foundations of their debilitating turmoil.[12]

The essence of Breuer's and Freud's discoveries was the idea that, with the help of the therapist, (1) our symptoms could be read, and (2) understanding the affective situation behind our symptoms would lead to an easing of psychological pain. During his brief collaboration with Breuer, Freud kept for the most part to his mentor's principle of deriving his views of mental pathology simply from experience. However, as Breuer himself observed in 1907, "Freud is a man given to absolute and excessive formulations; this is a psychological need which, in my opinion, leads to excessive generalization."[13] Indeed, Freud often attempted to find a pathology in his patients from which they did not actually suffer. Wanting to categorize, within a universally applicable framework, the stages of infantile psychosexual development, he came to work with ready-made patterns. He left behind the search for individual constellations of pain and used preconceived ideas that ultimately kept him from encountering the patient. Freud's clinical interpretations frequently rely on a handful of archetypal developmental traumas (such as the primal scene of observing parental intercourse, castration anxiety, seduction), typical "traumas" that are supposedly manifested in equally generalized scenarios of unconscious fantasy. It is as if Freud had asked his patients: At what point of your psychosexual development—whose inevitable stages I have already described in my theories of the Oedipus complex, penis envy, and so forth—did you suffer the most? This amounts to asking: What part of my psychosexual theory do you carry in you? Freudian psychoanalysis has long been threatened from within because it combines daring, even revolutionary methods of inquiry with a tendency to restrain unbiased exploration. This is a fundamental methodological contradiction, a clash between the remarkable spirit of openness—the desire to free us from our own emotional and psychosexual prisons—and the unforgiving rigidity of a predictable system for identifying universal sources of psychic turmoil.

I submit that if psychoanalysis has been assailed with renewed vigor these last few years, and with ever increasing success, this is not ultimately due to the widespread and effective use of drugs in the management of mental turmoil, the intrusive monitoring, exercised by most American insurance companies, of the reimbursement of outpatient psychiatric claims, or the stringent restrictions health management organizations have placed on the duration of talk therapy. It is equally uncertain that the depth of the dissatisfaction with Freudian theories can be conveniently blamed on the *mala fide* rejection of the very concept of the unconscious. My conviction is that anybody interested in a viable future for psychoanalysis would do well not to cast off criticism as a form of resistance but to take bittersweet inspiration from it and examine the disharmony inherent in Freudian theories as well as clinical practice.

At the risk of alienating friends and foes alike, I want to suggest that the genuinely useful core of contemporary talk therapy can be summarized in terms of the Aristotelian theory of catharsis as extended independently in the clinical and interpretative work of Breuer and the early Freud. In brief: therapists elicit the harmonious release of those oppressive or unconsciously stifled emotions that have been denied the soothing outlet of speech on account of traumas suffered; these traumas and the attendant affects can be accessed through the understanding of dreams, slips of the tongue, symptomatic compromise formations in language, body, and soul; thus talk therapy aims to reconstruct an individual's *specific* traumatic history from his or her own broken relics of pain, turmoil, and conflict. These vital aspects of psychoanalysis do and deserve to thrive in the myriad forms of verbal psychotherapy that have mushroomed wildly because orthodox psychoanalysis increasingly blocked pathways to satisfactory solutions.

How Should the Analyst Talk?

A significant debate erupted in the 1920s between Freud and his closest friend Sandor Ferenczi over the attitude of the therapist. The controversy focused on the quality of the analyst's speech—strict neutrality versus the analyst's supportive, even active, participation in the eliciting, understanding, and absorption of clinical material. Freud's stance is well known. Patients must be led back—through the lengthy anatomization of their transference and resistance within the analytic setting—to both loverly and hostile feelings as regards their early parental figures. It is important, Freud claimed, to adopt a strict, at times rigid form of neutrality so as to allow patients to extricate themselves from the shackles of their unconsciously transferred feelings of passionate love and/or hatred.

While it is clear that none but abusive or perverse analysts (and there have been more than a few) would generate transferred emotions for their own benefit or for the benefit of the psychoanalytic movement, rigid neutrality can also end up being a form of abuse. Ferenczi came to this conclusion as he reviewed what he called, in 1930, "the narrow-minded development of psychoanalysis." His disagreement with Freud, expressed in the same letter—"I do not agree with you . . . that the therapeutic process should be neglected or considered less important, or that, simply because it seems uninteresting to us, we have a right to neglect it"—stemmed from two separate yet related issues.[14] One had to do with fundamental theoretical concerns over the object of psychoanalytic treatment, the other with the psychological atmosphere of the analytic session. Ferenczi came to hold that psychoanalysis, as developed by Freud roughly after 1908, had neglected the traumatic origins of neurosis and, as a result, overvalued instinct-based psychosexual fantasies at the expense of traumatic reality. This issue of deciding what clinical psychoanalysis must address first and foremost—unconscious fantasies or traumas?—determined Ferenczi's promotion of a supportive role for analysts in the psychotherapy of their patients. Ferenczi criticized the tendency of many analysts to handle psychoanalysis as a mainly intellectual process. They tried to reconstruct the repressed causes of illness based on their theoretical knowledge and thereby really carried out an analytical reeducation of the patient. This kind of relation between analyst and patient was becoming far too much like that between teacher and pupil. True, patients were acquiring the Freudian view of mental life in the course of their analysis, but, Ferenczi asked, could that kind of intellectual knowledge lead to a lasting cure of their neurosis?

Ferenczi warned against the didactic and falsely godlike attitude of analysts. He felt that the cool inflexibility of the therapist can take forms that cause unnecessary and avoidable difficulties to the patient. He proposed empathy, even a sympathetic form of tenderness as opposed to the rigidity and coldness that often masquerade as neutrality and objective reserve. In his eyes, the latter mostly led to an unnatural banishment of all human factors from psychoanalysis.

Ferenczi based his revision of the Freudian rule of strict analytic neutrality on the clinical finding that traumatic shocks often result from or are accompanied by improper, tactless, hurtful, or outright cruel treatment of children by adults. Thus Ferenczi feared that the analyst's persistent silence, his or her stereotyped questions or systematic failure to react with any hint of emotion might actually lead to a repetition of the trauma that formed the basis of the patient's neurosis. The "cool aloofness on the analyst's part was experienced by the patient as a continuation of his infantile struggle with the grown-ups' authority."[15]

The terrifying effect of traumas and the state of lonely helplessness of someone recalling or reliving traumatic shocks precludes the attitude of cold objectivity. In these moments of the reemergence of trauma in particular, friendly good will and a comforting attitude or gesture are not only human but clinically sound. "The patient will then feel the contrast between our behaviour and that which he experienced in his real family, and knowing himself safe from the repetition of such situations, he has the courage to let himself sink into a reproduction of the painful past."

Ferenczi also reassures his colleagues that replacing the all-knowing and omnipotent analytic persona with a friendly attitude of open expectancy does not lead to a loss of authority, but quite on the contrary, to increased confidence from patients in the therapeutic relationship. The feeling of trust thus reaped— the analyst is actually joining forces with the patient—can help to overcome the strong resistance to relive and let go of devastating traumas. Fostering trust is a crucial element of verbal psychotherapy, according to Ferenczi, precisely because traumatic experiences often instill in us a profound sense of mistrust.

Talk Therapy's Vital Importance

More recently, the analyst Maria Torok has questioned the notion that theories can be applied to the psychotherapy of people. In "Theoretra: An Alternative to Theory" (1982), Torok calls for a psychoanalytic art of relinquishing theory—given that theory most often entails a separation from the actual life experience of patients. Theory can become a form of rigidly cold observation, even the instrument of subtly manipulative terror, as opposed to being the reflective by-product of a free-flowing and continuously open-ended process of sympathetic understanding. Torok provides a poetic allegory of psychoanalysis as the exchange of gifts between patient and analyst. Patients reveal the utmost recesses of their minds and hearts; the analyst gives the gift of listening. For Torok, listening means to summon and welcome the voices patients cannot hear in themselves. The psychotherapeutic dialogue then is a joint conjuring of dead voices, either the voices of dead relatives or the faint voices of dead secrets, nameless hurts, and stifled sufferings.

The description of verbal psychotherapy as the invocation and revival of unlaid ghosts, with the purpose of finally giving them their deserved psychic rest, condenses the substance of Nicolas Abraham's and Torok's joint discoveries concerning the burdensome psychological posterity of family secrets. Abraham's and Torok's entire conception of talk therapy rests on the necessity of giving a name—and thus a right to exist—to as yet nameless desires, undisclosable losses, and wordless hurts. However, it is in the realm of actual secrets—when there has been a stifling silence and a willful attempt to suppress communication in the family—that talk therapy acquires vital significance. In cases where children were never told of shameful illnesses, abortions, madness, crimes, or suicides in the family, the unfinished burdens of their parents' lives can, unbeknownst to all, cripple the children's existence. Here the analytic dialogue needs to become a collaboration, a partnership, if real contact is to be made with the silence clamped on past events that insidiously continue to haunt entire generations of descendants. The collaborative unearthing in the analytic dialogue, the gradual acceptance by patients of shameful and studiously shielded secrets and suffering in their families are dependent on the analyst's explicitly sympathetic embrace of the traumatic emotions experienced by uncommunicative ancestors.

The ancestors and their secrets are dead, yet:

> a tiny something survives, emerges from its hiding place. From under the veil, [the ancestor] lets me catch a glimpse, hear a whisper of some continuing faint movement or noise. There is a murmur, a ventriloquy, rising from the tomb in which [the patient] or someone else, either a contemporary or an ancestor, was buried alive, sequestered, with their desires cut out, deprived of both life and death, and above all, something has been left *unsettled*. . . .

Right there, the two partners [patient and analyst] will . . . dream the same word, the same image, for an instant, and for once have a real session, a seance, to summon the specter, the spirit of the spirit of Spirit itself, assassinated by some ghost. . . . The absent spirits arrive not so much through invocation as through a convoking summons. For them to rap, for them to want to rap, the spirits need to understand that their absence has always already been a presence in the form of unrecognized knowledge, a *nescience.* They must understand that we were able to surmise this. . . . [H]ow to bury the unburied, to settle in and for ourselves the lot of the unburied dead?[16]

The need for talk therapy arises whenever the enemies of life—for example, our ancestors' unspoken secrets, the loss of a loved one, social or religious persecution—overwhelm us, curtailing our capacity for happiness as well as our ability to absorb new crises and disasters. Such enemies of life drive a wedge within our selves as well as between us and our society. Psychoanalytic talk therapy can profitably formulate and attempt to answer the question: How can people be helped to discover the secrets, the individual, familial, or social traumas, that may often go unrecognized as such or be too painful, too shameful, to be embraced as part of life?

Notes

1. See Gregory Zilboorg, *A History of Medical Psychology* (New York: Norton, 1941), and Henri Ellenberger, *The Discovery of the Unconscious* (New York: Norton, 1970).
2. Jacob Bernays, *Grundzüge der Verlorenen Abhandlung des Aristoteles über Wirkung der Tragödie*, Eingeleitet von Karlfried Gründer (Hildesheim and New York: Georg Olms Verlag, 1970); unavailable in English.
3. For further discussion see Nicholas Rand and Maria Torok, *Questions for Freud: The Secret History of Psychoanalysis* (Cambridge, MA, and London: Harvard University Press, 1997), 24–44, 115–35.
4. Bernays, op. cit. The quote in the original German is as follows: *eine von körperlichem auf Gemütliches übertragene Bezeichnung für solche Behandlung eines Beklommenen, welche das ihn beklemmende Element nicht zu verwandeln oder zurückzudrängen sucht sondern es aufregen, hervortreiben und dadurch Erleichterung des Beklommenen bewirken will.*
5. Josef Breuer and Sigmund Freud, *Studies on Hysteria*, ed. and trans. James Strachey (New York: Basic Books, 1974), 6.
6. Ibid., 17.
7. It may be noted here that the patient herself, and not the doctor, first called this form of therapy the "talking cure." Breuer says of Anna O, "I used to visit her in the evening, when I knew I should find her in her hypnosis, and I then relieved her of the whole stock of imaginative products which she had accumulated. . . . She aptly described this procedure, speaking seriously, as a 'talking cure,' while she referred to it jokingly as 'chimney-sweeping'" (*Studies on Hysteria*, 30). These two phrases are in English in the German original. Freud later modified Breuer's approach of soliciting, under hypnosis, the patient's account of traumatic emotions and events. For Freud, the primary raw ma-

terial of the cure became disorderly talk in the form of so-called verbal free associations. At times, however, the body itself would do the "talking"—through paralysis, tics, aches and pains, or other sensations—while the patient sat or reclined in silence. Moreover, it was precisely the random nature of verbal and/or bodily free associations that presumably allowed insight—through gaps, unsuspected connections, inflections of the voice, and the like—into the underlying flow of unconscious processes.

8. Breuer and Freud, *Studies on Hysteria*, 16.

9. Ibid., 29.

10. Ibid., 28.

11. The reader may wish to know more about Jacob Bernays (1824–81). A German scholar of Jewish extraction, his training included both the biblical-Talmudic and the Greco-Roman traditions. Contrary to his brother, the literary historian Michael Bernays, he refused to convert to Christianity and so never received a professorship. He taught classical philology at the Jewish Theological Seminary of Breslau before being named chief librarian at the University of Bonn. The eleventh edition of the *Encyclopaedia Brittannica* includes a rather detailed entry on him. Theodor Gomperz, the German philosopher and classical scholar, wrote extensively of Bernays in his memoirs (*Essays und Erinnerungen*, 1907). Gomperz himself was an early mentor of Freud's and involved the latter in his supervised translation of J. S. Mill's complete works (12 vols., Leipzig, 1869–80). Whether or not Freud himself knew (of) Bernays is an open question. My visit to the library in the Freud Museum in London showed that Freud did not own a copy of Bernays's work on Aristotle.

12. For more on this, see Rand and Torok, *Questions for Freud*, 9–23, 47–94, 139–44.

13. Letter to Auguste Forel, November 21, 1907. In Paul F. Cranefield, "Josef Breuer's Evaluation of His Contribution to Psycho-Analysis," *International Journal of Psycho-Analysis* 39 (1958): 320.

14. Unpublished letter to Freud, dated January 17, 1930. I want to thank Judith Dupont, the executor of the Ferenczi estate, for permission to quote unpublished excerpts.

15. Sandor Ferenczi, *Final Contributions to the Problems and Methods of Psycho-Analysis*, ed. Michael Balint (New York: Bruner/Mazel Publishers, 1980), 118.

16. Nicolas Abraham and Maria Torok, *The Shell and the Kernel: Renewals of Psychoanalysis*, ed., trans., and with an introduction by Nicholas T. Rand (Chicago: University of Chicago Press, 1994), 254–55.

What to Say when You Talk to Yourself

14

The Tower of Psychobabble

Margaret Bruzelius

A student was referred to me, in my capacity as dean, because he had interrupted a class by asking his female instructor to dinner. His persistent attempts, in my office, to excuse and explain, finally concluded: "I have problems with my mother."

What we needed to discuss, my less than penitent charge insisted, was not so much the effect of this offensive behavior on others as its root in psychic pain—employing a form of narrative determined to turn our institutional encounter into a psychoanalytic one. To call this talk a "conversation" is to misrepresent it slightly, since to converse implies some form of equal exchange; given my position, he was not my equal. But if this meeting was devoid of conversation, it was full of talk. I talked to him—gave him a "talking to"; he talked to me, proffering a causal account of his conduct. I was struck by the ease with which he slipped into a pop-Freudian explication of his psyche.

Therapeutic talk, perhaps, has rendered conversation alien to the American twenty-first century. The word "talk," from the Danish *tal*, "count" or "recount," has a wide semantic range: to use the faculty of speech, to convey information or communicate by any means; to speak incessantly or idly, to chatter or prate; to transmit a rumor; to confer, reason, or consult; to make sounds suggesting speech; to express a sensible, reasonable, or otherwise commendable attitude, as in "Now you're talking!" The definition of talk seems to waver between its meaning as conversation and having no object beyond the chatterer himself. In contrast, the word "converse" is derived from the Latin *convertere*, "to turn around," which is also the root for "conversion," and means to "engage in familiar colloquy, to interchange thoughts and opinions in speech, to talk, especially in an intelligent and sustained manner; to communicate" (*Webster's Second*). "Converse" also has a sexual dimension, explicit in its archaic meaning of sexual intimacy. The word *talk* includes the idea of conversation, but acknowledges that, in fact, we who speak often descend from being conversable, to merely being talkative.

On the popular level, the large audience for public talk—from Oprah, to the self-conscious "intellectual" productions of National Public Radio, to Internet chatrooms—suggests a nation ready to bare its least opinion at the slightest provocation—a nation ready to talk—if not to converse. In most cases, the talker has a "presenting symptom" that the "talking through" process is expected to help him or her resolve. The informality of the process—"Hi my name is . . ."—disguises its essentially solitary nature: the effort to summon community suggested by this familiarity is counterbalanced (and emptied of value) by the fact that the named person is not known to or responsible to the listeners. A conversational community, pace Jürgen Habermas, is already a difficult ideal, generally based on the ruthless exclusion of others (think of the servants excluded from conversation in Austen's novels; the women and slaves excluded from Plato's gab fests; the difficulties we see now in communicating nonhegemonically across linguistic and cultural barriers). Our current talk communities seem to be based on a series of solitary voices obsessively "talking through" their problems if not precisely in a vacuum at least in contingently constituted and evanescent groups that endlessly, randomly form and disperse. We might document a shift in the expectations attached to the idea of talk—away from conversation, with its demands for listening, taking turns, and engagement, and toward just plain talk, a self-display that welcomes listeners only as audience, and suffers their interruptions into the stream of talk only in order to reassert the original flow. This is a "talking through" that can neither envisage itself as really being through, as being finished and moving on, or as conversation, with its possibility of taking turns and play.

The faculty of "talking through" one's problems is the distinct gift to the twentieth century of psychoanalysis and the therapies that analysis has generated. The phrase "talking through" implies an end, as in going through a tunnel, but in fact psychoanalysis never proposes that problems can be resolved or ended: they can be processed, partially understood, and accommodated, but never fixed. Like a bookworm, one talks through one layer only to achieve another, inner layer in an endless process of substitution, an endless movement through a self-replicating maze. The process of "talking through" that is therapeutic talk (even though "throughness" is debatable) changes the nature of talk itself. Rather than a commitment to community or social dance—the exchange of opinions and ideas envisaged to some extent by all theorists of talk—talk becomes an essentially solitary activity witnessed by a distant therapist who does not look back at the patient.

Woody Allen's *Deconstructing Harry* represents this hilariously in the self-absorbed analytic patient who continues to ramble on about his unsatisfactory relationships during his analyst's rip-roaring fight with her philandering husband: come hell or high water, the patient wants to "work it through." (Allen's oeuvre as a whole can be seen as a series of riffs on therapeutic talk and illustrates the essential solitude of the endless talker.) Talk is still erotic, in Carla Kaplan's term, but on the public front it has become a question of masturbation rather than intercourse. And talk in social situations often echoes the performance of a masturbatory erotics, a solipsistic exercise in self-display. The model of talk as endless, therapeutic self-narration is an inheritance of Freud's most important insight, which is that the patient already knows everything she needs to know, but that she cannot know consciously what she needs to know unless she has help. The therapist is essential for her to display what she knows to herself, but the process is a delving into the interior, an excursion into the heart of darkness through the medium of the patient's words. In his early work with Josef Breuer, *On the Psychical Mechanism of Hysterical Phenomena: Preliminary Communication* (1893), Freud declares that "I decided to start from the assumption that my patients knew everything that was of any pathogenic significance and that it was only a question of obliging them to communicate it." The elaboration of his procedure became a movement away from the physical pressure on the patient that he uses in this early work (Freud describes himself as "plac[ing] my hands on the patient's forehead or t[aking] her head between my hands" as though the woman were a tube of toothpaste who just needed a squeeze to produce the necessary information) to the scenario of analysis that has now become famous, where the client, on the couch, speaks while the analyst listens and, sparingly, responds.

For someone who listened to so much talk, Freud only rarely reports speech directly, but he does elaborate one dialogue in his essay *The Question of Lay Analysis*, an essay that can serve as a model for the nature of therapeutic talk itself: the talking comes to no conclusion and the dialogue is extremely one sided, courtesy of an interlocutor who seems remarkably cardboardlike and unresponsive. In this essay Freud conjures up an "Impartial Person" for whom he makes the case that a medical degree is not necessary for analytic training, and may in fact be a hindrance to such work. He begins by explaining that "Nothing takes place between them [the analyst and his patient] except that they talk to each other. The analyst makes use of no instruments—not even for examining the patient—nor does he prescribe any medicines. If it is at all possible, he even leaves the patient in his environment and in his usual mode of life."[1] The "instrument" that the therapist needs is the talk, the voice of the patient himself, who will display for the therapist the underlying conflicts that give birth to his symptoms.

The essay is about dialogue, but the dialogue is peculiarly nondialogic: Freud's Impartial Person is hardly a Bahktinian other who disrupts the flow of the master discourse. Rather, like most imaginary play fellows, he pipes up and says the expected thing in the expected place. He manages to swallow even the most shocking part of Freudian theory, the existence of childhood sexuality, without too much difficulty. (His only remark on it is a question that scarcely needs to be asked, "'What, then, is the nature of this "sexual activity" of children at an early age?'" To which Freud replies, unsurprisingly, "Children's sexual impulses find their main expressions in self-gratification by friction of their own genitals, or, more precisely, the male portion of them."[2] To be fair, Freud seems to leave the Impartial Person unconvinced of the value of lay analysts, although it is difficult to tell since the dialogue moves away from the necessity of medical training for doctors to the utility of analysis for children as a form of prophylaxis. The final image of the essay is a partly humorous evocation of a band of (American) social workers who are "trained analytically . . . [to become] helpers for combating the neuroses of civilization," which the Impartial Observer hails as a "a new kind of Salvation Army!" (Freud's response to this is "Why not?") Like the analytic procedure it recounts, the essay ends inconclusively: the question of lay analysis is still open, the position of the Impartial Observer still unclear, and the relation of the two professions, analysis and medicine, still unresolved.

The other facet of therapeutic talk revealed in this dialogue is the inherently fissionable nature of the therapeutic psyche. We know that the patient already has within him all he needs to know, but that he cannot access that knowledge because there are parts of his psyche that are, by definition, unknowable. Freud explains to the Impartial Person the "agencies" of the psychoanalytic self, the familiar ego, superego, and id. While he does not elaborate a drawing of the mind, as he does in *The Ego and the Id*, he clearly describes the same topography: the unconscious id, deep in the inner recesses of the mind, makes its demands for instinctual satisfaction; the ego, closer to the strictures of the real world, represses those demands because they are unsuitable, or because it knows that their satisfaction will cause problems; the ferocious superego "confronts [the] ego as the strict father confronts a child."³ Repressed material, betrayed by inconsistencies and divergences in the flow of talk, functions as something like a funnel, by the assistance of which the analyst and the patient can delve under the surface and come to an understanding of the patient's neurotic predicament, of the unmentionable drive deriving from the id that manifests itself in unsuitable ways. Freud's elaboration here is not complex, but it is worth emphasizing that the picture of the ego he draws is of a being beset by large and ferocious forces that it can neither name nor control. He also insists that there are neurotics who do not want to get well, the one assertion that seems to really agitate the Impartial Observer. Freud tells him, "Calm yourself! . . . the patient wants to be cured—but he also wants not to be. His ego has lost its unity. . . . If that were not so, he would not be a neurotic."⁴ It is the patient's "lack of unity," his desire to know and not to know, that most astonishes the Impartial Person, who asks Freud, "'What do you possibly mean by 'telling more than he knows'?'" Freud's response is to emphasize that a patient himself may notice that a "thought of his own [is] being kept secret from his own self."⁵ This sense of the unknown regions of the mind leads into a discussion of the various agencies of the mind, which Freud compares to the difference between the strict order of the front line of battle and the comparative laxness of regulation in the area behind the lines.

Freud begins with the fairly simple division between the conscious and the unconscious, associated respectively with the ego and the id. But he then continues to enlarge the realm of the unconscious to include parts of the ego and the superego, thus mapping a three-part "mental apparatus" on the original two-part topography. As Freud proceeds in his exposition, the already divided psyche splinters more and more, and drives, constitutional factors, traumas, and other elements complicate an initially simple structure. Nevertheless, the central fact of analysis remains that everything that the analyst needs to know is already in the patient somewhere: illustrations from literature can illuminate the patient's predicament, but nothing can be added to the patient's mind, no abstract knowledge can change his condition. The only way to understand the patient's behavior is to insist on the autonomy of various parts of his pysche. It is these semiautonomous agencies in Freud that will become the basis for the "conversations" between interior personae elaborated by later therapists.

The central condition of Freud's therapy is, of course, his insistence on the spoken word, which is saturated with meaning for him. In his essay, Freud models for us a dialogue in which there is none of the back and forth that one might imagine in a real dialogue on the nature on analysis. But the woodenness of Freud's dialogue is a testimony to the nature of therapeutic talk—it is talk, not conversation. The classic analytic situation, in which the patient speaks to the void, as it were, while the analyst listens, out of the line of sight, enshrines this idea of talk that needs no interlocutor—of talk with no possibility of conversation. Freud's avowed reason for not allowing the patient to look at him—that he disliked being stared at for eight hours a day—merely reinforces the idea that these sessions are not conversations, but displays. Moreover, the patient's talk reveals a psyche split into semiautonomous agencies that work independently and at cross purposes with each other. This splintering of the self has itself engendered an extraordinary progeny, first, of course, in the work of Jung, who elaborated a series of archetypal figures that the self could recognize in itself, and more recently in the work of American therapists who have described the process of healing the self as an encounter with an endless series of me's.

If Freud inaugurated a process with no endpoint, a potentially endless excavation of the psyche's archeology, one group of later talkers have elaborated a process in which the psyche is eerily populated by archaic figures derived largely from folklore, each of whom represents various emotional potentialities. One recent popular example of this is Robert Bly's *Iron John*. Bly's book is addressed to the wimpy men of the sixties and seventies, for whom he wishes to reclaim ancient models of testosterone-fueled masculine inner being. Just as Robinson Crusoe, shipwrecked on an island, talked to himself and drew up balance sheets (loss talking to profit) in order to discover how he was doing, Bly responds to the essential solitariness of the therapeutic talker by creating a continually proliferating number of inner selves—Wild Man, Grief Man, the multitalented Mythologist/Magus/Cook—drawn from the fairytale *Iron John*, with whom the talker needs to talk. (It is remarkable that in such inner conversations we never need to summon our grandmother in Hoboken, or Uncle George in Katonah—instead we talk to (or with) Alaskan shamans, or Tibetan saints, or characters out of *Grimms'*.) Ridiculed and parodied, *Iron John* remains extremely popular and influential.

Another, less literary, version of a self-improving talk-script is Shad Helmstetter's *What to Say when You Talk to Yourself*.[6] In Helmstetter, therapeutic talk very literally means self-talk, since Helmstetter elaborates a method for self-improvement by the constant positive reinforcement of the self. Al Franken's Stuart Smalley (from the show *Saturday Night Live*)—full of self-affirmation and concluding every conversation with his bathroom mirror by deciding, "Goshdarn it, people like me!"—encapsulates the mindless self-absorption of this method. Helmstetter's only similarity to Freud is his acceptance of the idea of the unconscious; however, his unconscious is not Freud's resistant past or even Bly's village of archaic types, but rather the programming of a self-computer—the unseen codes that determine the functioning of the machine. Helmstetter imagines that the brain has a "control center" that he imagines as a wall "completely covered with literally tens of thousands of light switches, much like the light switches in our homes. . . . Everything about us—our memory, our judgment, our attitude, our fears, our creativity, logic and spirit—is controlled by the switches in our mental control room."[7] As he develops this image he suggests that much of the "programming" in the mind works against the psyche, and then develops the idea that "you can *re*program. You can erase the old negative, counter-productive, work-against-you programming and replace it with a healthy, new, positive, *productive* kind of programming. And it's easy. *Erase and replace.* All you have to do is learn how to talk to yourself."[8]

Helmstetter's "erase and replace" (he seems serenely oblivious to the threatening undertones of this cheerful statement) consists of addressing to oneself a constant stream of self-improving remarks. For example, the list of "self-talk" for help to stop smoking begins:

> *I do not smoke. My lungs are strong and healthy. I am able to breathe deeply and fully. I like keeping myself fit and feeling good. I have more energy and stamina than ever before. I enjoy life and I am glad to be here.*[9]

This list continues for another page of self-affirmation, in which the conscious mind hectors (or reprograms) the unconscious. While the self begins by telling itself a lie, Helmstetter is quite sure that insistent repetition will just make the lie a truth. Helmstetter's fascination with a simplistic mental mechanics suggests that we can rescript the unconscious at any time. In a grotesque inversion of Freud, who postulated the unconscious as inaccessible no matter how it influences the conscious, Helmstetter sees the unconscious as an endlessly malleable entity that simply enacts whatever it is told. He advises his clients to make tapes to address their unconscious while they shave, exercise, and do the dishes—because "your subconscious mind will be listening—whether you are or not." Helmstetter sees the tape as a human invention on par with the "wheel, the printing press, motorized transportation, radio, television and the computer": "Never before in the history of the human race have we had a device which could, when used in the right way, literally *change* our own internal direction as rapidly, as effectively, and as effortlessly as can the audio cassette."[10] Indeed, the message need not be addressed to you to have effect. Helmstetter recounts several tales of wives or husbands overhearing tapes addressed to their spouses and themselves losing the weight, getting the job, or quitting the bad habit.

Helmstetter takes for granted that we have an unconscious and that the messages the unconscious receives control our daily life.[11] There is no moment in which the direct engagement with another human being is even envisaged. Every turn is a turn inward enabled by constant self-address. And indeed, as Helmstetter tells us in his concluding poem, we have no need for an other with whom to converse, since "You are everything that is, / Your thoughts, your life, your dreams come true. / You are everything you chose to be. / You are as unlimited as the endless universe."[12] Here Bly's village of inner beings is expanded to the universe, a universe curiously contained within the gizzards of a human computer. Improvement is obtained by merely hearing one's own self-talk—not by listening to it. Nothing could be farther from the ideal of conversation than this incessant inane self-address. As Helmstetter addresses himself when aggravated by traffic: "I enjoy relaxing when I am driving in the car. Traffic lights change *at their own discretion.*"[13] The focus on the striving self in Helmstetter is enough to make one nostalgic for the community in Bly, even if that community is an imaginary and internal one.

A more subtle use of therapeutic talk is elaborated in Michael White and David Epston's *Narrative Means to Therapeutic Ends.*[14] White and Epston propose a therapy deeply influenced not only by social theorists such as Bateson, Geertz, and Foucault, but also by literary critics such as Peter Brooks and Paul Ricoeur. Their method consists of externalizing the clients' "problem" in a narrative, and then, using evidence from the speakers themselves, suggesting to the clients a reworking of the narrative that will free them from the problem. In this approach to the self, editing is therapy: talk is turned into narrative, which is commented on and changed in order to accommodate the therapist's critique. This "new improved" talk is certified as better by the therapist in letters or certificates drawn up for the client. Although the therapists work with the clients, they preserve the power inequity that makes them editors, rather than fellow conversationalists. The supervised talk produced in therapy becomes a method for constructing a new self in a potentially endless series of reinscriptions.

White and Epston practice family therapy, the basic assumption of which is that a family (or sometimes other kinds of familylike groups) in distress will choose a member of the group to represent its collective malaise. Externalizing the "problem" in the form of a narrative gives the patient and the family the authority to rewrite it: their aim is not to describe the psyche by linking it to an ahistorical narrative or to address the patient's subconscious, but rather to help the patient control his or her story. White and Epston describe several rather literary-critical practices that characterize "narrative therapy": it

> invokes the subjunctive mood in the triggering of presuppositions, the establishment of implicit meaning, and in the generation of multiple perspective; encourages polysemy and the use of ordinary, poetic, and

picturesque language in the description of experience and in the endeavor to construct new stories; invites a reflexive posture and an appreciation of one's participation in interpretive acts; encourages a sense of authorship and re-authorship of one's life and relationships in the telling and retelling of one's story; acknowledges that stories are co-produced and endeavors to establish conditions under which the "subject" becomes the privileged author; and consistently inserts pronouns "I" and "you" in the description of events.[15]

In essence, narrative therapy represents a conscious effort to use the performative powers of mimetic talk toward liberation from unhappy life situations.

While White and Epson privilege the authority of the "sick" family member over the narrative, they never abandon the idea that the self is a tale told by a community. Indeed, their therapy consists in inserting themselves into the patient's life narrative—which for their purposes *is* the patient's psyche—and using their intervention to encourage its revised retelling.

One of the ways in which White and Epston participate in the narrative is by personifying the patient's problem. This character then joins the therapeutic throng, and triumph—or at least partial control—over the character is celebrated as a benchmark in the patient's healing.

The most interesting example of this process is "Sneaky Poo," the character invented with a young patient driving his family crazy by playing with his feces. His yen for fun with excrement was personified as "Sneaky Poo." Instances in which he was able to resist his urge to play with it (him?) were identified and then incorporated into his life story. Sneaky Poo, now a figure in the boy's life story, can be resisted and manipulated like any other human being. The process of resisting Sneaky Poo is memorialized in a certificate drawn up by White and Epston entitled "Breaking the Grip of Sneaky Poo." (The certificates are coauthored documents that certify the patient's progress.) "Sneaky Poo was messing up ——'s life, and often gave him a really hard time by sticking around when it wasn't wanted. Sneaky Poo even tried to trick —— into believing that it was his playmate."[16]

For White and Epston, the representation of the self achieved in the life story is endlessly malleable, and can be populated by an elastic number of figures. If Freud elaborates a bounded ego in bondage to early experiences that it can only marginally bring to consciousness, White and Epston imagine a world in which the ego can incorporate any new material by turning it into its account of itself with the help of a canny editor: every life is a novel.

Freud and his pop inheritors share certain basic values of therapeutic talk. Narrative is a form of healing not because one can talk "it" through—whatever it is—but because talk is the self. Therapeutic talk is an endless process—like all origins, the psyche recedes constantly before the talker.

Talk, in this context, is an inherently serious, almost excruciatingly mean-ingful, thoroughly self-centered activity in which content is always recuper-able from hesitations, lacunae, roughness—not only the words themselves but their method of delivery. Even silence is not the absence of anything to say, but a resistance that needs to be overcome or circumvented: the unac-knowledged ideal of therapeutic talk is an endless and untrammeled stream of itself. The idea of presenting oneself to the world in play in conversation simply doesn't exist in the therapeutic universe, for which primary narcissim is a central condition. Perhaps most startlingly, however, none of these ther-apists seem to envisage conversation, with the "turning" that it implies, as part of their notion of talk; there is no "conversation therapy" despite the fact that therapists talk all the time. We may think of "turning" in many senses here: as in taking turns, turning to face the interlocutor, turning in re-sponse to conversational cues. Freud absented himself from his client, sitting out of the line of sight and offering only occasional guidance as the patient talked himself into being. Bly evokes community, but the communities he invokes are archaic, ethnic, exotic, and are, finally, the community of one person talking to ("in touch with") his or her many selves. His books are full of stray remarks but bereft of conversation, give and take.

At roughly the same time that Freud was elaborating his early versions of "talk therapy" with Breuer, Joseph Conrad published *Heart of Darkness*, a novel that also interrogates the idea of "making" the self in talk. Conrad's tale is a written document obsessed with talk: the novel is told out loud by Marlow to his friends (with practically no interruption and certainly no con-versation); Kurtz himself is a figure of endless, self-obsessed talk. When Marlow describes himself as almost having made it to his goal, Kurtz's out-post, he realizes that what he wanted was to hear Kurtz talk: "I made the strange discovery that I had never imagined him as doing, you know, but as discoursing. . . . The man presented himself as a voice."[17] Kurtz exists as a rhetorical extravaganza that commands the attention of those around him: as the Russian vagabond Marlow meets along the river says, "you don't talk with that man—you listen to him."[18] Kurtz also shares the self-sufficiency of the therapeutic talker. The voice of "enlightened" Europe, Kurtz finds that what he did not know he knew is brought into his consciousness in the jun-gle like the patient who knows what he needs to know already, but can only bring it to consciousness with the help of the therapist. Marlow declares be-fore he meets Kurtz that "the mind of man is capable of anything—because everything is in it, all the past as well as all the future";[19] what Kurtz finds there is summarized by his final remark, "The horror! The horror!"[20] Kurtz's "ability to talk," is, in Marlow's words, "the gift of expression, the bewilder-ing, the illuminating, the most exalted and the most contemptible, the pul-sating stream of light, or the deceitful flow from the heart of an impenetrable darkness."[21] He embodies talk that wants no interlocutor—he ends as voice alone: "Kurtz discoursed. A voice! A voice! It rang deep to the very last."[22] But what is true of Kurtz is true of Marlow; he, too, is "A voice! A voice!" He too talks endlessly, repeating his tale to a group of disengaged listeners. Having once met the consummate, self-absorbed talker, he seems condemned to talk him through. There is no banter or conversation in *Heart of Darkness*: Marlow grabs the floor and hangs onto it just as Kurtz had grabbed the floor. Kurtz never converses with Marlow, he talks to him, about "my Intended, my ivory, my station, my river, my —."[23] The endless stream of talk is only mitigated for Marlow by his engineering training, his loyalty to the machinery of the steamboat that he must tend. And the story, like the therapeutic narrative, seems to be virtually endless and endlessly repeatable; one could imagine Marlow as a modern-day Ancient Mariner, stopping one in three and boring them to death with his old tale. Conrad's talk is also impregnated with seriousness; there is no play in *Heart of Darkness*. Marlow tells us that maintaining the steamboat—that is, the labor of fixing the rotting machinery—is the "surface-truth" that kept him sane while going up river—but every example of talk that we hear in the novel is either debasing, like the conversation between the station manager and his uncle about the probability that Kurtz is dead, or, like Kurtz's (or Marlow's) voice, an endless stream of sound that requires no response. There is no moment in this novel when conversation exists as a form of play, turn and turn about. Nor is there any moment in the novel when such play may be said to be possible. The doctor who measures Marlow's head before he sets out for Africa is amusing, but only for the reader: Marlow finds him annoying.

Both *Heart of Darkness* and the therapists assume that the talker encloses an entire world. Both assume that the tale told is the psyche. Both assume that there are parts of that psyche that are unknown and unknowable—the heart of darkness is within, not without. What is truly different is the deep seriousness with which Conrad suggests that talk may ultimately be meaningless. Therapy assumes that all talk is ultimately meaningful and that an understanding of that meaning will lead to the solution of or at least an accomodation to the patient's problem. Within the therapeutic universe meaning is always potentially recuperable. Freud describes a psyche that accomodates itself with difficulty to the real, a psyche that is never at ease and that faces real dangers. His followers have dropped his sense of the difficulty of the life of the psyche and retained its narcissistic self-importance. It is this bland assumption of safety that one feels in therapy-talk, the obsession with the ultimate importance of one's self, the middle-class security that allows Bly to assume that Iron John, once discovered, will not simply tear him apart. Conrad, perhaps precisely because he is a novelist whose medium is words, confronts the much darker possibility that one may talk and talk and talk and not mean anything, not get anywhere. Kurtz talks in the jungle; Marlow talks on the boat. There is nothing more.

We have as a culture been "talking through" for a century, and yet the central predicament of the talker has not moved far from Marlow: like him, we seem to be endlessly talking to the empty air. The promise of liberation, or at the very least new understanding, that seems to underlie Freud at least in his more optimistic moments is contradicted by the formulaic quality of what is discovered: the same Oedipus complex, the same iron man, the same old sneaky poo. We have assumed as a culture that when we follow the script for self-improvement we will be changed, we will become more creative— what we seem to be left with, on the contrary, is a legion of people constantly repeating the same narrative of the self over and over. Therapeutic talk offers an endlessly proliferating number of scripts (hysteria, the trauma of birth, the inner child) in which talkers can, at least temporarily, find themselves. What it seems completely unable to do is imagine a world in which we can find one another.

Notes

1. Josef Breuer and Sigmund Freud, *The Question of Lay Analysis*, in vol. 20 of *The Standard Edition of the Complete Psychological Works of Sigmund Freud*, ed. James Strachey (London: Hogarth Press, 1959), 187.
2. Ibid., 216–17.
3. Ibid., 223.
4. Ibid., 221.
5. Ibid., 188.
6. Shad Helmstetter, *What to Say when You Talk to Yourself* (New York: Pocket Books, 1987).
7. Ibid., 38.
8. Ibid., 46.
9. Ibid., 156; emphasis in original.
10. Ibid., 134.
11. If Helmstetter envisages any difference between the subconscious and the unconscious he does not articulate it.
12. Ibid., 255.
13. Ibid., 208; emphasis in original.
14. Michael White and David Epston, *Narrative Means to Therapeutic Ends* (New York and London: W. W. Norton, 1990).
15. Ibid., 83.
16. Ibid., 44.
17. Joseph Conrad, *Heart of Darkness and Other Tales*, ed. Cedric Watts (Oxford: Oxford University Press, 1990), 203.
18. Ibid., 213.
19. Ibid., 186.
20. Ibid., 209.
21. Ibid., 203–4.
22. Ibid., 237.
23. Ibid., 206.

Hearsay Booked

15

Fugitive Talk Brought
to Justice

Jan B. Gordon

All truths begin as
hearsay. . . .
—Matt Drudge in
an address to the
National Press Club

I
f talk—gossip, word-of-mouth, buzz—is the
foundation of truth and the rationality that informs it, the muckraker's elusive source of the
Nile, it has been a "suspect" discourse, in the
Anglo-American tradition, when brought to court.
For, though there may be no reason why secondhand utterances are *innately* less likely to be truthful than those of persons present, this sort of talk
is imagined to pervert justice in the same way "idle
gossip" has been imagined to subvert dominant
cultural structures and discourses.[1] As Martin
Heidegger imagined *Gerede*—the "idle talk" that
floats about modern civilization—to be a form of
deracinated or "uprooted" speech at a perilous remove from truth, so claims of free-floating orality
to material truth have been suspect under the law.[2]
Even etymologically, one suspects, this drift of a
discourse—which cannot be satisfactorily tracked
and whose origins cannot be firmly tied down—is
reflected in the transitivity of the verbs composing
the portmanteau noun: hear-say.

What is hearsay? The *Federal Rules of Evidence*
characterize hearsay, which is generally inadmiss-

able as evidence in a case, as a declarative, secondhand statement offered in evidence *as proof of a matter asserted.* In order for a declaration to be deemed hearsay, the statement must be established as *assertive* in *intention.* Though determination of intentionality is, of course, as problematic in jurisprudence as in literary criticism, comment in the absence of intention (whatever intention is perceived to be) escapes classification as hearsay. In other words, a statement unintended as assertion carries legal weight, while an actual assertion, oddly, does not. Neither an enquiry nor a photograph qualifies as a declaration; thus both are admissible as evidence in court.[3] Bettors telephoning in their bets engage in nonassertive verbal conduct; though it may be relevant to the question of whether gambling has occurred in a locale, it is not "intended assertion" regarding the fact that gambling has occurred, and thus is admissible as evidence.[4] This sort of testimony proves the existence of a matter asserted rather than embodying a claim to validity.

There are, however, exceptions to this rule; for instance, an assertion otherwise disqualified from evidentiary status is often admitted when it bears upon the *state of mind* of a defendant or is offered to establish a declarant's *belief at the time.*[5] Declarations antecedent to rational reflection—known in legal parlance as "excited utterance"—never qualify as hearsay, under the assumption that the precipitating event was so startling as to suspend the possibility of fabrication. This would extend not merely to the edge of the grave—deathbed utterances are exempt from hearsay status under the assumption that a declarant facing imminent death would have no reason to lie—but also from the cradle: the statements of an incompetent, because underaged, child also fail to qualify as hearsay.[6] In other words, prereflective utterance, because it is uncontaminated by a truth claim—or, concomitantly, the willed deceptions and justifications imagined to attend the operations of reason—evades the fugitive status with which the law has historically stigmatized hearsay testimony. As "voice," in Jacques Derrida's formulation, is the irrecoverable foundation to which writing or inscription always (in occidental thought) doubly defers, so some mental consciousness exhibiting spontaneity outside or beyond a reasoned truth assertion (yet somehow "informing" it, as voice may inform inscripted iteration) renders the testimony acceptable within the Anglo-American jurisprudential tradition.[7]

The secondhand nature of talk is very much at issue, of course, in determining inadmissibility. In a bank robbery case, for instance, testimony obtained by a police detective from people in the bank that there were eight people present at the time of the robbery was not adjudged hearsay, since the testimony was a consequence of the officer's *own* deduction, which could also be tested for accuracy under cross-examination.[8] In other words, once putative hearsay has been "rationalized"—rendered firsthand and purged of its authorless, originless, traceless character—through a mediate process by the declarant, it no longer qualifies as fugitive orality and is thus admissible. The suspicion that a hypostasized, presumably uncorrupted Origin must prequalify all admissible testimony—as it has historically grounded legal precedent and other legally ensconced ideologies of social acceptance—is perhaps noteworthy, but not surprising. The "orphaned" truth claim has traditionally had a difficult time gaining acceptance. And the hearsay exclusion, as numerous judicial decisions have affirmed, deals with questions of *admissibility* rather than the quality or reliability of the testimony.[9]

Like gossip, talk arising from a community is often disowned as alien to that community and its interests. In instances in which it is seen to benefit that community, however, select types of talk may be salvaged as admissible. In one landmark U.S. Supreme Court decision, for example, "victim impact" testimony was ruled constitutional. The majority judgment held that assertions, intended as assertions, by survivors—often highly emotional narratives of personal loss—were admissible on the grounds that each murder victim is a "unique" human being "in a community" and that this uniqueness was relevant to jury deliberations that can take the loss of that individual's contribution into consideration.[10] In effect, the admissibility of circumstantial belief or state of mind by a witness is extended to include effects that may never have been foreseen or intended by the accused. The ways in which a specific crime lives on in the emotional declarations of a community of victims, even though potentially deceptitious, are rendered part of an original criminal intent. Although the majority decision recognizes the impact of a crime upon a previously unacknowledged community of victims, that very act of recognition in one sense creates two separable classes of victims: those more impacted by a loss *or better able to articulate it* (circumstances possibly resulting in enhanced sentences for defendants) and those victims less impacted by the crime *or less skilled at narrating their loss* (circumstances that might prove partially exculpatory). Whatever the consequences, the community of victims is clearly defined post facto and only via a mechanism contingent upon erstwhile inadmissible discourse.

Another expansion to hearsay practices—more problematic because not merely the declaration but the declarant is marginally fugitive—is involved in the extension of the Supreme Court hearsay rule in cases of conspiracy. Coconspirators' utterances are to be admissible in both civil and criminal cases under an expanded application of "agency" law. The logic here probably involves the commonsense appreciation that a person who authorized another to speak or act to a joint end would be responsible for what is later said or done by his agent, whether actually in his physical presence or not.[11] One must note, however, that in many instances evidence of a conspiracy as a jointly intended and enacted deed exists only in the post facto narrative of a party who is often partially exempted from the criminal responsibility (in both senses of that word) that would accrue to other criminal investors in the activity. The talking coconspirator's contribution to a successful prosecution is dependent upon his ability to construct an antecedent *intention* in his narrative, after the culmination of the "plot." There could be no better example than this of the notion, long espoused by Stanley Fish, that *intention* is a fabrication, an attempt to re-petition the idea of a coherent narrative, whose structure (complete with beginning, middle, and end) compels a jury's belief that the context is correct, in the absence of a more responsible criminal author(ity).[12] Like Jane Austen's gossipy spinsters who bring news of eligible male arrivals in a neighborhood without a prayer of utilizing their specialized intelligence, the talking coconspirator is often believable in direct proportion to a jury's perception that he is not a direct beneficiary of his own narrative.

Both the victim impact and conspiracy cases define criminal *communities* as spatial and temporal *continuities*. Once so defined, all of this community's utterance—even when it appears to qualify as hearsay—tends to be caught up in the overall discussion as contributory and relevant, necessary to the maintenance of narrative continuity. By contrast, subversive discourse, like gossip, has traditionally been represented as lurking outside a community's narrative, in which it would purport to open a local channel. As the criminal community is progressively expanded, progressively less testimony is left outside judicial relevance. When the enlarged criminal community comes to be allied with, if not determined by, a discursive community, hearsay is no longer a synecdoche for idle gossip: a collective narrative hegemonizes the logic that had previously justified the hearsay exemption. Yet the status of hearsay remains contested by opposing parties and throughout the long history of Anglo-American jurisprudence.

What feature of hearsay renders it simultaneously necessary to certain prosecutions yet a potential repository of fabrications and lies—discourse at once inside and outside the law, law-enforcing and criminal itself? A partial answer to our rhetorical question might be found in the outburst of poor Gridley of Dickens's *Bleak House*, repeatedly brought before Chancery to be "purged" of contempt for *speaking* in his own behalf rather than through the inscribed affidavits and rejoinders of legal representatives. With some as yet unpurged residue, he fantasizes a last oral will and testament through which he would escape incarceration with the assistance of a Transcendent Judge:

> "If I knew when I was going to die, and could be carried there and had a voice to speak with, I would die there saying, 'You have brought me here and sent me out from here, many and many a time. Now send me out feet foremost!'"[13]

In a novel oversaturated with written wills, codicils, and inauthentic copies—spawned in a drift from the precedent repressing idle speech in legal praxis—Gridley's last will would dramatically advance the claims of a subversive orality against the incessant re-petitions that are the lifeblood of the law.

In Dickens's imagination, the legal community exhibits an operational "heaviness" that weighs upon society with "walls of word," "banks of advocates," procedural delays, smudged transcriptions, cross-references within other references, and even in the thick robes and wigs that lend the court some of the density of the foggy, rheumatic climate of *Bleak House.* The Gridley whose modus operandi has involved the strategic use of skylights to gain criminal access to private property, discovers that the institutional practice of the law leaves no equivalent "opening" for the "still, small voice of humanity," celebrated by Wordsworth. Any plea enunciated in his own voice (as a proper, in the sense of self-same, plaintiff), is invariably resisted as an interruption of the record, and hence "out of order." Like, one suspects, so many voices of the impoverished, his courtroom outbursts, delivered in ordinary speech rather than a legal language that privileges a chronological record, have no real materiality in the readerly eyes of the law.[14] Yet, paradoxically, they apparently have enough materiality to leave him open to the ritual purgings attendant upon repeated contempt citations in a novel saturated with oozing mud, antediluvian inky blackness, and other assorted moral and corporeal stains that mark those excluded from social acknowledgment and transcendent judgment.

For Dickens, fugitive orality, introduced into the courtroom, would thus seem to have a curious double life at the judicial margins. Albeit lacking in legal materiality sufficient to contribute to the weight of evidence, the historical resistance of the law would seem to lend this orality, or otherwise transfer to it, vestiges of materiality. For once the subversive utterance is resisted by the court, it assumes a material embodiment, open to the purgings that leave behind, as it were, the novel's (and perhaps Victorian culture's) characteristic residue: a stain that signifies the operational dematerialization accompanying the purged religious, criminal, or pathological body. Otherwise extraneous oral interpretation, hearsay testimony, and unsworn emotional response or opinion assume some of the characteristics of gossip. This fugitive orality may spread, as do other contagions in Dickens's novel, infecting the privileged classes that are largely defined, like the law itself, as a descendant progression derived from the recuperation of noble precedents. One "traces up" the applicable precedent as one traces up genealogical ancestry. Hence, like gossip and orphans, the unacknowledged "report" in a court of law challenges the foundationalism upon which the law is imagined to rest, with a discontinuity. And, retrospectively, the rigid controls placed upon the random introduction of orally based testimony and judgments in the history of British jurisprudence would seem to owe something to one of its putatively foundational moments.

In 1616 Sir Edward Coke, chief justice of the Court of King's Bench, was petitioned to grant relief from a judgment of a common law court by a plaintiff in a court of equity, thereby creating a de facto distinction between common law (based upon statute) and the court of equity (based upon the individual facts of a specific case). His eighteenth-century successors as scholars of the law, such as Sir William Blackstone, continued to maintain that the application of abstract common law knowledge—which depended largely upon identifying and tracing up the applicable precedent in a specific case—was alone sufficient guarantee of sound legal judgment, since variations from established precedent would be bewildering.[15] Yet, even while acknowledging the limitations of a system so heavily dependent upon the recuperation of an origin and a logic of legal succession, Blackstone was even more fearful of the "softer," liberal interpretations mandated by courts of equity that, in considering all judgments in an "equitable light," would replace statute law with the arbitrary order of a judge who would assume the voice of the legislator:

> Equity thus depending upon the particular *circumstances* of each individual case, there can be no established rules and fixed precepts of equity laid down without reducing it to a positive law. And on the other hand, the liberty of considering all cases in an equitable light must not be indulged too far, lest thereby we destroy all law, and leave the decision in the *heart of the judge*. And law without equity though hard and disagreeable, is much more desirable for the public good than equity without law which would make every judge a legislator.[16]

In trying to steer a typically British *via media* between the demands of common law and equity, Blackstone realizes that the latter threatens to subject the written law to determinations from an unforeseeable set of individually variable circumstances. This would have the effect of erasing law altogether by the facts surrounding (i.e., circumstantial to) a given transgression, which might include intentions, motives, mitigating factors, and unanticipated consequences, none of which could be legally prescribed. Any necessary relationship between judgments and their informing precedents would be diluted or even severed, as facts assumed a status equal to law.

Even more revelatory than Blackstone's thought is the imagery. The arbitrary judgments handed down by courts of equity are emitted from the "heart" of the judge, that internalized organ wherein, for Charles Taylor, the metaphoric "voice" of Western liberal humanism, exempt from institutional coercion and/or collusion with state authority, lies. If private property was made into a synecdoche of the individuated "self" during the eighteenth-century revolutions—exempt from state encroachment—the "heart" of the judge in cases of equity became a similar hypothetical refuge from the control of a system of (legal as well as political) governance based upon privileged antecedence. "Sacred" speech is often subversive: some "inner voice" necessary to preserve equity, in its very resistance to encoding, threatened—at least for some scholars of the law—to usurp that system. Blackstone forthrightly admits as much in his fear that "the heart of the judge . . . might rise above the law, either common or statute," were courts of equity to assume an expanded role. In Blackstone's structural model, the historical tradition of common or statute law comes to be identified with the traceable *letter* of the law, whereas its more elusive, arbitrary, and uncodifiable *spirit* resides both in equity law, and derivatively one might presume, in the unforeseeable outbursts of Dickens's Gridley, ever rising.

Furthermore, and to his credit, the author of the voluminous commentaries recognized early on that this fugitive orality, either from the bench or among the defendants caught up in the law, would be brought to book. For gradually, equity law acquired a literature in the form of case histories, which reduced the arbitrariness of summary decisions from a judge's heart in favor of the creeping codification that would eventually inscribe this vocal "spirit":

> a real court of equity is not bound by rules or precedents, but acts from the opinion of a judge, founded on the circumstances of every particular case. Whereas *our* court of equity is a laboured connected system governed by established rules and bound down by precedent.[17]

Individual circumstances are an insufficient foundation for common law precisely because they could never be commonly shared—until and unless inscribed as statutes bound by recuperable precedents. Once such a connected system of rules comes to inform equity judgments, any difference between common law and equity would effectively disappear. The unencodable voice would come to occupy a problematic legal position, lacking as it does any foundational claims of materiality that might ground admissibility.

The threat represented by an otherwise unrepresentable voice nonetheless has a historically continuous place defined by the resistance to its procedural or real presence in Anglo-American jurisprudence. When President Bill Clinton publicly complained that the office of the independent counsel had, after more than two years of scrutiny, uncovered only gossip and hearsay, he was tapping an aversion to all uncorroborated oral assertion. For William Starkie's general rule—"that all facts and circumstances, upon which any reasonable presumption or inference can be founded, as to the

truth or falsity of the issue or disputed fact, are admissible as evidence"—
found a notable exception in an early positing of the so-called hearsay rule.[18]
Uncorroborated oral accounts gained at secondhand under circumstances
where the declarant was not available were to be in all instances excluded.
Starkie's exclusion of hearsay evidence in the nineteenth century was entirely
consistent with legal precedent, for Lord Chief Baron Gilbert, the author of
the first treatise on evidence in 1760, had observed that hearsay declarants
were not sworn and hence their oral assertions could never be tested by cross-
examination.[19] Starkie concurred, while adding an amended concern that
hearsay would place an additional burden upon a jury by opening up questions such as the character of the declarant, and his possibly circuitous means
of knowledge. Yet how that burden would differ from that imposed on conflicting, yet admissible, written testimony was never indicated. Why, precisely, would orality be more innately burdensome for juries to sift than
would be comparable written declarations?[20]

For whatever reasons, both the historical attempt to bring courts of
equity under the precedent-privileging procedures of courts of common law
and the procedural exclusion of hearsay evidence would suggest a prejudice
against unregulated orality in Western jurisprudence. Perhaps the best example of this systemic procedural marginalization of the oral is to be found, ironically, in the very proceedings of the Court of Chancery. Until the Chancery
Procedure Act of 1852, only written evidence admitted by affidavit and then
read aloud by counsel was admissible in Chancery. Because all parties to a suit
were to have written copies of these myriad affidavits, considerable energy
and expense were dedicated to making written transcriptions by a virtual
army of impoverished and illiterate copyists, the "dirty hanger[s]-on and disowned relations of the law" whose smudged fingers mark the inky plot of
Bleak House.[21] Even procedurally, orality had to be booked, initially transcribed, and hence repressed as an independent procedure.

Thus during the last quarter of the eighteenth century and through the
first half of the nineteenth century, the oral/aural discursive register was ju-
dicially relegated to the status of gossip like the "idle talk" in a Jane Austen
novel.[22] Although all parties—if especially eligible women in need of information about newly arrived marital "prospects"—are dependent upon gossip in a closed society, they are never to reveal this dependency. Gossip is a
discourse that requests of its beneficiaries that it never enter discursive practice as a condition of the narration. Hence, the resistance to it in so many
nineteenth-century British novels often assumes contradictory strategies.
The need for gossip is often sublated or disguised in Jane Austen, Dickens,
and George Eliot by rival cultural repositories of historically acquired
"achievements" to be tested in after-dinner performance: skill at the spinnet,
sketchbooks, or cleverness with alternative syntagmatic communicative sys-

tems, like parlor games and conundrums. Writ large, many nineteenth-century British novels conclude with the recuperation of a potentially wayward son or daughter into inheritable family "interests" and dwellings and away from verbally (or economically) centrifugal "speculative" energies that would devalue their worth in gossip.[23]

Jeremy Bentham was the first to question the blanket exceptionalism historically accorded hearsay testimony. In his preliminary writings on the subject, Bentham's argument seems entirely traditional: *all* testimony not subject to cross-examination is extrajudicial, be it oral or written, no matter what the intention. Cross-examination alone provides the indispensable guarantee against incorrectness or incompleteness. Only the (legally) dialogic secures hearsay by framing its potential drift. But Bentham later commences to pose critical questions that will initiate his departure from the historical tradition that stigmatized hearsay testimony. Initially, exceptions to the exceptionalism of hearsay are provided by those whose testimony would be rendered physically (as by death or mental infirmity) or practically (as by virtue of expatriation) inaccessible to the cross-examination that would ensure its correctness and completeness. Once having identified such absentee-based exceptions, Bentham proceeds through a sequence of reflective questions to lay the foundation for a new law of hearsay:

> *Question*: Why give admission to evidence in a shape thus liable to be vitiated by incorrectness and incompleteness?
> *Answer*: Because, were it excluded whatsoever information were not attainable from any other source would thereby stand excluded. Here then, supposing that the information is necessary to a decision in favour of that side, here would be deception, and consequent misdecision, to a certainty.[24]

Whereas Starkie had distrusted the skill of juries to evaluate hearsay testimony, Bentham queries the haste of his legal predecessor's condescension by asking, literally, Why not "stay and see"? In other words, why not simply admit the evidence in all cases where the declarant is unavailable, hear out the resultant jury verdict, and then, if in a particular case deception is apparent, use "a remedy . . . [that is] as safe and gentle as it is infallible," namely the remedy of granting a new trial?[25] If hearsay is fallacious, errant, or fabricated, as it may be, those disqualifications must be identified, as with any other testimony.

Bentham offers a hearsay declaration unattainable from any other source: the instance of a wife's claim against the provisions of a dying spouse's will. The deceased is clearly inaccessible to cross-examination in court, where the sincerity of his intentions might be weighed. Common sense dictates that his dying declaration must be admitted as evidence, even though it would otherwise clearly fall under the category of hearsay. Dickens's Gridley, who demands that his dying declaration be admissible in Chancery without fear of being struck down as contempt of court, reveals more knowledge of the law than he may realize: the prospect of death, as the argument goes, metaphorically converts the overheard (hearsay) into an admissible *text*. To this day, though tested numerous times, dying declarations remain exempt from the exclusion traditionally due hearsay utterance. Whether or not the rule excluding the testimony of an unavailable declarant is potentially an instrument of injustice—as Bentham strenuously argued and traditionalists have denied—surely it should have been a crucial issue for debate during the nineteenth century, so receptive to other legal reforms. Yet, despite Bentham's influence upon legal reform, his critique of the hearsay rule fared less well than his several successful reforms.[26]

Similarly, in the United States, sincere attempts to remodel the hearsay rule, often modeled upon Bentham's critique, fell on deaf ears or were otherwise thwarted. In 1886 the Committee on the Amendment of the Law of the Boston Bar Association received a proposal from James B. Thayer to alter the law to include spoken declarations of the deceased.[27] Had it been adopted, such a proposal might have been a first step in a logical progression terminating in a position close to Bentham's. If written statements of a decedent are admissible, why not oral utterance? If written and oral, then why not statements of persons now of infirm mind? If statements from those now of infirm mind are admissible, then why not those from declarants who are indisposed, expatriated, at large, or unavailable for any other reason? Thayer's scheme would have left the determination as to the materiality of the content to judge and jury. In 1938 the American Bar Association made recommendations similar to those of Thayer, and the American Law Institute undertook the preparation of the Model Code of Evidence, which would among other things "treat jurors as normal human beings, capable of evaluating relevant material in a court room as well as in the ordinary affairs of life" during which they "hear, consider, and evaluate hearsay."[28] Under this assumption, hearsay would seem to have escaped its reputation for deception insofar as it warrants the same judicial evaluation as would other discursive registers. Yet the committee entrusted with drawing up the code found the familiar threat to justice if hearsay became a substitute for cross-examination, likely if the exceptions applied to hearsay were to be entirely abolished. Although the members found that guarantees of trustworthiness could be found in more conventional tests for sincerity, such guarantees were not applicable as tests for other qualities such as recalled details of perception or the completeness of the narrative, which only cross-examination could appraise.

Like gossip in everyday life, the sincerity of unsworn testimony delivered at secondhand might be checked for veracity in other ways, but because hearsay lacks totalization—it can never suffice as the "whole story"—cross-examination alone can complete what is, by its nature, fragmentary and discontinuous about unsworn testimony. And yet, procedurally, cross-examination exhibits nothing so much as the absence of closure: How and under what conditions, save arbitrary agreement, could cross-examination ever be considered as complete? Clearly, an institutionalized version of the "dialogic" administered by officers of the court is being imagined to frame an otherwise fugitive discourse, thereby lending it a fictional materiality.

This argument has an uncanny resemblance to that advanced for another discipline by Francis Jeffrey, an editor of the *Edinburgh Review,* and applied to the proliferation of other fugitive discourse: in this case that of the fashionable novels of "sensibility" in the first quarter of the nineteenth century. Fearful of the vogue of gossipy, sensational novels (often written by and for "vulnerable" women—i.e., domestic servants), Jeffrey advocated a number of "tests" of sincerity for that novel genre, the novel, perhaps forgetting that the genre had its beginnings in highly personal, unverified eyewitness accounts (many of which were clearly fictitious) in the early eighteenth century.[29] In both cases an unregulated discourse outside established institutional guidelines is imagined as corruptive: of judicial judgments on the one hand and, on the other, of an imaginary republic of letters—the assortment of (usually male) authors, editors of periodicals, members of learned societies, and representatives of academy and clergy—in sum, the self-appointed guardians of public taste and morality during the late eighteenth and early nineteenth centuries.[30] In Anglo-American jurisprudence as, apparently, in other institutions dedicated to cultural formation, inclusiveness is sacrificed for "tests" of veracity and "sincerity" in the hope of establishing inheritable standards of judgment or taste. The unregulated, absent, or uninitiated voice, potentially subversive of those presumably historically mandated standards, is precisely what is being sacrificed in both instances.

Is the so-called hearsay question, as it has evolved in Anglo-American jurisprudence, really a synecdoche of the relationship between *fact* and *law?* Scholars of the law have typically believed that cases are decided on the basis of belief in facts rather than questions of law, which are always more difficult for jurors lacking legal training to access. If, however, hearsay testimony, like gossip in common discursive practice, consists of incomplete, dimly recalled, unsworn, or for that matter entirely fabricated facts petitioning for legal recognition, the law would operate as an a priori exclusionary mechanism, forever confining its truths (no matter how fleeting) to intransitivity or absence. The law has historically been represented as a system of familial relationships, whereas uncorroborated facts and arbitrary enunciation are extrafamilial and discontinuous—yet, ironically enough, sufficiently threatening to warrant suppression in advance—not unlike the voices of other subalterns.

The historical identification of hearsay with rationalization (and thereby rationality) should be kept in mind. The more potentially irrational the utterance (dying declarations, a child's *res gestae* exclamations, "state of mind" descriptions, highly emotive victim impact testimony), the more likely it is, as we have seen, to be judged admissible under the assumption that deception is less likely in highly emotional, associational, or reflexive narrative. Hence, the existence of a judicial aporetic: *The traditional exclusion of hearsay testimony, no matter how effective its guardianship against deceptions and lies, is really a censorship of reason (for only reason could willfully deceive or lie), in the interests of justice.* Liars are rationally knowledgeable narrators—as Socrates reminded Hippias—and such knowledge may not be a universal virtue, despite the professed interests of justice.[31]

If indeed the American founding fathers devised the First Amendment not to protect individual self-expression, but to widen the range of public discourse (as communitarian free speech theorists suggest), the hearsay rule may be a kind of duty, a quasi censorship such as the judicial system has historically levied upon the flowering of individual autonomy.[32] Testimony that has historically been censored as extralegal has in the past two decades come to have a legal status, ironically, as long as it makes no pretense to truth. And surely, were the exceptional status that has marked hearsay to be abolished altogether, as Bentham envisioned and recent judicial decisions have tended to affirm, all testimony would be aligned on more or less the same plane, with no screening of derivative or deceptitious declarations of increasingly dubious authenticity. But, though a deceptitious statement might be admissible for a jury's consideration, so might an uncorroborated truth.

All testimony, like the varied goods on display in a modern department store—expensive oriental carpets, toys, cheap sunglasses, a fake–brand name handbag—come to form a collective assemblage from which a wary (or not so wary) consumer chooses. No declaration or product would be prima facie inadmissible. That Jeremy Bentham, the visualizer of a Panopticon that aligned discipline, social surveillance, education, and efficient capitalist production in a totalizing environment, should have anticipated the progressive enclosure of another enclave, that legal "still, small voice" of the nineteenth century by/in a judicial totalization that leaves no discourse outside the law, seems—well—a case of poetic justice.

Notes

The author wishes to acknowledge with thanks the generosity of Charles Clark of the Texas law firm of Clark, Walker, and Lea for gaining him admission to a law library—as well as access to Mr. Clark's own experience with recent applications of the hearsay rule.

1.   See Jan B. Gordon, *Gossip and Subversion in Nineteenth Century British Fiction: Echo's*

Economies (London: Macmillan, and New York: St. Martin's Press, 1986).

2. Martin Heidegger, *Being and Time*, trans. John Macquarrie and Edward Robinson (Oxford: Basil Blackwell, 1980), 212. Heidegger's description of *Gerede* imagines it as "floating" and hence lacking in materiality; its initial lack of grounds to stand on (*Bodenständigheit*) becomes a complete groundlessness (*Bodenlösigheit*). This concept encompasses a discourse in which people participate "without ever making the thing one's own," and, given Heidegger's embrace of National Socialism in Germany after 1933, a chilling connection between "deracinated" speech and "uprooted" minorities, both of which "long for" enclosure.

3. *United States v. May* (1980, CA9 Washington).

4. *United States v. Zenni* (1980, ED Kentucky). Similarly, notebooks recording drug transactions, found in an apartment, did not constitute hearsay when offered to show the "character" of the place and to corroborate witness testimony (*United States v. Wilson* [1976, CA8 Missouri]). The testimony of a customs agent that he strip-searched a defendant on the basis of a computer report was first challenged as hearsay, but then deemed admissible in that the evidence was not offered to prove the computer's response (*United States v. Brown* [1976, CA9 Arizona]).

5. The judicial protection of antecedent intention and "state of mind" descriptions—as opposed to assertions—has been criticized by Antonin Scalia (Tanner lectures, Princeton University, 1995). Scalia would presume to find intention embodied in (and thereby inseparable from) a "final" text in which the law is embodied, probably because he fears that extrajudicial advocacy groups might constitute part of the "shaping intention" of the legislation, though not the actual law as enacted.

6. *Jones v. United States* (1956, 97 App DC 291).

7. Derrida has addressed the ways in which the law is perpetually reempowered (derivatively, from its own lack of author-ity) in his "Force of Law: The 'Mystical Foundations' of Authority," *Cardozo Law Review* 11 (1990): 914–1047.

8. *United States v. Stout* (1979, CA8 Missouri).

9. No better illustration of this could be found than a judgment rendered regarding a witness's testimony that she had observed defendants in possession of heroin. The defendants in the case held, with substantial supporting evidence, that the witness was incompetent to distinguish heroin from tobacco, and that her testimony should be ruled inadmissible, involving as it did a truth claim. The judge, however, ruled that "her testimony goes to weight and not to the admissibility of evidence" (*United States v. Eubanks* (1979, CA9 Arizona), in ruling to admit it. The jury could weigh (i.e., contextualize) the testimony after its admissibility.

10. *Payne v. Tennessee* (1991, 111 S. Ct. 2597). In a dissenting opinion, Justice David H. Souter held that as a consequence of the enhanced considerations given to testimony from the surviving victims of a crime, some defendant might be arbitrarily sentenced to death on the basis of testimony that would otherwise be ruled inadmissible, both because of its irrelevancy to the determination of criminal culpability, and because such testimony is not open to refutation. The majority, however, apparently agreed with Justice Antonin Scalia that, there being no limitations upon what a defendant might introduce as mitigating circumstances (character witnesses, a history of substance abuse), so there should be no limitations upon the admissibility of narratives concerning the emotional circumstances surrounding the victims of the crime.

11. For legal purposes, a conspiracy once begun is presumed to continue until its purpose has been achieved or thwarted; declarations made before the conspiracy commences

and after its cessation, as well as declarations not made in furtherance of that conspiracy, remain inadmissible. Statements made by unidentified informants to a coconspirator would remain covered by the hearsay exclusion (*United States v. Abrahamson* [1978, CA8 Minnesota]), as would a statement made by an unindicted coconspirator who had become a government informant, the logic being that once one became a government informant, he could no longer be a coconspirator. In practice, however, prosecutors, while careful to maintain his contribution, "turn" a coconspirator during preliminary hearings, and then assure his continued narrative cooperation by tenders of leniency or limited immunity. In cases involving racketeering and organized crime syndicates sworn to secrecy, the questionable testimony of a coconspirator might be the only source of information, advocates might argue.

Questions of hearsay in conspiracy are particularly relevant to the Racketeering Influenced Corrupt Organization (RICO) Act, passed into law in the late 1970s in an attempt to thwart large-scale criminal enterprises after a number of cases had been dismissed due to a preponderance of hearsay testimony. In a famous application, statements recorded at the home of a deceased defendant were ruled admissible under the RICO exception to the hearsay exclusion, since the taped conversations concerned the expulsion of a member of a crime family. Thus internal gossip came to be used as evidence of the "nature" of the enterprise under RICO (*United States v. Gotti* [1986, ED New York]).

12. See Stanley Fish, *Doing What Comes Naturally: Change, Rhetoric, and the Practice of Theory in Literary and Legal Studies* (Durham, NC: Duke University Press, 1989).

13. Charles Dickens, *Bleak House*, ch. 15.

14. The strategies by which the law has traditionally repressed "voice" save as a "dying delaration" might be demonstrated by the actions of the various commissions established by Parliament to look into the so-called Condition of England questions in the first three decades of the nineteenth century These commissions chaired by men like Hutchinson gave a belated visibility—by way of the new discipline of statistics—to what had previously been politically invisible and often inaudible, the cries of the poor. Hearsay and rumor are simultaneously exposed (as a statistical "finding") and repressed (as number displaces "real" materiality): the audible is made acceptable, but only as an abstraction to be dealt with as government "policy" rather than through "local acknowledgment." Hearsay represents some intrusion of the "local," both experientially and legally.

15. Sir William Blackstone, *Commentaries on the Laws of England*, vol. 1, ed. William C. Jones (1765–69; San Francisco: Bancroft-Whitney, 1915).

16. Ibid., 62; emphasis added.

17. Ibid., III: 432–33; emphasis added.

18. Thomas Starkie, *A Practical Treatise on the Laws of Evidence*, 3rd ed. (London: Stevens and Norton, 1842), I: 17.

19. Baron Gilbert, *Evidence*, 2nd ed. (1760), 152. Bentham refers to Baron Gilbert's pioneering contribution to the "subject of evidence" (not entirely without the ironic recognition of their differences) in at least two passages of the *Rationale of Judicial Evidence*.

20. In Britain the exclusion of hearsay evidence is applicable only to secondary and uncorroborated oral testimony but not to identical written testimony. United States 804(c)— the relevant statute—makes no real distinction between oral and written testimony for the purposes of judging exclusions (DC 252). This was recently upheld (*United States v. Day* [1978, App. DC 252]).

21. Dickens, *Bleak House*, ch. 5. See Jeremy Betham, *Rationale of Judicial Evidence*, ed. J. S. Mill (London: Stodderl, 1827); in particular the first two chapters of book 6, entitled "Of Makeshift Evidence," especially page 433. Also note the greasy walls of Jagger's chambers in *Great Expectations*. Gareth Steadman Jones (*Outcast London: A Study of the Relationship between Classes in Victorian England* [Harmondsworth: Penguin, 1971], 21–22), suggests that this army of illiterate copyists and scribes comprised almost 20 percent of London's lowest-paid laborers at midcentury.

22. A court's finding that certain statements introduced were not simply "idle chatter," but were actually made in the furtherance of a conspiracy (the words had criminal intent) was declared "clearly erroneous" under appeal, because the initial trial court never identified the foundational moment of the association (*United States v. Williams* [1984, CA7 Illinois]). The "idleness" of gossip, hearsay, and other supposedly foundationless discourse in judicial rhetoric smacks of the biblical distinction between idle hands and those that do the Lord's work in the world. That which distinguishes a criminal conspiracy from "idle talk," rhetorically, then, is an *investment in a criminal enterprise* that, like that other child of the nineteenth century, the limited liability company, has a moment of "incorporation."

23. One way of reading the recuperative marriages that furnish closure for Victorian novels is to imagine them as inscriptive restorations of a historically antecedent idea of the family in contradistinction to the dangerous exogamous "speculations" of "matches" offered up by gossips and their protégés: "idle talk" (hearsay) is economically unstable, a gamble, rather than a genuine investment.

24. Bentham, *Rationale*, 407–10.

25. Ibid.

26. Bentham's reformist ideology tended to be consolidative, as illustrated in his advocacy for the amalgamation of courts of equity with those of common law, gradually accomplished much later, between 1853 and 1873. Bentham's other reforms included recommendations for witness disqualification and special pleading.

27. James Bradley Thayer, *Legal Essays* (Boston: 1908), 303, n. 1.

28. For a detailed account of the resistances to the Model Code of Evidence project, see Thomas Morgan's foreword to *The Model Code of Evidence*, *American Law Institute Proceedings* 19 (1942): 74–157.

29. Francis Jeffrey, "Maria Edgeworth's Tales of Fashionable Life," *Edinburgh Review* 14 (1809): 376–77.

30. See J. Paul Hunter, "The Young, the Ignorant, and the Idle: Some Notes on Readers and the Beginnings of the English Novel," in *Anticipations of the Enlightenment in England, France, and Germany*, ed. Paul J. Korshin and Alan C. Kors (Philadelphia: University of Pennsylvania Press, 1987).

31. Although the relationship between rationality and deception is almost a refrain in Plato's thought, the debate between Socrates and Hippias regarding the "compatible/incompatible "virtues" of Achilles and Odysseus in the early "Hippias Minor" is exemplary. See "Hippias Minor," in *Early Socratic Dialogues*, ed. and with a general introduction by Trevor B. Saunders (Harmondsworth: Penguin, 1987), 275–93.

32. This argument receives one of its best contemporary articulations in Owen M. Fliss, *The Irony of Free Speech* (Cambridge, MA, and London: Harvard University Press, 1998).

Talking on the Telephone

16

Avital Ronell

The telephone splices a party line stretching through history. Since Moses has served as a privileged inducement to figure telephony, originating the legendary speech defect which tuned his special hearing, it is only in the interest of fairness that we mention the pharaoh's side of the coin deposited into the art of telephony.

When the French scientist Gaspard Monge followed the army of Napoleon Bonaparte into Egypt on its campaign of general decipherment, he explored the Temple of Mehmet Abn, where he made a discovery. He came upon a coil of wire in which were tangled several objects of ivory and bone, shaped somewhat in the fashion of the later drinking horn. These wires had been lying for ages in the place where they were found, a stone chamber in the temple. Later, on Monge's arrival at the pyramid of Gizeh, he discovered in a vault of about the same dimension as the chamber in the temple some of these ivory and bone objects and more coiled wires. At the time, scientists could make nothing of the manner in which the wires and their attachments might have been serviceable.

Were these funereal accompaniments, works of art, utensils of some unfathomable sort? The French publicist M. Henry Paccory has asserted that these objects were used for the transmission of speech "and that the chambers in which they were found were nothing less than ancient telephone booths. . . . Two miles, he thinks, was the limit of the distance over which the subject of the pharaohs could project his voice" (*HT*, 5).[1] This history seems a bit fanciful—so much so that one would want to enlist the counsel of a contemporary Egyptologist to secure an argument of these proportions. But like Bell's inability or unwillingness to confirm the receivership of the early telephone, we are caught in the same theoretical bind. So why introduce the possibility of a hookup to the pharaoh's Egypt? Only to suggest that the entire Mosaic intervention can be read according to telephonic protocols; a Heideggerian competition of the earth and sky, the pharaoh's vaulted pyramid booths pitted against the open lines of monotheism's suppression and abolition of divine party lines ✸ The Telephone Wars of the Egyptians and the Hebrews ✸ The electric flash that announced to Moses that God was on the line ✸ The transcription of that person-to-person call ✸ Moses was the only mortal to have seen the Mouthpiece. But here we are heading toward a dead sea of speculation, at which point it is always safe to attempt an exodus ✸ At the same time, we do not wish to limit our ventures, however precarious and telephonically unverifiable in the end, to Western phenomena. Again, in the interest of fairmindedness, ancient telephony among the Chinese deserves mention, if only to encourage others to pursue in greater detail this line of inquiry. As with any newborn archaeology, it needs time to develop, and many teachers.

Consider the communication made to a meeting of the Royal Asiatic Society in Shanghai, when it was shown that the Chinese had produced a rudimentary form of telephone consisting of two bamboo cylinders, from one and a half to two inches in diameter and four in length. A tympanum of pig bladder closes one end of each; the bladder is perforated for the transmitting string, the string kept in place by being knotted. This instrument, the "listening tube," as dependent on an organ transplant as ours once was, conveys whispers forty or fifty feet. It is unknown in many parts of the empire, Chih-chiang and Kiangsu being the only provinces where the listening tube was employed (*HT*, 39). Almost two centuries ago the Chinese are said to have produced the "thousand-mile speaker." The implement consists of a roll of copper, likened to a fife, containing an artful device; whispered into and immediately closed, the confined message, however long, may be conveyed to any distance; and thus, in a battle, secret instructions may be communicated. The inventor of the "thousand-mile speaker," Chiang Shun-hsin of Huichou, flourished during the reign of K'ang-his, in the seventeenth century. He left behind a text on occult science and astronomy.

In his book on the history of inventions, Johann Beckmann (1739–1811), generally considered to be the founder of scientific technology, devotes a chapter to speaking trumpets. The chapter includes reference to early "monstrous trumpets of the ancient Chinese," a kind of speaking trumpet or instrument by which words could not only be heard at the greatest distance possible, but also understood (*HT*, 6). "This invention," Beckmann adds, "belongs to the 17th century, though some think that traces of it are to be found among the ancient Grecians" (*HT*, 6). The speaking tube, the effort to extend the distance over which sounds could be sent by direct transmission through the air, was also of ancient origin. Beckmann supplies the following translation of a passage from Giambattista della Porta, presumably from his *Magia naturalis*, published in or prior to 1558. The figures of occult, magic, and friend gather together around this passage:

> To communicate anything to one's friends by means of a tube. This can be done by a tube of earthen ware, though one of lead is better—; for whatever you speak at the one end the words issue perfect and entire as from the mouth of the speakers and are conveyed to the ears of the other, which in my opinion may be done for some miles—. We tried it for a distance of two hundred paces, not having conveniences for a greater, and the words were heard as clearly and distinctly as if they had come from the mouth of the speaker (*HT*, 7).

Now back to modernity, where we discover Dr. Robert Hooke's preface to the first edition of his *Micrographia*, which the English philosopher had published in 1665. Exploring the propagation of sound waves through bodies other than air, and particularly through the distension of a wire, he brings us up-to-date on the prosthetic supplement to which we here aspire:

> The next care to be taken, in respect of the Senses, is a supplying of their infirmities with *Instruments*, and as it were, the adding of *artificial Organs* to the natural; this in one of them has been of late years accomplisht with prodigious benefit to all sorts of useful knowledge by the inventing of Optical Glasses. . . . And as *Glasses* have highly promoted our seeing, so 'tis not improbable, but that there may be found many *Mechanical Inventions* to improve our *other* Senses, of *hearing, smelling, tasting, touching*. 'Tis not impossible to hear a whisper . . . for that is not the only *medium* I can assure the Reader, that I have, by the help of a *distended wire*, propagated the sound to a very considerable distance in an *instant*. Or with as seemingly quick a motion as that of light (*HT*, 7).

According to the menu of artificial organs, the prosthetic olfactory device would still remain to be thought in order to give a sense of the projectile that Hooke throws into the waters of invention. What we know as the ear trumpet was exhibited at the Royal Society in London in 1668, under the name "otacousticon." It was portrayed in the diaries of Samuel Pepys, in his entry of April 2, 1668, as follows: "I did now try the use of the Otacousticon, which was only a great glass bottle broke at the bottom, putting the neck to my ear, and there I did plainly hear the dancing of the oars of the boats in the Thames to Arundel Galley window, which, without it, I could not in the least do" (*HT,* 9). What may elicit some interest in this portraiture is the telephone's acquisition of a new bodily part, the neck, which in subsequent memoirs of its anatomy was to be more or less decapitated, or let us say, shrunk to the abstraction of multiple displacements. The fractured neck originally had a lip which raised itself to the ear. In this scene of its operation the ears listen to the oars, the aquatic sound waves near the channel of dance music.

The speaking trumpet, as distinguished from the ear trumpet, came into prominence about 1670. A dispute arose among rival claimants regarding its invention. In 1671 a treatise on the invention was drawn up in which one of the claimants designated it as the "Tuba Stentoro-Phonica." The telephone is due to arrive a couple of centuries later, announcing itself by gradual degrees. In 1851 a speaking tube was exhibited at the London Exhibition under the name of "telekouphononon." The same manufacturer also displayed at the time an object thought to be a speaking trumpet, which he called the "Gutta Percha Telephone." The word "telephone" does not seem to have been applied to speaking tubes in English, but there are at least two cases, in 1869 and 1871, where it was applied to ordinary speaking tubes in the German language. All these devices, whether speaking trumpets, ear trumpets, or speaking tubes, worked on the principle of directly transmitting sound through air. One Captain John Taylor in 1845 invented an instrument "for conveying signals during foggy weather by sounds produced by means of compressed air forced through trumpets" (*HT,* 9). No thought of speech transmission informed this instrument, which only produced powerful sounds derived from blasts of compressed air. This aerial soundboard was called the "telephone"—one of the very early uses of the word.

The electromagnetic telegraph, introduced in 1837, was the opening wedge for the development of instant communication. In 1851 Dr. S. D. Cushman of Racine, Wisconsin, developed an "Electrical Talking Box," which he neglected to patent. Years later the Bell System defeated him in a lawsuit over this device. Still, theoretical telephonics always preceded empirical testing grounds. In 1854 the Frenchman Bourseul created the theory of the present-day telephone, leaving a blank for the switch, which awaited invisaging. In the early 1860s J. W. McDonough of Chicago invented, with the help of a Reis transmitter, a "teleloge." A New York newspaper tele-scripted a warning to its readers against buying stock in a newfangled device called the "telephone." Here goes the rumorous stock market again, switched on by telephonic speculation. As in *The Trial* of Kafka, rumor and arrest are part of the same performative experience:

> A man about 43 years of age giving the name Joshua Coppersmith has been arrested for attempting to extort funds from ignorant and supersti-tious people by exhibiting a device which he says will convey the human voice any distance over metallic wires. He calls the instrument a "tele-phone," which is obviously intended to imitate the word "telegraph" and win the confidence of those who know the success of the latter instru-ments. Well informed people know that it is impossible to transmit the human voice over wires, as may be done by dots and dashes and signals of the Morse Code. The authorities who apprehended this criminal are to be congratulated and it is hoped that punishment will be prompt (*HT*, 9).

In a crisis of small narcissistic difference, the newspaper presses charges against the parasitical instrument upon which it will develop addictive de-pendency. Pitting dots and dashes against the voice, the tele-graph against the tele-phone, the newspaper forms an agency with the police authorities of small-time writing. However, the logic of opposition informing the differ-ence between writing and vocal systems, phonetics and telephonetics, has no conceptual sanctuary to shelter it.

There remain perhaps only two orders of facts still to be recorded before we observe visiting rights with the Bell family. While they may in their un-natural setting appear segmented, isolated utterances, unprotected like the gash separating two schizoid remarks, they will have adopted a kind of long-distance semanticity spread over the body of our argument. First, a docu-ment from Frank Hall Childs, from which this passage has been clipped, indicates the extreme uncanniness assigned to the telephone: "One day the veteran showman, Phineas T. Barnum, came in to see the wonderful inven-tion, and I gave him his first introduction to the telephone. It seemed more of a curiosity to him than his freaks had been to the public" (*HT*, 26). Even through the hyperoptics of a sensibility comparable to that of a Diane Arbus, the telephone, as far as Barnum was concerned, presented itself as a curious counterpart to his freaks. In fact, Barnum was loath to display the telephone, because he didn't wish to freak out his audience with this voiced partial limb, no doubt, whereas limbless figures were still held to be digestible. A second point concerns the genderized voice that inhabits the telephone, and whose implications fill the slates we have accumulated. "In 1878, the first telephone exchange opened in New Haven, Connecticut. . . . Boys operated these early exchanges. The boys shouted at the customers, and it took several boys and many minutes to make a call. Girl operators later replaced the boys. The girls had softer voices, more patience, and nimble fingers" (*HT,* 29). Softer voices, more patience, and nimble fingers; the birth of a supple kind of texture, fortune's spinning wheel at the controls newly connecting voice to fingers. A digital combination for signing a destination. The invisible voices conducted through the tips of her fingers. The voice, entering the intimate borders between inner and outer ear, was soon feminized, if only to disperse the shouting commands of a team sport. Nowadays, it is said, when a military aircraft finds itself in serious trouble, the voice command switches to the feminine. The vocalized response to an S.O.S. signal was tuned in the emergency feminine—the maternal cord reissued.

Note

1. This and further such references are to A. W. Merrill et al., *Book Two: History and Identification of Old Telephones* (La Crosse, WI: R. H. Knappen, 1974).

TechnoTalk

17

E-Mail, the Internet, and Other "Compversations"

Sherry Turkle with S. I. Salamensky

S. I. Salamensky: Sherry, you write about people who converse with strangers—even "bots," or robots—over the Internet.[1] Many talk under assumed identities or different genders. Some live out fictional stories or lives within MUDs—online "communities," often set in other periods or worlds.[2] Some "have sex." You've interviewed hundreds of techno-talkers in the course of your research, and have even experimented for your research with these alternate modes of being. You seem to feel e-talk offers some rather revolutionary possibilities.

Sherry Turkle: Well, as we know, in traditional theater and role-playing games that take place in physical space one experiments with identity, stepping in and out of character. Online communities take this a step further to offer, in some sense, a parallel life. One's self-presentation as another can provide a second, rival identity. The boundaries are fuzzier; in a certain sense, virtual games don't have to end. Playing them may become part of the player's daily life.

For some people, life on the screen provides what Erik Erikson would have called a "psychosocial moratorium" similar to the identity development that occurs in adolescence. Although the term "moratorium" implies a "time out," what Erikson had in mind was not withdrawal. On the contrary, the adolescent moratorium is a time of intense interaction with people and ideas. It is a time of passionate friendships, experimentation, and significant experience. "Moratorium" refers not to a hiatus in experience but rather a hiatus in the consequences of that experience. During this time one's actions "don't count." Freed from consequence, experimentation becomes the norm rather than a brave departure. Consequence-free experimentation facilitates the development of a "core self," a personal sense of what gives life the meaning that Erikson called "identity."

Erikson developed these ideas about the importance of a moratorium during the late 1950s and early 1960s. At that time, the notion corresponded to a common understanding of what "the college years" were about. Today, thirty years later, the idea of the college years as a consequence-free "time out" seems of another era. College is largely preprofessional, and AIDS looms as a threat. But if our culture no longer offers an adolescent moratorium, virtual communities do. It is part of what makes them seem so attractive.

SS: So through e-talk we'll learn to crawl again?

ST: Well, rather than rigid sequences, Erikson's ideas describe what the individual needs to achieve before easily moving ahead to another developmental task. For example, he pointed out that successful intimacy in young adulthood is difficult if one does not come to it with a sense of who one is—that's the challenge of adolescent identity-building. In real life, however, people frequently move on with serious deficits. With incompletely resolved "stages," they simply do the best they can. They use whatever materials they have at hand to get as much as they can of what they have missed.

The MUD provides a dramatic example of how technology can play a role in these dramas of self-reparation. Time in cyberspace reworks notions of moratoria because they're now on offer in always-available "windows."

SS: I'm struck by your use of the word "window" here to denote both the computer setup and a means for categorizing experience. I'm hearing so many electronic terms enter everyday talk. These were introduced to naturalize and market the virtual world for the earthbound; now, in turn, they seem to respatialize our more abstract real-life concepts. No?

ST: It is interesting. The development of the windows metaphor for computer interfaces was a technical innovation motivated by the desire to get people working more efficiently by "cycling through" different applications. But in practice, windows have become a potent metaphor for thinking about the self as a multiple, distributed, "time-sharing" system. The self is no longer simply playing different roles in different settings, something that people experience when, for example, one wakes up as a lover, makes breakfast as a mother, and drives to work as a lawyer. The life-practice of windows is of a distributed self that exists in many worlds and plays many roles at the same time.

This notion of the self as distributed and constituted by a process of "cycling through" undermines many of our traditional notions of identity. Identity, after all, from the Latin *idem*, literally refers to the sameness between two qualities. On the Internet, however, one can be many and usually is. If, traditionally, identity implied oneness, life on today's computer screen implies multiplicity, heterogeneity, and fragmentation.

For instance, online, many people experiment with "playing" someone of the opposite gender. By enabling people to experience in some small—that is, purely textual—way what it "feels" like to be the opposite gender or to have no gender at all, the practice encourages reflection on the way ideas about gender shape our expectations of others and ourselves. Virtual cross-gendering teaches the first lesson of gender studies: the difference between biological sex and gender—the social construction of gender. When a man goes online as a woman, he soon finds that maintaining this fiction is difficult. To pass as a woman for any length of time requires understanding how gender inflects speech, manner, the interpretation of experience. As one woman who went online as a man said, "You have to think about it, make up a life, a job, a set of reactions."

William James called philosophy "the art of imagining alternatives." Online communities are proving grounds for an action-based philosophical practice that can serve as a form of consciousness-raising about gender issues. For example, in some online communities, offering technical assistance has become a common way for male characters to "purchase" female attention. In our physically embodied lives, our expectations about sex roles (who offers help, who buys dinner, who brews the coffee) can become so ingrained that we no longer notice them. On the Internet, however, expectations are expressed in visible textual actions, widely witnessed and often openly discussed. When men playing females on MUDs are plied with unrequested offers of help, they often remark that such chivalries communicate a belief in female incompetence. When women play males on MUDs and realize that they are no longer being offered help, some reflect that lifelong offers of help may have led them to believe they needed it. As a woman, says a college sophomore, "first you ask for help because you think it will be expedient. Then you realize that you aren't developing the skills to figure things out for yourself."

SS: You've compared online cross-gendered talk to the talk in *As You Like It.*

ST: Shakespeare provides the classic example of gender-swapping's potential to reveal new aspects of identity and permit greater complexity in relationships. In the play, Rosalind, the Duke's daughter, is exiled from the court of her uncle Frederick, who has usurped her father's throne. Frederick's daughter, Rosalind's cousin Celia, escapes with her. Together they flee to the magical forest of Arden. When the two women first discuss their plan to flee, Rosalind remarks that they might be in danger because "beauty provoketh thieves sooner than gold." In response, Celia suggests that they would travel more easily if they rubbed dirt on their faces and wore drab clothing, thus pointing to a tactic that frequently provides women greater social ease in the world: becoming unattractive. Rosalind then comes up with a second idea: becoming a man.

Rosalind and Celia both disguise themselves as boys, Ganymede and Aliena. When Rosalind flees Frederick's court, she is in love with Orlando. In the forest of Arden, disguised as the boy Ganymede, she encounters Orlando, himself lovesick for her. When Rosalind, as Ganymede, and Orlando meet "man to man," they are able to speak more freely. Their conversations about love are quite different from those that would be possible if they followed the courtly conventions constraining communications between men and women. In this way, the play suggests that donning a mask, adopting a persona, can be a step toward reaching a deeper truth about the real—a position many MUDders take regarding their experiences speaking as virtual selves.

To break a certain kind of conversational boundary, Shakespeare had to send his characters to the idyllic forest of Arden. Where do we have to go to open up new conversational possibilities? I believe that for many people, the answer to that question is to go on the Internet. A new kind of conversational space opens.

SS: And you've experienced self-revelation through e-talk.

ST: Yes. I remember the first time I had an experience of going online as a "man." It happened when I was at a virtual "party." I was new to this MUD. I had never been to a party in a MUD and I really didn't want to be part of the action. I didn't want to be picked up; I didn't want to dance.

SS: But you only dance on the linguistic plane, no? It's all narrative. To dance in a MUD, you type in: "ST dances."

ST: Right, but I didn't want to exert agency of any sort, just to watch, be a fly on the wall, observe others' choices.

So, on that party MUD, when you present as a character you are supposed to specify your gender. I forgot to do this, and at some point I realized that people seemed to assume I was male. And what surprised me was that there was something very liberating, very relaxing about this. People treated me differently. I didn't feel that accustomed social pressure to be, well, social. It was a potent reminder, in a way that brought theoretical gender studies down to earth, that gender is discursively coded. That experience made me painfully aware of how I bring my expectations of what I need to do and to be as a woman into every situation. As a man, being aloof from the action seemed acceptable. I wasn't a wallflower; I was simply reserved.

It was also very striking how little bits of virtual flirtation, done with a pretty teenage tone, brought me back to all the anxieties about flirting I had as a teenager. If only briefly, I had an experience of the thirteen-year-old me. There I was, sitting at a computer terminal, a woman in her mid-forties, with no interest in being on the make in this MUD—and yet, there was the experience of being anxious about not knowing how to flirt that brought me back to a junior high school dance.

And then, suddenly, somebody said, "There is a hot tub here—do you want to get naked?" I experienced such an awkward, get-me-out-of-here feeling! It would be something of an exaggeration to say I felt sexual panic, but it was something like that. And of course, the part of me that was observing my own reactions was quite surprised. Because the person with whom I was having this sexualized conversation was probably sixteen years old.

SS: So you reconfronted coming-of-age at a virtual frat party. Does revelation always lead to growth?

ST: For some. One man I interviewed enjoyed representing himself online as strong women. He felt that assertiveness as a man was acting as a bully. But he found assertive women powerful in a totally acceptable way. He used gender play to experiment with assertiveness. He said that in his "rest of life," he didn't feel he had the capacity to experiment as he could in online life. He used his life on the screen to get in touch with an aspect of himself that he wanted to know better. He told me that after years of experimenting in this way, he was able to bring some of this assertive capacity into the rest of his life.

SS: You describe a lonely student with a depressing, undecorated room who devotes all his energy to constructing virtual fantasy mansions in which to entertain virtual friends. Adults who spend twelve or eighteen hours per day in medieval-themed MUDs, pretending to be medieval. A married man who carries on an Internet affair because his wife "doesn't understand" him as well as a stranger whose real identity, location, and even gender are unknown to him. Perhaps this talk reflects the talker, but it doesn't compel self-reflection.

ST: No. Self-reflection is not compelled. Some people use online life to act out, to simply express their needs or seek to fulfill them through fantasies. But there is no question that the people who make the most of their lives on the screen are those who approach it with a spirit of self-reflection. And there is something about being able to look at a transcript of one's whole relationship with another that encourages reflection on what elements of the interaction gave rise to certain feelings, emotions, reactions.

These "archives," these logs of online conversation, are fascinating. In the research I've done, I find that people quite often describe online relationships as very intense, very powerful, very important. But then, we look at the logs and they can't see where or why there seemed to be so much going on. This phenomenon is related to the notion of transference in psychoanalysis. We project meaning, we experience the thickness, the consistency of relationship. But it is not because of what literally is being said. I think that this notion of what we bring to relationships and the ways in which they are constructed out of our desires is becoming more real for people through online experiences.

It's becoming a quite common occurrence to be in an online relationship and experience it as compelling—but when one examines its literal sum and substance, it comes across as totally flat! People realize through that how much of a relationship lies in the realm of fantasy—in what we bring to the relationship, in what we want from the relationship.

Having these archives, these logs, is also interesting in itself. It gives people something very concrete to refer to as they try to sort out what seems important in a relationship. We have a new tool, a new object-to-think-with for thinking about memory and transference. People look at what's on the screen, they look at the textual history of what has been on the screen and they're able to say, "You know, how I feel about this relationship comes in large part from what I am bringing to this relationship, it's not what the other person said to me." Of course, it's not enough to recognize the transference; you have to analyze the transference and make something of it, work it through, in order for it to be helpful to you. So I'm not at all arguing that life online is one big analytic session. And you were of course right when you said that self-reflection in this environment is in no way "compelled." But it is important that online life gives people powerful material for at least recognizing the fact of transference.

But let me say something about the very notion of the distinction between the virtual and the "real." In most conversations, people seem to want to divide the virtual from real life, RL. I don't like this distinction. I prefer to talk about the virtual and rest of life, R-O-L, to avoid the use of the word *real.* I think that, increasingly, we are not going to feel the necessity to oppose them so starkly; in the future it's the permeable boundaries that will become the most interesting to understand and study. People will always want face-to-face contact with other people, people will always want the immediacy of human contact, will always want to talk over the cup of coffee, will always want to see where somebody lives, physically, with their body. You learn a lot about a person by coming in, seeing the way they live, the kind of art they like, how the light comes in, whether they work in a dark room or a light room. People will always want to form relationships that contain information about our bodies and the bodies of those we talk to. But people will also always want—now that we've developed the taste for it—the possibility of meeting in the virtual, will always want the speed, the global reach, and yes, even the special kind of intimacy that comes from e-communication.

SS: So many of the people you describe are so addicted to incessant virtual conversation they find it increasingly difficult to talk to real people, real people who might dislike or reject them. Wouldn't the student with the ugly room be better off spending his energy painting? Or at least, you know, e-mailing Martha Stewart?

ST: I don't find the notion of addiction helpful in this context. The term *addiction* is most usefully saved for experiences with substances like heroin, which are always dangerous, always bad, always something to turn away from.

The Internet offers experiences in which people discover things about themselves, good and bad, usually complicated and hard to sort out. People grow and learn and discover good and new potential. People also discover preoccupations and fantasies that they may have never dealt with before and which may be very troubling. If you call the Internet addicting, then you have to call all powerful, evocative experience addicting.

This is very different from saying that the online world is one of "truth and beauty." It simply offers powerful, evocative experience that provokes self-reflection and self-discovery. This is not always positive, it just sometimes is. But it is not an addiction. The term *addiction* closes down the interesting questions about online life and ourselves that we need to explore.

SS: But e-conversation—with that plasticity you seem to value—can be engineered, fabricated, manipulated. So much of the e-talk you describe—

for instance, in the case of the Internet adulterer—involves idealized, idealizable interlocutors constituted solely in talk. Solipsistic self-affirmation seems pretty easy to find in this vacuum. That still seems to me intoxicating—as in, addicting, vertiginous, toxic.

ST: E-talk has its specificity, but at the most basic level, it is just talk. If you try to measure the impact of talk on people, you might say that some conversations are exciting. Most conversations are small talk, some conversations are depressing, some are toxic, and some are powerful, constructive, and life-transforming. If you try to average them, you might come up with the notion that "conversation" is, overall, mildly depressing. But we know that this "finding" would tell us very little about conversation and people. When it comes to human relationships, not much is gained from looking at the averages. What we need to study are the specifics: What kinds of interactions, what kinds of people make what kinds of match? What are the dynamics of different styles of interacting? I believe that these are the kinds of questions we need to be looking at for the online world.

What is specific about e-talk is that it often takes place in environments where people who have come to a talk-site—a chat room, a discussion group—have, by their very presence on that site, expressed a desire to talk to you about a very specific thing. Right now, I'm studying children and their relationships with the new generation of pet: the Furby.[3] If I really wanted to talk to you about, say, the details of how Furbies are programmed, at some point you are probably going to look at your watch and say that you have to go. But if I'm chatting on a website devoted to Furbies—and there are many—I'm surrounded by people who have self-selected to be there. I'm very likely to find someone willing to engage with me and be engaged by me. And if that person leaves, someone else will most likely appear, also ready to talk. So I think that one very new conversational habit that comes with e-talk is that people become used to the availability of sites where they can talk about exactly what they want to talk about—and to have these spaces available at all times.

If you happen to be obsessively working on something you'll find a space for it, that is for sure.

SS: And if you're working on nothing, talking for the feel of talk, the sake of talk, just chewing the fat?

ST: That too. I think that the extraordinary popularity of the seemingly extraordinarily banal chats has to do with people experiencing the pleasures of the feel of talk.

SS: It strikes me that a lot of the talk you describe is merely the parroting back of received narratives. Like the couple who courted in a medieval MUD, using quasi-medieval language. Or the sex talk that sounds like a bad movie. Is that talk or narrative? Have received forms of narrative—through media, perhaps—become more real to us than talk, more real than the narratives we can make?

ST: I think that the Internet takes many of the phenomena of postmodern life and makes them concrete. The postmodern experience of living in simulacra—of having our conversations take place in these artificial environments—is concretized online, writ larger than life, so to speak. It is not just on the Internet that you have the phenomena of people thinking of romance in terms of Sleeping Beauty or Cary Grant and Grace Kelley or Cinderella's blue ballgown. These images become part of our cultural bricolage offline and on. I think that we see these things more clearly online. We may find them sad, but people do create intense, personally meaningful, developmentally important relationships using this material.

People who use the Internet to express different aspects of self than might be possible in the physical real can learn things, can sometimes even work through things that they can bring back to the rest of their lives. And I think a more general sensitivity to the question of conversational context can emerge. It can make people more aware of the structuring context of every conversation. It makes the question "What can I change here?" more present in the rest of communication as well.

In the best of cases, looking at one's life on the screen causes one to reflect on the self, and on what one seems to desire, what seems to be missing, what seems to be gratifying. In the best of cases, experiencing multiple aspects of self facilitates greater communication among parts of the self. That is why I become so frustrated when I feel that people are trying to get me to say that we are moving from a psychoanalytic to a computer culture. Perhaps it seems fashionable to think that we no longer need to think in terms of Freudian slips but rather of information-processing errors. But the reality is more complex. Our need for a practical philosophy of self-knowledge—one that does not shy away from issues of multiplicity, complexity, and ambivalence—has never been greater as we struggle to make meaning from our lives on the screen. I like to insist that it is time to rethink our relationship to the computer culture and psychoanalytic culture as a proudly held joint citizenship.

SS: What makes these e-conversations so compelling?

ST: Well, it's interesting. I often like to compare e-mail with the *pneumatique* in Paris. In 1968–69, I was living with a traditional family in France who'd just had a telephone installed, but only for emergencies. For writing a significant letter, a significant apology, an important rendezvous, marking a moment of congratulations or thanks, they sent a *pneumatique*. You wrote something on special paper, you took it to the post office where they put it into a canister, the canister went into a pneumatic tube, which in turn went on the underground system of tubes through all Paris and got sucked out in another post office, taken out of the canister and put into the hands of a *facteur*, who delivered it to the *destinataire*. In other words, an extraordinary amount of industrial age technology, the tubes, the gas, the suction, went into this correspondence. What made it seem so intimate, I think, was the experience people had of writing something and being able to fantasize that in the space of perhaps only an hour the other person would sense both the writing and the intensity of their desire to communicate quickly. There was this fantasy that I write it, you read it, not instantaneously, but almost instantaneously. With significant correspondence by e-mail or other forms of electronic communications there is, on the one hand, the intensity and fantasy of that kind of "instantaneous communication." But unlike conversation, we can read and reread our e-mail. That gives it the power of conversation and a supplement of layered meaning as well.

There is an instrumental side to online conversation—it can be frequent, it facilitates planning among different and geographically dispersed people. But there is another side to electronic conversation. A subjective side. The subjective side of technology is not what the computer does for us, but what the computer does *to* us. I'm talking about the sense that in an online discussion group, I write and then, right away, someone is able to pick up my idea, get excited, and send me something in return. These gratifications are heady and build a sense of belonging.

Another way to say this is that online communities give people very powerful experiences of being responded to. Perhaps this is where the comparisons with the physical real become invidious. I belong to online communities and of course I belong to a community of colleagues at MIT. My colleagues at MIT are every bit as interesting, as smart, as well read as anyone in any of the virtual communities to which I belong. But when I encounter my MIT colleagues in the hall, for example, we are not there to be there for each other. We are off doing our jobs. But when people go online to participate in a virtual community, they are there to respond to others. It is this sense in a virtual community that people are there to be there for you, that people are there to respond to you, that becomes a powerful source of the "holding power" of such places.

Virtual communities can be like bars, bistros, coffee shops. They don't have the intimacy of the family, but nor do they have the anonymity of the street. They are poised between the private and the public. At least in

America, these spaces are hard to come by in the physical "real." We have many Starbucks, but they are not the neighborhood meeting places that the French café can be.

I live in a physically beautiful neighborhood—Back Bay in Boston—that is not a neighborhood. I don't know anyone in my neighborhood. I love walking on the street, I love the architecture of the homes, I'm hooked on the buildings, but there's no community. The playground is used by preschoolers in the area, but as soon as they start school, they are bussed away or carpooled away to different places. The bistro is a Starbucks, frequented by tourists, shoppers, the people who are staying at the big hotels.

Let me return to the online fantasy, which has some reality, that when people are there, they are there for you. Even in the neighborhood coffee shop, when people say "Hi," they may want to chat, but they're not there for you. Online, people have made a joint decision that they are there for each other, and that is extraordinary. It's a different kind of human experience and that's what gives these new communities a lot of their power. When seniors, for example, log on to the many, many communities that are now organized for them, it's not like the old days when my grandmother sat in the park where people she knew would say hello to her. She didn't expect to have intense conversations there, she just wanted to feel she was part of the neighborhood. You log on to "senior.net," you're there, and right away it's let's talk, let's chat. It's a heady experience. In the past I think we have been comforted by comparing online experiences with what we had in the physical real. These analogies only took us so far. I think it's time to move beyond these analogies.

SS: Don't you think that e-talk simply conveys the illusion of projecting one's voice into the public sphere? Isn't there a sense, with e-talk, of amplification, that your chatter is marked, recorded, inscribed, published all over the world—your Warholian "fifteen minutes"—and thus more valuable than real-life chatter?

ST: I think that this sense of broadcast is far more true of the personal web page. The web page text is more like talk than writing—but it is a broadcast talk. People put their journals on them. People tell what they did today, and in the retelling I think they experience their day as more important because it is broadcast. And now this talk/text broadcast is increasingly amplified by images—sometimes video images of the person as they are living a life—in the phenomenon of the video camera in the bedroom broadcasting onto the web. Here again, what we see in the online experience is a kind of amplification of what is in the culture. People feel validated by sharing their experiences on Oprah, and people feel validated when they watch

Oprah and see echoes of their experience. Of course the danger is that we will only feel authentic when we are broadcasting. But this is, again, a crisis about authenticity and what makes us feel "real" that predated the web.

SS: Won't all this talking into the ether even further pacify us as, like, late-capitalist fodder?

ST: I did a study of twentysomethings who consider themselves "politically active on the Internet" but who didn't vote in the 1992 election. It is stunning to hear people talk about how exciting it is to feel politically active and involved—indeed potent—in the online world, and yet not feel the need to bring that sense of potency offline—into the world of social crisis, poverty, class, race.

But I think that I see an evolution here. As people spend more and more time in virtual places, there is a push, a kind of expression of human desire, to make the boundaries between the physical and the virtual more permeable. To have communities on the screen and to bring them into the physical surrounds, to have communities in the physical and bring them into the virtual, and in so doing, to enhance their possibilities for action and communication, and political power. In other words, I think just as experts continue to use the language of the real and the virtual, people are building lives where the boundaries are more and more permeable. I think there is a lot of activity at the border of the virtual and the physical—expressing the desire to have both at the same time.

Over the past few years, we've seen a change in the model of what is most exciting about the web. As little as five years ago, there were a lot of people saying things like, "Oh my God, what's exciting about the web is that I can talk to this guy in Australia who has my exact same stamp collection," to the feeling that what is most exciting about the web is that it can also enhance relationships with people you see face to face. It has been a movement from global to local. I think things are going to continue in this direction. So, the web will be valued both for what it does to our global reach and to our local possibilities. Including to our local political possibilities.

I am very impressed by the work of Alan Shaw, who did his doctoral work at the MIT Media Lab. What he does is take a community and give it extra leverage by putting it online and giving it communications and organizing tools. His perspective is stunning. He shows that many communities think they're lacking in community resources due to poverty—because they're not counting the strengths of community members. If you have easy ways to organize and share information online, you might find that several members of the community can teach basketball, and several can teach mahjongg, and others can teach bridge. The communication tools allow them to get together with others, to create networks—and they end up with the functional equivalent of community centers. Alan is trying to conceptualize virtual community enhancers that allow people to see the resources of their communities more easily. Alan tells what I think is a classic story of a hospital that couldn't get federal funding unless it provided community outreach programs. So the hospital put up signs for an outreach program on prenatal care, but nobody came. Yet, almost at the same time, a group of pregnant women learned of each other on the community network. They got together online and decided that they needed help. As a group, formed online, they went to the hospital and said, "What can you do for us?" The hospital said, "What? We're the ones who need you!" So the community developed resources just by being able to mobilize its members. This is a good example of a great deal being accomplished when people cross boundaries from the physical to the virtual and back to the physical.

SS: Still, most of the interactions you describe seem circumscribed to the nonthreatening realm of the computer screen.

ST: I think that I began studying this phenomenon in its very early days. Increasingly, people are starting to realize that when they have an e-encounter there is an embodied person behind that encounter. Of course, they always knew this intellectually—they knew that they were not talking to computers but people, but the computer's novelty and other mediations masked the reality. Now, increasingly, people on a mailing list or a web chat will say, "Can we meet, perhaps in June, in California?" And they will. And people begin relationships online, but pretty soon it is as though a hand reaches out from the computer and asserts that we are two physical, vulnerable people and it is time to meet.

There is another very rapidly changing aspect of e-talk and this is the increasing realization that it is never really anonymous. Psychologically, even when people know that users of a particular system can easily find out their "true" identities, when people see a name other than theirs on the screen and "their" words are being assigned to this "other" name, they feel anonymous. There is a very powerful illusion of anonymity, if increasingly challenged by our greater technical understanding. But I think that even with this increased understanding there is something about that illusion of anonymity that will remain. It has the appeal of a masked ball—that ritual of anonymity without true anonymity. There is something liberating, something desirable in being at once you and not you. The mask at the ball only covers the eyes. But the fiction created by the ritual context gives a sense of anonymity in which certain things are accessible that would be prohibited without it.

SS: What about the MUD "rape" scenario you describe—where one MUD participant took over another participant's female character, altered her speech and actions, and engineered a sexual encounter against her author's will? You say that words are deeds and treat this as seriously as a physical rape in the material world. I'm afraid I can't buy that.

There is apparently a raging Internet debate over virtual rape. I don't know whether that is pathetic or tragic.

ST: There are lot of people, like you, who dismiss virtual rape as inconsequential. They say, "It's just words," "You can always log off," "You can turn off the machine."

SS: And they're right!

ST: But there are many things that make the story less simple than it might be.

First of all, you do have bodily experiences when you interact in a MUD. It's uncanny, but watching your virtual persona be stroked on the head by another virtual persona is a powerful—a physical—experience. Sometimes people say it is erotic, or comforting, or maternal, but it is not nothing. We experience our bodies in all sorts of ways. It makes me think of Freud and hysteria: the discovery that you can say the right word and a paralyzed arm can move again. So MUDs dramatize the power of the word.

The second thing, and this relates to one of the reasons that MUDs are so fascinating and complicated, is that participants spend months, maybe two or three years, developing their virtual personae. To have to destroy your persona because it has been made to do obscene actions that others on the MUD cannot recognize as unintended is a very big deal. The terrible thing that happened in this particular rape was that the rapist, using "voodoo doll" programming, had found a way to get the attacked virtual persona to behave in certain ways, while the person who felt they owned the virtual persona could just look on.

Let me make this concrete: We're in a MUD together, your, Shelley's, character is called Goldie, and my, Sherry's, character is called Brunette. A third party has used software that has Goldie performing obscene gestures on Brunette. I'm watching as my virtual body is violated by Goldie and so are sixty other people who have come to know you and me—or rather who have come to know Goldie and Brunette—over the years. Of course, at some point you can move out of character and say: "Excuse me, it's not me doing this because someone else has stolen the body of Goldie." But essentially, in the terms of the virtual world, Goldie is a rapist.

So what would made this case so disturbing is that you lost control of your character, her words, her relationships, and you were doing horrible things to a variety of people who were all watching, thinking it was really you. So it is not rape but it is not "just word" either.

SS: I can accept that words wound, if not as clearly as attacks to the body, but even verbal attack seems adherent only to the degree that the hurtful words are identity-based. A stranger who tags me with a generic epithet hurts me a bit, as all violent language is hurtful. A stranger who makes a gender- or ethnicity-based remark hurts me more. But words directed at a known "me" carry—at least for me—much more destructive power.

In the MUD rape case, it's pretty hard for me to see what power is exercised. Because the characters are fictional, and both the source of the insult and the insulted party are unidentified—even as to their real-life genders: a male character fictionally rapes a female character, but the male might well be authored by a woman and the female by a man. Maybe even a group. There's no knowing who is behind the character.

There's power, of course, in speaking as an unlocatable source; but here the victim, too, is unlocatable. Symbolically, there's an attack on all women, as with misogynist graffiti, and it does seem, on that level, upsetting and ugly. But really. Rape?

ST: You didn't have a relationship over many years with the stranger. You talk about attack by a member of your community; the people who are playing characters in MUDs have chosen to invest in what they thought were safe communities. I think it may also be hard to appreciate from the outside that when you participate in this community, you do fantasize a virtual body. You identify with the actions of your character. You care about others' regard for your character. So to appreciate the violation—and perhaps rape is not, finally, the right word for this violation—you have to imagine, to be in the moment with your character, whatever you have called yourself, you have to imagine watching this character—you!—doing something obscene to somebody else. Until you can imagine that your reaction would be physical—a revulsion, a nausea, an impotent rage—until you can imagine that, it is hard to understand the way people experienced this event. Perhaps it is easier to think of less violent examples. Like, for instance, if a mischievous hacker contented himself with causing your character to fart in public. You might well feel humiliated, even though it might seem silly—"just words" or, beyond that, "just computer code."

SS: So: conversation with manufactured characters. Calvin Klein has run a billboard campaign with pictures of models assigned fictional names, personalities, and e-mail addresses. For instance, one was called Anna and was thirteen. If you e-mailed her she'd e-mail you back—not regularly, but sporadically, like a real person—about her school, dates, parties, et cetera.

ST: That example's very rich. It seems strange, yet not so strange, that we create fictional characters tied to real faces in a real advertisement who live fictional lives that we want to know about. And with whom we want to correspond.

It highlights the degree to which we live in a culture of simulation. It is important to always remember that the phenomenon of e-talk we are discussing is taking place in this broader context. It makes me think of something my daughter said last summer. She was seven and I took her to Italy. She was sitting, watching the water from a little boat, and up swam a jellyfish. And she said, "Oh, mommy, look, a jellyfish. It looks so realistic."

A friend who works for Disney told me that when they opened the Animal Kingdom—a nature park in Florida with real animals—they got a lot of negative feedback from adult visitors to the park who complained that the animals weren't "realistic" enough! Because the gold standard there is what you expect of an animatronic Disneyworld animal: that it should look perky, that there should be continual motion.

What is the gold standard here? Is responsiveness and interactivity becoming the gold standard for "realism"? The e-mail from fictional people seems to bridge a gap between the imaginary and the real. Again, we are having our conversations on the boundary.

SS: Speaking of the boundary, I recently saw someone walking around at MIT wearing a computer headset. One eye trained onto the street, the other onto a little screen.

ST: I believe that you saw someone who belongs to what is known as the Wearables group at the Media Lab. Sometimes they call themselves cyborgs. They are in fact wearing portable computers. Some of them are broadcasting video to the web—broadcasting everything they see—and some are connected to the Net but not broadcasting.

Imagine that I'm one of them. I wear a headset, I shake your hand and type your name onto a small one-hand keypad. I'm wearing glasses—which are also my computer screen—and onto my screen pops your web page and I go to your c.v. So, as we're talking, I can be scrolling through your last paper. In the view of the Wearables group, our social interaction can on some level be enhanced by technology. The cyborg project has to do with the ways in which people can expand their minds by using technology as prosthetic. I want to understand the changes in identity when people experience much more fluid boundaries between themselves and technology. I've always thought of the computer as an intimate machine, but in the cyborg project, for instance, we can see that intimacy becoming concretized in very dramatic ways.

SS: When I first began to look at e-conversation I thought it might signal a new cultural focus on talk over text. But in your Wearables scenario, text supplements talk; for you as a Wearable, I seem to be less my present, real-time talk than my text: it's what you can look up that counts.

ST: I suppose I agree. To capture the kind of social interaction you can have with people who are simultaneously reading your last paper—well, the term "small talk" comes to mind.

SS: Speaking of small talk, you've described a virtual date you made to meet a virtual friend at a virtual bar—that is, a MUD themed as a bar. He says, "I'll have a martini." You say, "I'll have an herbal tea." A user playing the waitress takes your order and spills a glass of water. Your date excuses himself for the restroom. What's the sense of a parallel world if it's equally banal?

ST: There's small talk and there's big talk; I think what's important is the presence of both. One of my favorite examples of the range and levels of e-talk is observing students in a computer cluster. They're close together physically, and sometimes they get up and chat, and sometimes they sit down and send each other e-mail. And sometimes they send each other instant messages, which pop up immediately on the screen in real time. And then there are Internet chat rooms, where you can be anonymous or semianonymous, with other people around. And then there are MUDs, where you interact as an avatar of yourself, and even your friends may not know which character you are. So these students have five ways to talk, five different kinds of talk. And the question is, how do people decide in practice what modality of talk is most appropriate to their current purposes?

SS: For me, this also recalls classical debates: Which is more authentic, speech or writing? Which most closely represents the self?
In the end, is e-talk talk, or writing?

ST: Well, perhaps the old categories don't serve us well here. New and hybrid forms are being developed. Some think that this new writing, the texts of MUDs, are a new kind of literature. But it is not exactly literature. It has the immediacy of talk. It borrows the conventions of talk. It is a form of talk, and yet it is written talk.

I think that e-mail is a curious kind of resolution in that you get the immediacy of speech and trace as in writing. I've recently been studying handwriting and people's feelings about handwriting as opposed to typing. If you're used to composing on a computer, and you have a significant love letter to write, do you compose it on your computer and then rewrite it? A love letter, above all things, feels like something that might need the trace of the body. But now they have these handwriting fonts, and that is very interesting, because in a sense you're turning yourself into a kind of computer.

Students have written me beautiful papers on objects like a letter they wrote in third grade or a letter their mother wrote them in third grade, and finding the paper, the thrill of seeing this trace of the body. What would you feel if you only found your mother's e-mail to you? What is it that we're gaining and losing in this? The significance may lie less in the moment of use and more in our feelings about our history and our material culture.

The MIT architecture department was one of the first places to adopt computerization enthusiastically and wholeheartedly. But when I was interviewing members of that department, one architect, who was very positive about the use of computers in architecture studios, also had very grave reservations because he felt that he had lost the power of the trace of his body. He said, "I could be walking along the street and look down and see a piece of paper with a drawing on it and know it was mine; now, with pieces of printout, I don't recognize my designs." There is a sense of alienation from the writing. And one might also ask whether the e-mail is an alienation of the conversation.

SS: You don't seem overly alienated.

ST: I end *Life on the Screen* on a fairly dark note, writing about the Wim Wenders film *Until the End of the World*. At the close of the film, the characters are introduced to a technology that can record their dreams in such a way that they can view them on video screens. They walk around with blankets on their heads so that they can better view the little screens they hold in their hands. They have fallen in love with their dreams. I think that our ability to live on fantasies in "real" online relationships carries something of this danger.

Still, I think that what is worrying me most now has to do with how children are growing up into a new cyborg consciousness. I find that today's children speak with increasing ease about factors which encourage them to see the "stuff" of computers as the same "stuff" of which life is made. To take a noncomputer example, the seemingly ubiquitous "transformer toys" shift from being machines to being robots to being animals, and sometimes people. Children play with these plastic and metal objects and, in the process, they absorb a notion that boundaries are fluid between mechanism and flesh.

I once observed a group of seven-year-olds playing with a set of plastic transformer toys that can take the shape of armored tanks, robots, or people. The transformers can also be put into intermediate states so that a "robot" arm can protrude from a human form or a human leg from a mechanical tank. Two of the children were playing with the toys in these intermediate states—that is, in intermediate states between people, machines, and robots. A third child insisted that this was not right. The toys, he said, should not be placed in hybrid states. "You should play them as all tank or all people." He was getting upset because the other two children were making a point of ignoring him. An eight-year-old girl comforted the upset child. "It's okay to play them when they are in-between. It's all the same stuff," she said. "Just yucky computer 'cy-dough-plasm.'"

My current work with children focuses on the nature of this "cy-dough-plasm." Today's children have a tendency to see computer systems as "sort of" alive, to fluidly cycle through various explanatory concepts, and to willingly transgress boundaries. Most recently, the transgressions have involved relationships with virtual "pets." The first and most popular of these was the Tamagotchi, who asks its owners to feed it, play games with it, inquire about its health and mood, and, when it is still a baby, clean up its virtual "poop." Good parenting of a Tamagotchi will produce a healthy offspring; bad parenting will lead to illness, deformity, and finally to the pet's virtual death. The Tamagotchi is only the first in a series of computational objects designed for children that teach a new lesson about the machine world: computational objects need to be related to as another life form. The Furby goes beyond the Tamagotchi: the Furby is cute and lovable. Children say, "My Furby is sort of alive because he loves me. My Furby is sort of alive because I take care of him."

People are increasingly willing to take computational objects as companions. I call this "taking things at interface value." For example, when the interactive psychotherapy computer program Depression 2.0 first came out, people asked, "How can I confide my feelings in something that doesn't have any? How can I discuss my mother with something that never had one? How can I talk about my sexuality with something that doesn't have flesh?"[4] But people started taking things at interface value; that is: if it's helpful, let it help me. And now, we are starting to see the beginnings of objects designed to be electronic companions.

The Furby is only the first stage of development in a whole line of computational objects that will be able to chat with you. They won't be very smart, but they'll know enough to hold an intelligent-sounding conversation. In terms of emotional intelligence, the computer will know if you're upset. And it will modulate its way of being with you depending upon what it perceives.

What is talk with something that doesn't even make a pretense of understanding? You talk to it, and it doesn't just reflect back what you have said. It replies. The object is put into the position of a thinking subject, the subject "presumed to know."

SS: You've discussed a competition to create the most effective bot. The measure of this bot's intelligence will be its ability not only to respond to human statements but to carry on half of a random, freewheeling conversation. One bot you've described, Julia, is particularly successful in this, in part because she replicates humor—seemingly a higher plane of talk, in transcending the literal. For instance, she tells a man whose verbal codes suggest he's propositioning her to "take a cold shower."[5]

Artificial intelligence, as you describe it, seems predicated on talk. Which would imply that real intelligence, or measures of humanness, or humanity, are also predicated on talk.

ST: One of the interesting things about AI today is that when you increase the degree of sociality that programs can show, when you increase the sense that they are responding to people, you get a very powerful response. If a robot is able to capture your gaze and move its eyes to keep in contact, that has a stunning effect. I believe that when we meet such an object, we are programmed—and here I mean biologically programmed—to feel that we are in the presence of a kin. We meet this object and we say, "I'm home. I'm with my people." Today, the AI researcher asks, "What is it that I have to give people so that when they interact with this object they are willing to take it as a subject?" The computer is not a thinking subject, but comes to function like one through the human codes that put it in that subject position and, yes, through its talk. If talk is the measure of intelligence, it also seems to be the measure of consciousness.

SS: Our satisfaction with virtual conversation, perhaps, raises questions of what we want out of talk in the rest of life.

ST: In e-life you get pure talk. I think that, talking as we are, in the same room, the presence of the body really makes a difference. We're surrounded by so many cues that situate us as people, in ways that can be comforting or stimulating or upsetting.

When we were planning to have this talk, you said: "Actually, I'm down the street, but if you like we could talk over e-mail."

SS: We could have had multiple conversations under multiple identities in your MUD café.

ST: I have a lot of online conversations, and it's not the same as sitting here with you. I do feel that a lot of what you get out of face-to-face conversation you don't get out of e-talk. A lot of energy is certainly spent in MUDs creating word atmospherics to get even the smallest sense of that. But in the end the words cannot capture the presence of the body.

And as I've said, when people make transcripts, archives of their conversations from the MUD, they so often look at the transcripts and say, "*This* is the wonderful conversation I had? *This* is the man, the woman I fell in love with? The virtual touch that actually felt erotic? This looks completely different!" That feeling's so familiar to me. As I do my research, I tape most of my interviews. So often, leaving, I say to myself, "That was a fascinating conversation! I loved meeting that person!" And then I look at the transcript and say, "Where is it? Where did it go? Look at this transcript. There's nothing here!"

As they say: You had to be there.

Notes

1. Bots, from "robots," are conversational artificial intelligences—that is, programmed "personalities" with whom one may "converse" via computer. Bots' replies, based on grammatical and other cues, are in the best cases so lifelike that one may talk for some time without realizing that one's conversational partner is not, in fact, human. For more information on bots and related artificial intelligence phenomena, see Turkle's *Life on the Screen: Identity in the Age of the Internet* (New York: Simon and Schuster, 1995; New York: Touchstone, 1997).

2. MUD stands for "multi-user domain," a themed site in which multiple users, generally unknown to each other in real life and potentially from all parts of the world, participate as characters or "avatars" with fictional names and identities. A number of "online communities" have been in existence since the inception of net communication, with some stability of population. Physical environments—for instance, a "house" in which the virtual e-talk party "takes place," are "built" in words. "Sex," "affairs," and "marriages" occur, often between people who have no plan to meet in real life. Many users take their online lives quite seriously, feeling these lives, friendships, and loves to be in some manner more authentic than offline existence. See *Life on the Screen*.

3. The Furby, like the Tamagotchi, is a popular computerized or "animatronic" toy.

4. Depression 2.0 is a computer program that carries on an "analytic" conversation, based on syntactical codes. For instance, if the user types in "I'm depressed about my job," the program answers with the prefix "Why do you say . . ." attached to the suffix ". . . you are depressed about your job?" In Turkle's research, many users have not only reported feeling helped by the program, but have seemed to attach human qualities—generally against their will—to the program. See *Life on the Screen*.

5. See *Life on the Screen* for more discussion of Julia.

Gossip

Homi Bhabha holds the Chester D. Tripp Chair in the Humanities at the University of Chicago and is Visiting Professor in the Humanities at University College, London. Among his recent books are the edited collection *Nation and Narration* (1990) and *The Location of Culture* (1994). He is currently working on *A Measure of Dwelling*, a theory of vernacular cosmopolitanism.

Margaret Bruzelius teaches in the Program for Degrees in Literature and serves as a dean at Harvard University. She is working on a book on modern permutations of the romance.

Judith Butler is Maxine Elliot Professor in the Department of Comparative Literature at the University of California, Berkeley, as well as in the Department of Rhetoric, of which she is chair. Her books include *Gender Trouble: Feminism and the Subversion of Identity* (1990), *Bodies That Matter: On the Discursive Limits of "Sex"* (1993), *The*

Psychic Life of Power: Theories in Subjection (1997), and *Excitable Speech: A Politics of the Performative* (1997). She is currently at work on a manuscript on *Antigone.*

Stanley Cavell is Walter M. Cabot Professor of Aesthetics and Ethics at Harvard University. He is the author of *Must We Mean What We Say?* (1969), *The World Viewed: Reflections on the Ontology of Film* (1971), *The Claim of Reason: Skepticism, Morality, and Tragedy* (1979), *Pursuits of Happiness: The Hollywood Comedy of Remarriage* (1981), and *Disowning Knowledge in Six Plays of Shakespeare* (1987), among many other works in philosophy, language, American studies, drama, and film.

Tom Conley teaches French and film at Harvard University. He is the author of *Film Hieroglyphs* (1991), *The Graphic Unconscious* (1992), and *The Self-Made Map* (1996). His current project in cinema is a study of the early films of Raoul Walsh.

Steven Connor is Professor of Modern Literature and Theory at Birkbeck College, London. His most recent books include *Postmodernist Culture: An Introduction to Theories of the Contemporary* (1989), *Theory and Cultural Value* (1992), *The English Novel in History, 1950–1995* (1996), and the forthcoming *Cultural History of Ventriloquism.*

Marjorie Garber is Walter R. Kenan, Jr., Professor of English at Harvard University, where she directs the Center for Literary and Cultural Studies. She is the author of several books on drama and culture, including *Coming of Age in Shakespeare* (1981), *Shakespeare's Ghost Writers: Literature as Uncanny Causality* (1987), *Vested Interests: Cross-Dressing and Cultural Anxiety* (1992), and *Symptoms of Culture* (1998).

Deborah R. Geis teaches drama, postmodern literature, and women's studies at the University of Tennessee, Knoxville, and has also taught at Queens College of the City University of New York. Her books include *Postmodern Theatric(k)s: Monologue in Contemporary American Drama* (1993) and, as coeditor with Steven F. Kruger, *Approaching the Millennium: Essays on Angels in America* (1997).

Alexander Gelley teaches in the English and Comparative Literature Department at the University of California, Irvine. He is the author of *Narrative Crossings: Theory and Pragmatics of Prose Fiction* (1987) and the editor of *Unruly Examples: On the Rhetoric of Exemplarity* (1995). He is currently working on further studies of idle talk and on the idea of criticism in Walter Benjamin.

Sander L. Gilman is the Henry R. Luce Distinguished Service Professor of the Liberal Arts in Human Biology and Chair of the Department of Germanic Studies at the University of Chicago. He is a cultural and literary historian and the author or editor of more than fifty books, including *Seeing the Insane* (1982), *Jewish Self-Hatred* (1986), *Love + Marriage = Death* (1998), and *Creating Beauty to Cure the Soul* (1998).

Jan B. Gordon is Professor of English at the Tokyo University for Foreign Studies and the author of *Gossip and Subversion: Echo's Economies* (1996).

Alec Irwin teaches the study of religion at Amherst College. He is coeditor, with Jim Kim, Joyce Millen, and John Gershman, of *Dying for Growth: Global Economics and the Health of the Poor.*

Carla Kaplan is Professor of English at the University of Southern California. Her works include *The Erotics of Talk: Women's Writing and Feminist Paradigms* (1996).

John K. Limon, Professor of English at Williams College, is the author of *Writing after War: American War Fiction from Realism to Postmodernism* (1994) and *The Philosophy of Standup, or Abjection in America* (forthcoming).

Paul Rabinow is Professor of Anthropology at the University of California, Berkeley. He is the author of *Essays in the Anthropology of Reason* (1997), *French DNA, or Trouble in Purgatory* (1999), and many other well-noted works on science, society, ethics, and philosophy.

Nicholas Rand is Professor of French and Senior Fellow of the Humanities Research Institute at the University of Wisconsin, Madison. Most recently, he is coauthor, with Maria Torok, of *Questions for Freud: The Secret History of Psychoanalysis* (1998). He is also consultant at large for the intellectual estate and archives of Sandor Ferenczi. He has published widely, in many languages, on literature and psychoanalysis.

Avital Ronell is Professor and Chair of Germanic Languages and Literatures, and Professor of Comparative Literature, at New York University. Her books include *The Telephone Book: Technology, Schizophrenia, Electric Speech* (1989). She is currently completing an investigation into the body, the sacred, and "stupidity."

S. I. Salamensky is Visiting Assistant Professor of English at the University at Albany, State University of New York. She has taught at Harvard University and the University of Essex, England, and is completing a book entitled *The Wilde Word: Talk and the Performance of Modernity.*

Sherry Turkle is Professor of the Sociology of Science at MIT. She holds a Ph.D. from Harvard in sociology and psychology, and is also a licensed clinical psychologist. Her recent books are *The Second Self: Computers and the Human Spirit* (1984) and *Life on the Screen: Identity in the Age of the Internet* (1995).

Index